Students' English Grammar

Jake Allsop

Prentice Hall
New York   London   Toronto   Sydney   Tokyo   Singapore

PRENTICE HALL INTERNATIONAL ENGLISH LANGUAGE TEACHING

Published 1993 by
Prentice Hall International (UK) Limited
Campus 400, Maylands Avenue
Hemel Hempstead
Hertfordshire HP2 7EZ
a division of
Simon & Schuster International Group

First published 1983 by Cassell Publishers Limited

Printed and bound in Great Britain by
The Bath Press, Avon

British Library Cataloguing in Publication Data

Information available from the British Library

ISBN 0-13-856089-7

2 3 4 5   97 96 95 94

Contents

Introduction

I have written this book to help foreign learners of English, especially those from elementary up to post-First Certificate levels who need to be able to check up on points imperfectly understood during the lesson, or to get a more complete picture than they can get from their Course Book. At the same time, my experience of using the material in class with groups of teachers of English encourages me to believe that it can help teachers as well, not so much with their own understanding of the language, as with finding useful ways of presenting or reviewing points of grammar in class.

There are three features which may at first sight seem startling in a grammar book. The first is the number of diagrams and line drawings. Every teacher knows the value of a quick sketch on the blackboard, using 'pin men' to demonstrate actions and relationships without the interference of words. Over the years I have been impressed with the illumination these simple sketches provide, and for this reason I have included a lot in this book. The second feature is the number of word lists. Such lists, and the sections on word formation, may stretch the definition of 'grammar', but they are here because they have proved useful to students, and because such things do not seem to be dealt with elsewhere. The third possibly startling feature is the use of traditional grammatical terms. Despite the inadequacy of the analysis of the language which they represent, I have continued to use them because they are still universally used and understood by teachers and students. I hope that, under these labels, users of this book will find insights and explanations which are more exciting than the labels might suggest.

In the preparation of this book, I have gone to the masters to check on points here and there, but I must acknowledge two other sources of inspiration which I regard as even more relevant to my purpose in writing this book: firstly, the generations of foreign students from many different language backgrounds whose searching and often awkward questions have forced me, willingly, to try to get to the bottom of things; and secondly, the teachers I have worked with, who are the richest source of good ideas for tackling age-old problems of grammar in fresh and illuminating ways.

I wish to acknowledge in particular the following people: Brian Graver, whose skilful surgery on the first draft undoubtedly saved the patient's life; Roger Scott, who untied a number of knots that I got myself into when trying to tell the truth about problems like the difference between *needn't* and *don't need to*; Evelyn O'Neill for helping me to get the shape of the book right during the early stages; John Walsh, of the Bournemouth English

Book Centre, for his valuable advice on such things as presentation and format; Mione Ieronymidis, who undertook the formidable task of preparing the index, and also helped in many ways to make the text more readable; and Joy McKellen, who is the ideal editor, for she knows exactly how to wield the velvet fist in the iron glove to get books out of her authors.

People from a number of teaching institutes have helped in various ways by working either on the material or on the author, as a result of which at least the former has improved considerably. I am particularly grateful to colleagues from King's School and King's College, Bournemouth; York House and ESADE in Barcelona; and staff of the Escuelas Official de Idiomas in Valencia.

The book is dedicated to my family, who put up with a lot during its production with no certainty that it would all be worthwhile in the end.

Jake Allsop
Bournemouth
August, 1982

Abbreviations

adj.	adjective
adv.	adverb
advbl	adverbial
conj.	conjunction
n.	noun
np	noun phrase
prep.	preposition
vb	verb
vi	intransitive verb
vt	transitive verb
Ø	empty category

1 Contents

1 Nouns

The Blackbird and the Beautiful Apple

The birds of the world realized that there was too much fighting, so they decided to hold a peace conference on the top floor of a large office block in London. Many species came from all parts of the world to discuss how they could learn to live together. At one o'clock on the first day, the group stopped to have their lunch. One of them pointed to a large object in the centre of the table.

'What is that?' he asked.

'Une pomme,' said the French partridge.

'Una manzana,' said the Spanish Imperial eagle.

'Ein Apfel,' shouted the bird who represented Germany.

Soon every delegate was shouting out the name of the object in the centre of the table. Of course, all the names were different. Suddenly, an English blackbird flew in through the window, landed on the table and began to eat the object.

'What are you doing?' the others cried angrily.

'I am eating this beautiful apple,' replied the blackbird between mouthfuls.

'*What* did you call it?' they all asked in one voice.

'I called it *an apple*.'

'Why?' they asked, astounded.

'Because that is what it is,' replied the blackbird, continuing to eat contentedly.

Moral: Eat first, and ask questions afterwards.

1.1   Introduction

We use **nouns** to *identify* (put names to) people, things and qualities in the world around us
e.g. student, man, house, sky, Monday, France, hope, information

> A noun answers the question *'Who is it?'* or *'What is it?'*

We may need to use several words with a noun in order to identify which person, thing or quality we mean. These groups of words are called **noun phrases (np)**.

e.g. *a foreign* student
   the student *at the back of the class*
   the student *who asked the question*

1.2   Use of capital letters

The capital letters are: ABCDEFGHIJKLMNOPQRSTUVWXYZ

The small (lower case) letters are: abcdefghijklmnopqrstuvwxyz

In modern English, most nouns are written with an initial small (lower case) letter.

However in the following cases we use capital letters.

a *Names of particular people, places or things*
John, Anna, Mr Smith, the Rolling Stones, the United States of America, the *Daily Express* (a newspaper), the *Jupiter* Symphony

b *The titles of particular people*
Mr and *Mrs* (or *Ms**); *Miss* (or *Ms**) Cynthia Brown, the *Duke* of Edinburgh, *Princess* Anne, the *Duke* of Royston, the *President* (i.e. the present holder of the office), the *Prime Minister*.

*Ms is a currently accepted neutral form which can replace Mrs or Miss.

c *Days of the week, months of the year and public holidays*

Monday	Tuesday	Wednesday	Thursday	Friday	Saturday	Sunday

January	February	March	April	May	June
July	August	September	October	November	December

Easter	Good Friday	Christmas Day	Boxing Day	New Year's Eve/Day

d *Nationalities*
the English, a Frenchman (also adjectives, → Section 4.7).

Notes

1 We also use a capital letter to start the first word of a new sentence:
The children looked out of the window.
It was snowing outside.
The personal pronoun *I* is always written with a capital.

2 Titles of books, plays and films are also written with initial capitals (usually only the important words – nouns, adjectives and verbs) e.g. *Great Expectations*, *A Student's Grammar of English*, *The Mousetrap*, *Gone with the Wind*. Chapter headings may be written with capitals or small letters.

e.g. *Chapter Three: The Management of the Economy*
Chapter Three: The management of the economy

1.3 Formation of the plural   singular = one: a student   plural = more than one: students

A   Regular plurals

1.3.1   The usual way to form the plural

Add **-s** or **-es** to the singular.

-s	-es
Most nouns	**Nouns ending in -s, -ss, -sh, -ch, -x, -z**
e.g. book books seat seats lip lips rope ropes bed beds car cars home homes	e.g. bus buses fuss fusses wish wishes match matches box boxes buzz buzzes
including	
Nouns ending in -ay, -ey, -oy, -uy	**Consonant + y → consonant + ies**
e.g. day days key keys boy boys guy guys	e.g. fly flies country countries party parties baby babies (except family names e.g. the Kennedys)
Nouns ending in -o except (Mostly abbreviations like *memo* for *memorandum* and words which were originally foreign like *concerto*)	the following nouns in -o
e.g. memo memos photo photos video videos kilo kilos piano pianos dynamo dynamos solo solos soprano sopranos studio studios	cargo cargoes domino dominoes echo echoes hero heroes potato potatoes tomato tomatoes
Nouns ending in -f except	the following nouns in -f → ves
e.g. belief beliefs chief chiefs cliff cliffs handkerchief handkerchiefs* roof roofs scarf scarfs* (*or handkerchieves, scarves)	calf calves self selves half halves shelf shelves knife knives thief thieves life lives wife wives loaf loaves wolf wolves

1.3.2 **The pronunciation of the plural endings -s and -es**

The plural ending -(e)s is pronounced in one of three ways:

[ɪz] after -s, -ss, -sh, -ch, -x, -z, -se, -ge and -dge

[z] after vowel sounds and other voiced consonants

[s] after other unvoiced consonants

e.g.

[ɪz]			[z]		[s]	
buses	(horse)	horses	days		books	
kisses	(wage)	wages	cars		seats	
wishes	(bridge)	bridges	beds		lips	
matches			dogs		ropes	
boxes			(home)	homes	cliffs	
buzzes			(line)	lines	(cake)	cakes
			(hill)	hills		
			halves			

The following table lists the voiced and unvoiced consonant sounds, and the way they are usually written at the end of a word:

Sound		Written as		Examples	
voiced	unvoiced	voiced	unvoiced	voiced	unvoiced
[b]	[p]	-b(e)	-p(e)	pub, tube	cup, hope
[d]	[t]	-d(e)	-t(e), -ght	lid, side	lift, night
[g]	[k]	-g, -gg	-c, -k, -ck	dog, egg	disc, look, back
[dʒ]	[tʃ]	-ge, dge,	-ch, -tch	wage, edge	beach, match
[v]	[f]	-ve	-f(e)	cave	wife, belief
[ð]	[θ]	-th(e)	-th	lathe	tooth
[z]	[s]	-ze, -zz	-s, -ss, -ce	size, buzz	bus, kiss, dance
[ʒ]	[ʃ]	*	-sh	–	wish
[h]	–	–	–	–	–
[m]	–	-m(e), -mb	–	home, comb	–
[n]	–	-n(e), -gn	–	pain, sign	–
[ŋ]	–	-ng	–	song	–
[l]	–	-l(e), -ll	–	fool, hill	–
[r]	–	-r(e)	–	war, share	–

*Occurs as a final consonant sound only in some words of foreign origin, e.g. *mirage* [mirɑːʒ], *garage* [gærɑːʒ]

The plural of **house** [haus] is pronounced [hauzɪz]

The ending -**th** is usually unvoiced, [θ], and the plural ending -**ths** usually remains unvoiced, [θs], e.g. depth→depths, month→months, fifth→fifths. In a few cases, the [θ] of the singular becomes voiced in the plural, so that the plural ending -**ths** becomes [ðz], e.g. bath→baths, mouth→mouths, path→paths, youth→youths

1.3.3   Plural of compound nouns

(See Section 1.7.8 for compound nouns).

a Most compound nouns form the plural in the usual way, i.e., by adding -(e)s to the second element,
   e.g. office block→office blocks boyfriend→boyfriends grown-up→grown ups lay-by→lay-bys (notice the spelling) sergeant-major→sergeant-majors

b Nouns ending in -*in-law* add the plural -**s** to the noun,
   e.g. father-in-law→fathers-in-law sister-in-law→sisters-in-law etc.

(Notice, however that we refer to the family of a wife or husband as *his/her in-laws*).

c Compound nouns which come from phrasal verbs (→Chapter 11) usually add an -**s** to the end of the compound,
   e.g. flyover→flyovers, lookout→lookouts

But note: passer-by→passers-by hanger-on→hangers-on

d Nouns ending in -**ful** usually add -**s** to the end,
   e.g. basinful→basinfuls, cupful→cupfuls handful→handfuls spoonful→spoonfuls

e If the first element is *man* or *woman* (plural *men* and *women*→Section 1.3.4), both elements are made plural,
   e.g. woman driver→women drivers
        manservant→menservants

B   Other plurals

1.3.4   Irregular plurals

The following ten nouns are completely irregular:

man→men	foot→feet	louse→lice
woman→women	tooth→teeth	mouse→mice
child→children	goose→geese	penny→pence ox→oxen

Notes

1 Notice the pronunciation of woman–women and child–children
   ['wumən] – ['wɪmɪn]   ['tʃaild] – ['tʃɪldrən]

snow
money
pence

snowballs
coins
pennies

2 The noun *penny* has a regular plural form, *pennies*. Use *pennies* to talk about the number of coins, as in

There are *five pennies on the table.*

Use *pence* to talk about the value of something, as in

The small apples are *five pence each.*

Compare this with the difference between mass and count nouns (→ Sections 1.6 and 2.3.1 **a**):

1.3.5 Words of foreign origin

A lot of words borrowed from Latin and Greek now form their plural in the regular way, i.e., by adding -s. A few have kept their original Latin or Greek plural endings.

	Ending	Regular plural	Latin/Greek plural
1	-us	-uses	-i
2	-a	-as	-ae
3	-um	-ums	-a
4	-ex	-exes	-ices
5	-ix	-ixes	-ices
6	-is	-ises	-es
7	-on	-ons	-a

The commonest words which have kept the original Latin/Greek plural endings are:

1 cactus, fungus, radius, stimulus (note also *genus*, plural *genera*)
2 alga, formula (in science), larva, vertebra
3 addendum, bacterium, curriculum, datum, erratum, medium, memorandum, stratum (These words are more often used in the plural anyway, and it is not unusual to hear people treating *data, media* and *strata* as if they were singular nouns.)
4 index (The plural *indices* is used in mathematics; the regular plural *indexes* is used in books.)
5 appendix (*appendices* in books; *appendixes* in medicine), matrix
6 analysis, axis, basis, crisis, diagnosis, hypothesis, oasis, parenthesis, synopsis, thesis (Note the difference in pronunciation between the plural nouns *analyses* and *diagnoses*: [əˈnæləsiːz], [daiəgˈnousiːz]; and the forms from the verbs *to analyse* and *to diagnose*, i.e., *he analyses* and *he diagnoses*: [ˈænalaizɪz], [diəgˈnouzɪz].
7 criterion, phenomenon

1.3.6 Nouns which do not change in the plural

a The nouns **series** and **species**:
e.g. He gave *a series* of lectures about birdwatching.
There have been several *series* of programmes on television about microchip technology.
The white rhinoceros is *an endangered species.*
There are less than *sixty species* of butterfly in the British Isles.

b Names of nationalities ending in -**ese**: (→ Section 4.7)
e.g. He *is a Chinese* and his name is Lee Yung.
The Chinese are very industrious people.
Similarly: Japanese, Lebanese, Maltese, Portuguese, Sudanese, Vietnamese. We also use nationality adjectives (→ Section 4.7) ending in -**ish** with a plural meaning
e.g. *The Spanish* are very proud of their country.

c Some animals and fish, especially those which are often hunted, or which are thought of as something to be eaten.

e.g.   *Birds*: duck, grouse, partridge, pheasant, snipe (and other game birds)
Fish: carp, fish, herring, pike, plaice, salmon, trout (and many others)
Mammals: deer, reindeer, sheep (and a few others)

Most other animals have a regular plural.

1.3.7 Nouns which look singular but are in fact plural

The commonest nouns in this group are:

cattle   clergy   dice   people   police

His *cattle are* the finest in this part of England
The Roman Catholic *clergy are* looking forward to the Pope's visit.
Dice are used in many board games.
I only want to see *those people* who *have* done all *their* work.
The police *have* admitted that *they are* baffled by the crime.

(See also → Section 1.5.)

1.3.8 Nouns ending in -s which are in fact singular

Some words *look* plural, but are in fact singular. The commonest are:

a The word **news**:
No news *is* good news. (proverb)
Bad news travels fast.   (proverb)

b The popular names of some common diseases:
measles, mumps, rickets, shingles

c The names of some games:
billiards, bowls, darts, dominoes, draughts

d The names of some activities or branches of study in -**ics**:
athletics, ceramics, classics, economics, ethics, gymnastics, linguistics, mathematics (often shortened to *maths*), phonetics, physics, politics

Note the two uses of the word *statistics*
i) Statistics is the study of probability. (statistics=a branch of study)

ii) Statistics are often misleading. (statistics=sets of figures)

1.4 Nouns which occur only in the plural

1.4.1 Names of objects (tools and clothing) which have two parts

Tools: binoculars, glasses, pliers, scales, scissors, shears, spectacles, tweezers
Clothing: braces, knickers, pants, pyjamas, shorts, tights, trousers, underpants.

Note
These objects can be expressed in the singular by using the expression **a pair of**:
e.g. a pair of glasses, a pair of trousers, a pair of pyjamas
(compare *a pair of stockings* and other items of clothing which are in two separate parts)
To express the plural of these nouns you must use the expression **X pairs of**.
e.g. I need two shirts, *three pairs of underpants* and *two pairs of pyjamas*.

1.4.2 Other nouns which occur only in plural form

There are about 50 of these. The commonest are:
arms (=weapons), clothes, contents, customs (i.e., at the frontier), earnings, goods (as in *a goods train*), lodgings (popularly called *digs*, i.e., rented accommodation with a resident landlord, often with meals provided), means, minutes (the written record of a meeting), odds (in betting), outskirts (of a town), premises, headquarters, regards (as in *Give my kind regards to your mother*), stairs, surroundings, thanks.

1.5 Words which can be either singular or plural nouns

Words which refer to *groups of people* can be considered as either singular or plural.
If you think of the group as a *single body*, that is, with everyone in the group *acting as one*, it is singular.
e.g. The new Labour government *has* announced *its* programme.
The committee *has* produced *its* final report.

If you think of all the individual people who make up the group, it can be treated as plural:
e.g. The team (=the members of the team) *are* celebrating *their* victory tonight.
The staff (=all the people who work in the place) *are* going to buy a leaving present for *their* supervisor.

The commonest words in this set are:

association	crew	majority
class (in a school)	crowd	minority
club (e.g. sports club)	family	the public
committee	gang	staff
company	government	team
council	group (e.g. pop group)	union

(Remember: the nouns *cattle, clergy, dice, people* and *police* are always plural)

1.6 Nouns which occur only in the singular form

Things which you cannot count, or cannot easily count (i.e., you cannot say there are two, three or four of them) usually occur only in the singular.

e.g. bread, coffee, cheese, milk, sugar (and many other kinds of food)
air, grass, soap, snow, water (and many other substances/ materials)
fun, happiness, hope, laughter, sleep (and many other abstract nouns)

We call these nouns **mass** (or *uncountable*) **nouns**. The characteristic of a **mass noun** is that you can only say that there is *more* or *less* of it, i.e., you can only ask the question *How much is there?* (but not *How many are there?*) about such things as bread, cheese, soap, water, fun and happiness.

Things which you *can* count (i.e., you can say there is one or there are two, three or more of them) occur in both singular and plural.

e.g. *a slice* (of bread)   three *loaves*
a cup (of coffee)   a lot of *coffee-beans*
a piece (of cheese)   many *kinds* of cheese
a pint (of milk)   several *bottles* of milk
a kilo (of sugar)   plenty of *sugar lumps*

We call these nouns **count** (or *unit* or *countable*) **nouns**. The characteristic of a **count noun** is that you can say how many there are, i.e., you can ask the question *How many are there?* about such things as slices, cups, coffee beans, bottles and lumps of sugar.
(See also → Section 2.3.1 a).

Notes

1 Be careful of words which are mass nouns in English, but which may be count nouns in other languages. The following words are **mass nouns**, i.e., *they cannot be used in the plural*:
advice, baggage, furniture, hair, homework, information, luggage, news, progress, rubbish, work
To talk about a particular example of these things, we use such expressions as:
a piece of advice, an article of luggage, a piece of furniture, a strand of hair, a piece of information, a news item
and, of course, *a lot of, plenty of* and other quantitative expressions (→ Section 3.1).

2 The word *hair* describes the uncountable mass of hair on the head or the body. You can use the plural *hairs* to refer to individual strands of hair:
He has got a good head of *hair*.
You have got several blond *hairs* on your jacket. Whose are they?

3 Be careful of words which can be either **mass** or **count** nouns depending on what they mean.

e.g. A window made of *glass*   A *glass* of wine

Would you like some *cake?*   How many *cakes* have you made?

I haven't got much *time.*   We had *a good time* at the party.

What beautiful *hair!*   Waiter, there's *a hair* in my soup!

1.7 Formation of nouns

1.7.1 Masculine and feminine

a *Different words*

bachelor–spinster	king–queen
boy–girl	lad–lass
brother–sister	landlord–landlady
cock–hen (and other common animals)	man–woman
	Mr–Mrs (Miss, Ms)
father–mother	nephew–niece
gentleman–lady	son–daughter
grandfather–grandmother	uncle–aunt
grandson–granddaughter	
husbar.d–wife	

b *Change of ending*

The commonest are:

actor–actress	manager–manageress
duke–duchess (and some other titles)	prince–princess
	usher–usherette (in a cinema)
emperor–empress	
god–goddess	waiter–waitress
hero–heroine	widow–widower

c *No distinction*

There are many words where you do not know whether the person referred to is male or female until you hear a pronoun (he/she) or possessive adjective (his/her). The commonest are:

cousin   friend   foreigner   guest   neighbour
parent   person   stranger

and many professions such as

cook   doctor   journalist   judge   lawyer   scientist
student   teacher

To make a distinction, you can use the words *male* or *female*.
e.g. a male cousin   a male nurse   a female student

In the case of professions, use *lady* or *woman*.
e.g. a lady doctor   a woman driver   a woman journalist.
(Nowadays, most people use *woman*, or do not make the distinction at all.) Notice the plural forms: *lady doctors* but *women drivers*.

Special note
Words in **-man** have the feminine form **-woman**, as in businessman–businesswoman, policeman–policewoman, salesman–saleswoman, spokesman–spokeswoman.

1.7.2   Endings to describe size

English has very few such endings:
-let = something small, as in *leaflet* and *booklet*

-ling = something small, as in *duckling*

-ling = something we have a poor opinion of, as in *weakling, hireling*

But we usually use adjectives:
for something small: *little, nice little* or *tiny little*
for something big: *big, great big, huge.*

In recent years, especially in advertising, the prefix **mini-** and the suffix **-ette** have become very popular ways of describing a small version of something:
e.g. minicab, mini-computer, miniskirt; cigarette, kitchenette, launderette, lecturette, maisonette (a sort of flat).

Even scientific prefixes like **micro** (very small) and **macro** (very big) are beginning to be used, at least by the media:
e.g. microchip technology   macro-economics.

1.7.3   Endings which describe small and/or repeated actions and small objects

You can sometimes get a feeling for the meaning of a word by looking at such endings as *-inkle, ingle, -ggle, -tter, -mble, -bble, -ddle* and *-ttle,*

e.g. **-inkle**: twinkle, winkle
-ingle: jingle, tangle, tingle
-ggle: giggle, wriggle
-tter: chatter, flutter, mutter, pitter-patter, stutter
-mble: mumble, ramble, rumble, stumble, thimble (from *thumb*)
-bble: bubble, pebble, quibble, rabble, rubble, stubble
-ddle: cuddle, muddle, paddle, puddle
-ttle: little, tittle-tattle

(There are a number of nouns with these endings where the idea of smallness or repetition is not present, e.g. *ankle, letter, single, middle*)
(See also → Section 7.7.2.)

1.7.4   Professions

To describe the person who does something, we use various suffixes:

(e)r
The suffix **(e)r** may be attached to a verb or a noun, or to a word which no longer exists separately:

VERB+(E)R: bake→baker, build→builder, design→**designer**,
manage→manager, speak→speaker,
teach→teacher

NOUN+(E)R: engine→engineer, football→footballer,
garden→gardener, law→lawyer,
photograph→photographer*, trumpet→**trumpeter**.

Others: butcher, carpenter, grocer, plumber, usher

*Note the stress: 'photograph→pho'tographer

-or
The commonest are:
   actor, author, director, doctor, editor, professor, solicitor,
   surveyor, tailor.

-ist, -ian, -ant *and* **-ent**
(Notice where the stress moves from one syllable to another)

-ist
a *players of some instruments:*
   e.g. 'cello→'cellist, pi'ano→'pianist, 'violin→vio'linist,
   trom'bone→trom'bonist

b *-ology   -ologist:*
   e.g. ge'ology→ge'ologist, orni'thology→orni'thologist

c *-ics   icist:*
   e.g. 'physics→'physicist, eco'nomics→e'conomist

d *others in -ist:*
   e.g. 'science→'scientist, 'telephone→te'lephonist,
   'chemistry→'chemist, 'art→'artist

-ian
a *-ic(s)   -ician:*
   e.g. mathe'matics→mathema'tician, 'music→mu'sician,
   'politics→poli'tician, sta'tistics→statis'tician

b *others in -ian*
   e.g. 'history→his'torian, 'library→li'brarian

-ant
   e.g. a'ccount→a'ccountant, a'ssist→a'ssistant,
   a'ttend→a'ttendant, con'sult→con'sultant
   Also the words de'pendant, in'formant, in'habitant

-ent
   e.g. 'resident, superin'tendent

1.7.5 Abstract nouns

An **abstract noun** describes a quality or an idea like *hope, beauty*
or *information*, in contrast to a **concrete noun**, which describes a
real thing or person, such as *an egg, a house* or *a girl*.

Here are the commonest endings of abstract nouns, which are added to **nouns**, **verbs** (see Chapter 7) or **adjectives** (see Chapter 4):

-tion (pronounced [ʃn] or possibly [ʃən])
e.g. inform→information situate→situation solve→solution
define→definition promote→promotion;
Also, nation, station

-sion (pronounced [ʒn] or possibly [ʒən]
Verbs ending in **-de** form nouns in **-sion**.
e.g. explode→explosion persuade→persuasion
invade→invasion conclude→conclusion decide→decision

-sion and **-ssion** (pronounced [ʃn]
Verbs ending in **-vert** form nouns in **-version**.
e.g. convert→conversion pervert→perversion

Some verbs in **-d** or **-de** form nouns in **-ssion** pronounced [ʃn])
e.g. succeed→succession   proceed→procession
recede→recession

-ment
Mostly formed from verbs:
e.g. amuse→amusement judge→judgement excite→excitement
argue→argument state→statement arrange→arrangement

-ness
Mostly formed from adjectives:
e.g. sad→sadness ready→readiness useful→usefulness
red→redness busy→business (prounouced ['bIznIs]).

-ance, -ence, -ancy, -ency
e.g. independent→independence attend→attendance
account→accountancy efficient→efficiency
Also, nuisance, conscience, emergency

-y, -ty, -ity, -iety
Many of these abstract nouns have a related adjective:

- **-y:** 'comic(al)-'comedy, har'monious-'harmony, 'jealous-'jealousy, 'rival-'rivalry, 'tragedy-'tragic.
  Also, systems of government like au'tocracy, de'mocracy, plu'tocracy, 'monarchy, 'oligarchy, 'anarchy.
- **-ty:** 'pity (*adj* 'pitiful), 'beauty (*adj* 'beautiful), 'loyalty (*adj* 'loyal).
- **-ity:** 'dense-'density, 'equal-e'quality, hi'larious–hi'larity, 'scarce-'scarcity
- **-iety:** 'anxious-anx'iety, no'torious-noto'riety, 'proper-pro'priety (compare '*property*) 'social ('sociable)-so'ciety, 'various ('variable)-va'riety

Adjectives ending in **-able** or **ible** form nouns in **-ability** or
-ibility respectively. For example:
  -able **-ability**: 'probable→ proba'bility re'spectable→ **respec-
ta'bility**
  -ible **-ibility**: 'possible→ possi'bility
  re'sponsible→ responsi'bility

Examples of other endings

-t and -th
-t: height (*adj.* high), weight (*verb*, weigh)
-th: formed from adjectives, often with a change of vowel
        sound and/or spelling: broad→ breadth deep→ depth
        long→ length wide→ width

-ship
  relation→ relationship scholar→ scholarship
  workman→ workmanship

-ism
Used to describe all sorts of philosophies and other systems of
belief. For example:

Adjective	The person	The belief
classical	classicist	classicism
communist	communist	communism
conservative	conservative	conservatism
defeatist	defeatist	defeatism
liberal	liberal	liberalism
optimistic	optimist	optimism
pessimistic	pessimist	pessimism
realistic	realist	realism
romantic	romantic	romanticism
socialist	socialist	socialism

Various
-al: arrival (*vb* arrive), committal (*vb* commit), denial (*vb*
        deny), dismissal (*vb* dismiss), proposal (*vb* propose),
        refusal (*vb* refuse), withdrawal (*vb* withdraw)
-dom: kingdom (*n* king), wisdom (*adj* wise)
-hood: likelihood (*adj* likely), neighbourhood (*n* neighbour)
-our: behaviour (*vb* behave), candour (*adj* candid),
        demeanour, endeavour, humour (*adj* humorous),
        favour, flavour, rancour, valour.
-or: horror (*adj* horrible), terror (*adj* terrible)
-ure: departure (*vb* depart)

1.7.6 Gerunds (verbal nouns)

Many useful nouns to describe an *activity* can be formed by
adding **-ing** to a verb. For example:

Sporting/healthy activities
climbing, dancing, fishing, horse-riding, gliding, jogging,
potholing, skiing, skating, shooting, surfing, **swimming**, **walking**

Other activities and habits
birdwatching, drawing, drinking, eating, hitch-hiking, painting, sketching, smoking, stamp-collecting, touring, typing

The language skills are: listening, speaking, reading and writing

1.7.7 Noun or verb?

There are many words in English which can be nouns or verbs without any change of form.
e.g. I've got a lot of *work* to do. (*noun*)
I *work* in a factory. (*verb*)
Other common examples are:
charge, comment, copy, cut, dance, design, diet, drink, hope, hurry, lift, look, love, offer, notice, paint, plan, post, promise, queue, reply, shout, sleep, smell, stay, stock, stop, study, swim, taste, travel, visit, walk, welcome, worry.

Notes

1 There are about fifty words in English where the stress is on the first syllable when they are used as nouns, and on the second syllable when they are used as verbs. For example:

noun – *stress on the first syllable*	**verb** – *stress on the second syllable*
I have a present for you	May I present Mrs
'present	Kennedy? pre'sent

The commonest words of this kind are:
export, extract, import, increase, permit, present, protest, record, survey, suspect

You might also meet:
abstract, conduct, conflict, digest, discount, escort, insult, perfume, produce, progress, rebel, refill, refund

2 There is a change of pronunciation between *use* as a noun and as a verb: *use* (noun) [jus]   *use* (verb) [juz]

3 In British English, there is a change of spelling between *practice* (noun) and *practise* (verb)

4 There is a change of both spelling and pronunciation between the noun *advice* and the verb *advise*; and the noun *device* and the verb *devise*:
advice(noun)   [əd'vaɪs]   advise (verb)   [əd'vaɪz]
device (noun)   [dɪ'vaɪs]   devise (verb)   [dɪ'vaɪz]

1.7.8 Formation of compound nouns

Words like *policeman, bedroom, swimming-pool* and *steam engine* are compound nouns. Compound nouns are very common, and new ones are being invented all the time.

a *Meaning of the two parts*
The second part (man, room, pool, engine) identifies the object or person we are talking about. The first part (police, bed, swimming, steam) tells us what kind or type of object/person, or describes the purpose of the object:

A *policeman* is a man who works in the police force.
A *bedroom* is a room with a bed, i.e., a room for sleeping in.
A *swimming-pool* is a pool for swimming in.
A *steam-engine* is a type of engine which is driven by steam.

	man		police	
	room		bed	
	pool		swimming	
	engine		steam	

<table>
<tr><td>this tells us
who or what</td><td>this tells *what type* or *what purpose*</td></tr>
</table>

Thus, for example, a house*boat* is a kind of boat, but a boat*house* is a kind of building.

 tea cups

 cups of tea

Note:
Notice the difference between such similar expressions as
a teacup, i.e. a cup designed to contain tea, and
a cup of tea, i.e. a cup filled with tea.

a milkbottle and *a bottle of milk*

 a matchbox and *a box of matches*

a cigarette packet and *a packet of cigarettes*

 a flower vase and *a vase of flowers*

b *Pronunciation*
The stress in compound nouns falls on the first part:*
 po'liceman   'swimming-pool
 'bedroom   'steam engine

*In a few cases, there may be equal stress on both parts, e.g. 'head'master as well as 'headmaster. Most compounds from phrasal verbs (→ Chapter 11) are regular, i.e., they have the stress on the first part, but note 'passer-'by and 'hanger-'on.

In this way, you can distinguish a compound noun like
'greenhouse (i.e., a place where we grow plants) or 'blackbird
(i.e., a species of songbird, *Turdus merula*) from a simple noun
with an adjective like green 'house (i.e., a house painted green)
or black 'bird (i.e., any bird with black plumage):

Compound	Adjective + noun
a 'greenhouse	a green 'house
a 'blackbird	a black 'bird

Note: It is important to distinguish between nouns used as the
first part of a compound or as simple adjectives:

COMPOUND NOUN   a 'woman-hater = someone who hates women
ADJECTIVE + NOUN   a woman 'driver = a female driver
COMPOUND NOUN   a 'ladybird = a species of beetle, *Coccinella X-punctata*
ADJECTIVE + NOUN   a lady 'doctor = a female doctor
COMPOUND NOUN   a 'schoolboy = a pupil
ADJECTIVE + NOUN   school 'premises = the buildings and grounds
of the school
(The same distinction occurs in such pairs as
an 'English teacher = someone who teaches English and
an English 'teacher = a teacher who is English.)

c *Spelling*
The two parts of a compound noun may be written
  i) *as one word* e.g. bedroom, armchair
  ii) *with a hyphen* e.g. swimming-pool, air-brake
  iii) *as two words* e.g. steam engine, waiting room.

Very common compounds, especially those which are long-
established or which consist of two short words, are written
as one word,
e.g. breakfast, cupboard, homework.
All others may be written as one word or with a hyphen or
as two words. Unfortunately there are no clear rules about
this – even dictionaries do not always agree!
We advise you to write common compounds (ones you know)
as one word. In other cases, or when you are not sure, write
the compound as two words.

d *Patterns*
The table gives examples of various combinations of noun,
verb, adjective and adverbial in compound nouns (see
opposite):

A list of common compound nouns is given in Appendix I p 30.
A list of common compound nouns formed from phrasal verbs
(→ Chapter 11) is given in Appendix II p 31.

	Noun		Verb	Adverbial
Noun	history teacher motorcycle oil well bedclothes girlfriend	daylight goldfish fire engine snowball babysitter	rainfall haircut book-keeping horse-riding	'passer-'by 'hanger-'on
Verb	turntable washing machine punchcard chewing gum swimming-pool			throwaway cutout lookout
Adjective	greenhouse blackboard shorthand heavyweight highbrow blueprint		'dry-'cleaning	
Adverbial	onlooker bystander		offset outlet income	

1.8 The possessive form of nouns

1.8.1 Meaning

The possessive form is used mainly with *people, groups of people* (including *countries*) and *animals* to show their relationship to someone or something. *Possession* is only one of the relationships which this form describes. For example:

Possessor		Object related to possessor		Expressed in possessive form
	Michael +		*some books* which belong to him	= They are *Michael's books*
	Anna +		she goes to *this* *school*	= This is *Anna's school*
	the boss +	EVERYONE MUST WORK HARDER	*an idea* which he has had	= It is *the boss's idea*
	the boys +		this is *the bedroom* where they sleep	= This is *the boys' bedroom*
USA	+		*nuclear missiles*	= *USA's nuclear missiles*

1.8.2 The formation of the possessive

The rule is:

> Add 's to the noun.
>
> If the noun is a plural ending in -s, just add '

For example:

+'s	Michael → Michael's	women → women's
	Anna → Anna's	children → children's
	the boss → the boss's	
	the boys → the boys'	the Smiths → the Smiths'
	ladies → ladies'	(the Smiths = Mr and Mrs
	men → men's	Smith and their family)

Notice the construction of possessive phrases:

Michael	+	some books	→ [Michael + 's]	+	[s~~ome~~ books]	=	Michael's books
Anna	+	this school	→ [Anna + 's]	+	[t~~his~~ school]	=	Anna's school
the boss	+	an idea	→ [the boss + 's]	+	[a~~n~~ idea]	=	the boss's idea
the boys	+	the bedroom	→ [the boys + ']	+	[t~~he~~ bedroom]	=	the boys' bedroom
USA	+	nuclear missiles	→ [USA + 's]	+	[nuclear missiles]	=	USA's nuclear missiles

Notes

1 Compound nouns and short noun phrases (see Section 1.1) usually add 's:
mother-in-law → his mother-in-law's opinion
sergeant major → a sergeant major's duties
the Duke of Edinburgh → the Duke of Edinburgh's latest speech

2 *Names ending in -s*
There are a few first names which end in -s (e.g. Thomas) and quite a lot of surnames or family names (e.g., Davies, Edwards, Jones, Marks) which end in -s. In speaking we indicate the possessive by adding the sound [ɪz] to the end of the name:

Thomas ['tɒməs] ['tɒməsɪz]
Jones ['dʒoʊnz] ['dʒoʊnzɪz]

Although the written form may be either 's or ', we advise you to write 's: Thomas's   Jones's

1.8.3 Pronunciation of the possessive ending

When you have added 's to a noun, pronounce it according to the rules for the pronunciation of plural -s (← Section 1.3.2.):
unvoiced [s] e.g. cat's, Philip's, the staff's
voiced [z] e.g. the dog's, Alan's, Anna's, the council's
voiced [ɪz] e.g. the horse's, George's, the boss's, Selfridge's

1.8.4 Other uses of the possessive form

a The possessive form is also used with some expressions of time, and in a few fixed expressions:

a day's work	For heaven's sake (and other
a month's salary	expressions with *sake*)
a fortnight's holiday	at the water's edge
yesterday's newspaper	a stone's throw from here (=not far
tomorrow's	from here)
programme	a pound's worth of stamps
in two years' time	

It can also be used with ships, boats and other vehicles (e.g. *the ship's crew, a car's top speed*), but we advise you to use the construction THE X OF THE/A Y to describe the relationship between things (i.e., not people), as in *the crew of the ship* and *the top speed of a car.*

Reminder: With things, possession is often expressed by compound nouns of the pattern NOUN+NOUN, e.g., bedclothes (=the clothes of the bed), doorbell (=the bell of the door), television screen (=the screen of the television).

Note: Use the **of**-construction (THE X OF THE Y) with people in cases where you might be misunderstood. For example:

This is a photograph of the woman I love.

is easier to understand than

This is the woman's photograph I love.

(which could mean that I love the photograph rather than the woman!)

or

This is the woman I love's photograph.

(which is ungrammatical and unclear).

b *Expressions like 'at the grocer's'*
We often refer to shops, churches, restaurants, colleges, etc., by the name of the owner, the founder, etc:

Shop	*Surgery/office*	*Church*
the butcher's	the dentist's	Saint Joseph's
the florist's	the doctor's	
the greengrocer's	the optician's	*College*
the grocer's	the vet's	Saint John's
the ironmonger's		
the jeweller's	*Restaurant*	
Harrod's	Luigi's	
Macy's	Tiddy Dol's	
Marks and Spencer's	Wheeler's	
Selfridge's		
Woolworth's		

Examples
I bought it at Woolworth's.
I've got to go to the doctor's at four o'clock.
He was at Saint John's.
Is Saint Joseph's a Catholic church?
We had dinner at Luigi's last night.

1.9   Appendix I: A list of common compound nouns

adding machine
air-conditioning
aircraft
airport
armchair
armpit
ashtray
baby clothes
baby-sitter
backache
bank clerk
bathing costume
bathroom
bath towel
beachbag
bedroom
blackbird
blackboard
bloodstain
blood test
blueprint
boardroom
boiling point
bookcase
book-keeping
booklist
bookshop
boyfriend
bricklayer
briefcase
building site
building society
bus stop
campsite
carving knife
cassette recorder
chairman
chessboard
chess set
cigarette lighter
cleaning lady
coalmine
coat-hanger
coffee cup
coffee pot
credit card

crossword puzzle
dance hall
daybreak
daylight
deckchair
dining room
dinner jacket
diving board
doorbell
drawing board
dressing gown
dressmaking
drinking water
dustbin
earache
earrings
earthquake
exit visa
eyebrows
eyelashes
eyelids
filing cabinet
film star
finger nail
fingerprints
fingertips
fire engine
fireplace
fireworks
flashlight
flower bed
football
freezing point
frying pan
girlfriend
goldfish
golfball
golf club
graveyard
greenhouse
hairbrush
haircut
hairdo
hairdresser
hair style
handbag

handshake
handwriting
headache
headlamp
headquarters
hold-all
homework
horse riding
houseboat
housekeeping
housemaid
housewife
ice-cream
ice-cube
lampshade
landlady
landlord
landslide
letter-box
letter-head
letter writing
lipstick
living room
machine gun
man-eater
mantelpiece
mincemeat
motorbike
motorcycle
motorway
mudguard
nailfile
nightdress
nightgown
notepaper
notice board
office worker
oil well
orange juice
pain-killer
paintbrush
paperback
parking meter
payday
penknife
photocopy

pipeline
playboy
policeman
policewoman
pocket book
postcard
post office
power station
railway
rainbow
raindrop
rainfall
record-player
rush hour
safety belt
salt cellar
saucepan
scrapbook
screwdriver
self-control
sewing machine
shoelace
shopkeeper
shoplifting
shopping bag
shopping list
sideboard
side road
sightseeing
signet ring
sitting room
sleeping bag
snowball
snowflake
space ship
sports car
sports jacket
staff meeting
step ladder
stomach ache
stop watch
sunbathing
sunglasses
sunrise
sunset
sunshine

sweetheart	tennis ball	travel agent	window-shopping
swimming pool	tennis player	turntable	windscreen-wiper
swimsuit	toenails	typewriter	word processor
tablecloth	toilet paper	waiting room	workbench
talcum powder	tongue-twister	washbasin	workbook
tape measure	toolbox	walking stick	working hours
tape recorder	toothache	wallpaper	wrapping paper
teacup	toothbrush	washing machine	writing paper
teapot	toothpaste	weightlifter	yearbook
teaspoon	toothpick	wet suit	yes man
telephone call	traffic lights	windfall	zip fastener
television set	traffic warden	windowpane	zero hour

1.10 Appendix II: Common nouns (and adjectives) formed from phrasal verbs

a breakdown (of a machine or a system)

a breakdown (=an analysis of accounts or statistics)

a break-in (a burglary)

a breakthrough (e.g. a scientific advance)

the break-up of a relationship

an outbreak (=an epidemic)

a build-up

an outburst (=a violent explosion of emotions)

cast-off clothing

to make a comeback

the outcome (=the result)

a comedown (=reduction of status or standard of living)

an outcry (=a strong protest)

the cut-off point

a cutback (e.g. in costs or expenses)

a drawback (=a disadvantage)

a drive-in cinema or bank

a drop out (someone who rejects the social system by e.g., not completing his/her education)

a drop-off (e.g. in interest or attendance)

a fall-out shelter (*fall-out* is the radioactive dust from a nuclear explosion)

feedback (the information you get back from a computer; response to something you have done)

a flyover (a road over another road for fast-moving traffic)

the getaway car (used by thieves)

a giveaway remark (=a remark which reveals too much)

a go-between (=an intermediary)

an ongoing process (=continuing)

a hand-out (something given as an act of charity) or (an information or publicity leaflet)

a hold-up (=a delay, or an armed robbery)

a hangover (something, often unwanted, which has survived from an earlier time)

the layout (e.g. of a page)

the outlay (the money you need to spend to start a project)

an overlay (used with an overhead projector)

a letdown (a disappointment)

an outlet (e.g. a market for your goods)

an inlet (e.g. the place where something is drawn into a machine)

the outlook (=the prospects for the future)

a lookout (=a man on guard)

'it's your own lookout.'=it is your fault or your responsibility

makeup (=lipstick, powder, etc., to beautify the face)

the payoff (=the benefit or profit from an enterprise)

an underpass (=a road for through traffic under another road. Compare *flyover*)

a pull-in (e.g. a roadside shop or cafe)

a pullover (a sort of sweater which you 'pull over' your head)

output (=production)

input (=e.g. the effort put into a project, or the information initially fed into a computer)

a put-up job (an action intended to deceive)

offputting (discouraging, unattractive)

a runabout (e.g. a small town car)

the run-up (e.g. the time just before an important event such as an election)

a runaway success (outstanding, greater than anyone expected)

a rundown (usually a verbal analysis of a situation to inform another person)

a see-through blouse (=transparent)

a send-up (=a satirical representation of someone or something official)

a wonderful send-off (=a farewell ceremony for, e.g. newly-weds)

a set-back (=an interruption to the progress of a project)

the set-up (=the way things are organized; the situation)

at the outset (=at the very beginning of a project)

the shutdown (=the time a plant or factory is closed for maintenance)

a sit-in (=the illegal occupation of a building as a form of protest)

a slip-up (=a mistake or an accident which interrupts a plan)

a stand-in (=a substitute)

on standby (=a method of getting a cheap flight by arriving at the airport without a booking in the hope that there will be an empty seat)

(or=being ready to do something if necessary, e.g. replace a sick colleague)

outstanding (excellent, remarkable)

a takeaway (a place where you can buy and take away ready-cooked food)

the intake (=the new students at the beginning of a course)

the takeoff (=the departure of an aeroplane, the moment of leaving the ground)

a takeoff (=a send-up, i.e. a satirical impersonation)

a takeover (in business, the method by which one company gains control of another)

a throwaway razor

a downturn (in business, a decline)

an upturn (in business, an improvement)

a good turnout (=a good attendance at a meeting or other event)

a walkover (=an easy victory)

a washout (slang=a total failure or disaster)

2 Contents

2 The articles (*a(n)/the*) and the demonstratives (*this/that*)

The Elephant and the Mouse

An elephant and a mouse fell in love and decided to get married. When the elephant told her father, he said: 'Don't be silly, an elephant can't marry a mouse.'

When the mouse told his mother, she said: 'Don't be silly, mice don't marry elephants.'

So the elephant, who was very musical, became a pianist, and the mouse, who had a very good voice, became a singer. They toured the world together for many years, giving concerts and bringing pleasure to everyone who heard them.

Moral: There is more than one way to live in harmony.

A The articles

2.1 Form and pronunciation

A, the indefinite article, is pronounced [ə] before words beginning with a consonant or a consonant sound. **A** becomes **an**, pronounced [ən] before words beginning with a vowel or a vowel sound.

> [ə]: a mouse   a new school   a university
> [ən]: an elephant   an old school   an umbrella   an hour*   an honest* man

There is no plural form of the indefinite article. The plural of *a dog* is *dogs*, without an article.

The, the definite article, is pronounced [ðə] before words beginning with a consonant or a consonant sound; it is pronounced [ði] before words beginning with a vowel or a vowel sound.

It is used with both singular and plural nouns.

> [ðə]: the town   the towns   the new school   the union   the house
> [ði]: the eye   the eyes   the old school   the Underground   the hour*

*In a few words, the initial 'h' is not pronounced: *hour, honest, honour, heir*, and their derivatives (*hourly, honesty*, etc.)

Note

a or **one**? Think of *one* as a number, in contrast with two, three, and so on. *One* also contrasts with *another* and *the other(s)*:

e.g. There is more than one way to live in harmony.
There are three telephones in the office. I've got one, and the boss has got the other two.

| **2.2 The uses of the articles:** *the* or *a(n)?* | We use **a(n)** when the object is not specified; we use **the** when the object is specified. (*To specify* is to say which particular one you mean out of a group of objects.) |

A Not known and not specified a(n)	B Known but not specified a(n)	C Known and specified **the**

A I always like to have *a* book by my bedside.
  → any, we don't know which one

B I received *a* book about gardening for my birthday.
  → a particular one, but not (yet) specified

C 'I have a book about carpentry and a book about gardening.
  Which do you want to see?'
  'Could I see *the* book about gardening, please?'
  → A particular one, and specified

(ALL) BOOKS

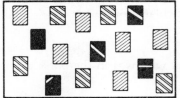   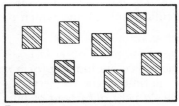   

A any one of these   B a particular one of these   C this one!

2.2.1 A Not known and not specified

a a(n) = *any, it doesn't matter which:*
I've never seen *an elephant.* (=any elephant)
I'm looking for *a man* to help me with my work. (=any man)

b a(n) = *any member of the class to which the member belongs*
A(n) in the sentence *an elephant cannot marry a mouse* means:
it is not possible for **any** *elephant* (it does not matter which
elephant) *to marry* **any** *mouse* (it does not matter which
mouse).
In such sentences, A(N)+NOUN... =ANY MEMBER OF THE CLASS
It is most often used in definitions, i.e., in statements which
tell us who or what something is:
e.g. *a ruler* is an instrument for drawing straight lines.
  a screwdriver is a tool for driving in screws.
  a butcher is a man who sells meat.
  a bird is an animal with feathers.

It can also be used in statements of facts or rules about any
member of the class, i.e., to say what is always true:
e.g. An elephant cannot marry a mouse.
However, in such cases, it is more usual to use the plural
(→ Section 2.3.1)
e.g. *Mice* do not marry *elephants.*
  Cars must be fitted with *safety belts.*

Note

When you are talking about specific objects, rather than objects *in general* (→2.2.3d), you must use the plural, as in the notice in car parks which reads:

Cars are parked at owners' risk. (i.e., specific cars in a specific situation).

For this reason, we advise you always to use the plural when you want to make statements of fact or rules about things or people (see also→ Section 2.3.1a concerning generalizations).

c a(n) = per

60 mph (or *60 m.p.h.*) means *sixty miles per hour*, but we often say *sixty miles **an** hour*. Similarly, *three times **a** week, twice **a** month, ten pence **a** kilo*, etc.

2.2.2 B Known but not yet specified

a a(n) = *a particular one, not yet specifically identified*

A(n) in the sentence ***An** elephant and **a** mouse fell in love* means *a particular (individual) elephant and a particular (individual) mouse . . .* , but we do not know yet which particular elephant and which particular mouse.

Other examples are:

I've got *a good job* at last.

The police are looking for *a man* who was in the bank at the time of the robbery.

She's *a very old friend* of ours.

A Mr Smith called to see you this morning, sir.

In the last sentence, *a Mr Smith* (i.e., a man called Smith) means that the man who called can be identified from the limited number of men called Smith who might call to see you.

b a(n) = *a kind of or an example of*
  e.g. The mouse had *a good voice.*
     Polignac is *a French brandy* that I haven't tried yet.
     We have *a good climate.*
     What *a beautiful day!*
     What *a strange man* he is!
     I've never heard of *such a thing!*

c a(n) = *a particular member of the class*
  e.g. The elephant became *a pianist*, and the mouse became *a
     singer.*
     My father is *an engineer*, but I want to be *a lawyer* when
     I grow up.
     To be *a good MP* you must be *a good speaker.*

**2.2.3 C Known and
specified**

The characteristic meaning of **the** is that the object is known and
specifically identified.

a the = *the one(s) already referred to*
  e.g. An elephant and a mouse fell in love. When *the elephant*
     told her father . . .
     I've got an orange and some apples. Who wants *the
     orange?*
     All right, you have *the orange*, and I'll have *the apples.*

Titles of books, plays and films may also use **the** to introduce the
people or objects dealt with in the story: *The Elephant and the
Mouse; The Longest Day; The Mousetrap.*

Note: Sometimes, for dramatic effect, stories begin with **the** even
though the people and things referred to are not known to the
reader:
     The old man sat in *the* corner, his eyes fixed on *the* body on
     the floor . . .
The effect is to make you want to know what is going on (Who
is the old man? Why is there a body on the floor? Where is all
this taking place? **The** = somebody knows all these things, but ·
you do not – you feel 'left out', and so you read on in order to
find out.)

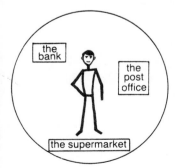

my universe or
sphere of interest

b the = *the one(s) which can be identified from the situation (the
context)*
Every person has a personal 'universe' or 'sphere of interest' in
which everything is known and identified. I say:
     'I must go to *the bank* and *the post office.* Then I'd better
     call in at *the supermarket* on *the way back.*

If my listener knows or shares my universe (e.g. he lives in
the same town), he will know which bank, which post office
and which supermarket I mean.

Other examples are:

> There's a funny-looking animal *in the garden.*
> You look ill: you ought to go and see *the doctor.*

Common expressions from different spheres of interest:

A building	**A town**	**A country**
in the bedroom	on the ground	in the country
in the kitchen	in the street	on the beach
at the door	at the cinema	in the mountains
in the garden	at the station	across the sea
on the landing	across the road	at the seaside
in the corridor	in the (town) centre	in the South
on the second floor	on the Underground	all over the
down the stairs	in the supermarket	country
in the lift	over the bridge	

Within our local or national sphere of interest, we use **the** to refer to institutions and individuals that have authority:

Institutions   the Police, the Church, the Law, the Clergy, the Establishment, the Government

Individuals   the Prime Minister, the President, the Managing Director, the Principal, the Captain, the Head(master), the Doctor

(Notice that we leave out *the* when we use the individual's surname or when we address him/her directly: *I want to speak to the Captain*, but *I want to speak to Captain Brown* or *Good morning, Captain.*)

c **the** = the only one(s)

The widest sphere of interest is, literally, our Universe, which contains objects which we regard as unique, e.g. the earth, the sun and the moon:

> They toured *the world* together.
> *The earth* goes round *the sun.*
> She lives in *the United States* now.
> 'Fly me to *the moon* and let me play among *the stars*' (Popular song)

We also use **the** to refer to **superlatives** (→ Section 4.5.1) and **ordinal numbers** (→ Section 4.6)

Superlatives   The best ...   The lowest ...   The most recent ...   The only ...

Ordinals   The first ...   The second ..., etc. (Also, The last ..., The next ...).

d **the** = *one (imaginary) member of the class to represent the whole class*

When we wish to talk or think about a class of objects *in the abstract*, we can use THE + SINGULAR NOUN. It can be used in definitions (e.g., *The horse is a domestic animal*), but it is best

Abstract The Hawaiian goose

Concrete Hawaiian geese

used in statements of *opinions or facts which have not always been true*:

> e.g. *The Hawaiian goose* is in danger of extinction.
> *The tractor* has replaced *the horse* on *the modern farm*.

Note: We can also make such general statements using the plural (without **the**); in case we are thinking *in the concrete*, i.e. we picture the objects in our mind:

> e.g. *Hawaiian geese* are in danger of extinction.
> *Tractors* have replaced *horses* on *modern farms*.
> (→ Section 2.3.1)

(See also note on *cars are parked at owners' risk* ← Section 2.2.1b.)

e THE + ADJECTIVE = *the whole class of people described by the adjective*
(Adjectives → Chapter 4).

> e.g. We have made special arrangements for *the handicapped* and *the disabled*.
> Our aim is not to make *the rich* poorer, but to make *the poor* richer. (F. D. Roosevelt)
> *The young* do not listen to *the old*.

Note that *the rich, the poor, the handicapped* are *plural* in meaning: *rich people, poor people, handicapped people*. To refer to one such person, you would have to say: *the rich man, the poor man, the handicapped person*.

2.3 The uses of the articles: with *the* or without *the*?

2.3.1 General and particular statements

Count nouns

a dog

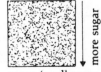

dogs (= all dogs, dogs in general)

Mass nouns

sugar

sugar (= all sugar, sugar in general)

As we have seen (← Section 2.2.3), the article **the** is used to specify or identify *which particular object* we are talking about: it is associated with *particular statements*. So, when we leave out **the**, we are making *general statements* about objects which have *not* been specified or identified.

a *General statements involving* **mass** *and* **count** *nouns*
To make generalizations, we use:
> the plural of **count nouns** without **the**, e.g. dogs
> **mass nouns*** without **the**, e.g. sugar.

> e.g. *Dogs* make good *pets*.
> *Sugar* is bad for you.
> *Englishmen* make good *husbands*.
> *Money* cannot buy *happiness*, but it's nice to be miserable in *comfort*.
> *Death* is *Nature's* way of telling you to slow down. (graffiti on the London Underground)

Notice particularly that abstract nouns like *happiness, death, nature, comfort, life*, are used without the article in such **general** statements.

*Mass nouns have no plural form (← Section 1.6).

b *Particular statements*

As soon as you specify *which particular thing(s) or person(s)* you are talking about, you will need to use **the**:

e.g. *The dogs in our street* are very noisy.
The sugar I like best (=the kind of sugar I like best . . .) is called Demerara sugar.
The Englishmen we met at the conference were all married.
What about *the money you owe me*?

The phrases *in our street, I like best, we met at the conference,* restrict and identify (specify) what we are talking about. They answer the question *Which particular one(s)*?

Notes

1 Adjectives and adjectival phrases (→ Chapter 4) added to nouns do not necessarily restrict and identify (specify):

dogs	*working dogs*	= a class of dogs distinct from *pet dogs* or *show dogs*
sugar	*white sugar*	= a kind of sugar distinct from *brown sugar* or *Demerara sugar*
music	*classical music*	= a kind of music distinct from *pop music*, etc.
history	*classical history*	= history which deals with the classical period, as distinct from *modern history*
mothers	*mothers who go out to work*	= *working mothers*

The words *working, white, classical* and *who go out to work* in these examples do not answer the question, *Which particular dogs? Which particular sugar? Which particular example of music?* etc., but the question *What kind of . . .* ?

For example:

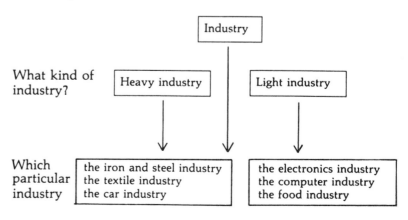

2 When you want to distinguish one particular *example* of the thing from another, you will need to use **the**. For example: in this pair of sentences, A and B are talking about French wine and Italian wine in general:

A 'Which do you prefer, *French wine* or *Italian wine*?'
B 'Generally I prefer *French wine*.'

But in this pair of sentences, they are talking about *particular examples* of French and Italian wine:

A 'Now, try a glass of this French wine, and a glass of this Italian wine, and then tell me which you prefer.'
B 'Oh, *the Italian wine*, definitely. I find *the French wine* rather acid.'

Note: **The** is also used in this way to express the idea *the right kind of*
e.g. This snow is just *the* snow for skiing.

2.3.2 Other cases where *the* is used

a *Geographical and other place names*

Use **the** in place names which contain a count noun.

Union	the Soviet Union the Union of South Africa
Kingdom	the United Kingdom the Hashemite Kingdom of Jordan
State(s)	the United States of America the Gulf States
Republic	the Republic of Panama the German Democratic Republic
Sea	the Red Sea the Black Sea the North Sea the Mediterranean (Sea) the Caspian (Sea)
Ocean	The Indian Ocean the Atlantic (Ocean) the Pacific (Ocean)
Gulf	the Gulf of Mexico the Gulf (=the Persian or Arabian Gulf)
Canal	the Suez Canal the Panama Canal the Kiel Canal
Channel	the English Channel
Straits	the Straits of Dover
River	the River Thames* the River Nile
Mountain range	the Rocky Mountains the Himalaya(n) Mountains
Desert	the Sahara (Desert) the Kalahari (Desert)
Islands/Isles	the British Isles the Virgin Islands

*The word *River* is usually omitted i.e., the Thames the Nile the Danube the Rhine the Amazon

Notes

1 The names of *individual* mountains and islands, **and the names** of lakes are written without **the**:

Mount Everest, Sugar Loaf Mountain, Table Mountain,

Ben Nevis, Long Island (but *the Isle of Skye*, using the pattern THE /X/ OF /Y/ → Section 2.3.5), Lake Balaton, Lake Erie, Lake Garda

2 Use **the** in plural place names e.g.
the Netherlands the West Indies the Tropics the Azores (and other island groups) the Alps the Pyrenees
the Rockies the Himalayas (and other mountain chains)

3 Various other place names are written with **the**, e.g.
the North Pole the South Pole the Arctic the Antarctic
the Sudan the Gambia the Gold Coast the Riviera
the Costa Brava the Hague the Middle East the Far East

But notice: Asia Africa Australia Europe America
North America South America Great Britain

b *Names of pubs (inns), hotels, theatres, cinemas*
e.g. the Red Lion (inn)   the George and Dragon (inn)
the Randolph (hotel) the Hilton (hotel)
the Old Vic (theatre) the Playhouse (theatre)
the Odeon (cinema)   the ABC (cinema)
The names of famous ships have the article, as in *the QE2*, *the Victory*.

c *Titles and dates using ordinal numbers*
(ordinal numbers → 4.6.).
e.g. Elizabeth II =(Queen) Elizabeth *the Second*
Louis XIV   =(King) Louis *the Fourteenth*
13 April   =April *the thirteenth*
            or *the thirteenth* of April

Notes
1 We usually use the ordinal numbers without **the** when we are talking about prizes and competitions, such as races:
e.g. She won *first prize* for her essay on natural history.
The Spanish contestant was in *second place*.
2 We do not use **the** in the pattern TITLE+NAME,
e.g. President Wilson Major Thompson Mr and Mrs Smith
Admiral Nelson

2.3.3 Other cases where *the* is left out

a *Fixed expressions*
There are many fixed expressions where **the** is omitted. The commonest constructions are VERB+NOUN and PREPOSITION+NOUN. (prepositions → Chapter 6).

VERB+NOUN
Verb+singular
count noun   to take place   to have breakfast
Verb+plural noun to make friends   to shake hands
Verb+mass noun   to make progress to make love
(→ Appendix II for a comprehensive list)

PREPOSITION+NOUN

e.g. on time   for example   in turn   after lunch
in harmony

(→ Appendix III for a comprehensive list)

Notes

1 We say *at night* but *in the morning, in the afternoon, in the evening*.
2 **The** may be omitted in expressions with the names of the seasons: *in (the) spring, during (the) summer, in (the) autumn, before (the) winter*.

b TO/IN/AT+*school, work, bed, etc.*

There are a number of expressions on the pattern TO+NOUN and IN/AT+NOUN which refer to the activity or function associated with the noun:

e.g. to go *to school*=to be in full-time education
to be *in hospital*=to be a patient, i.e., you are there because you are ill
to send someone *to prison*=to imprison him for doing something wrong

to:	go to bed	**in:**	be in bed
	go to church		be in church
	go to hospital		be in hospital
	go to prison	**at:**	be in prison
	go to school		be at school
	go to sea		be at sea
	go to work		be at work
	but		
	go home		be at home

Although there is no good reason, we use **the** in other cases: *to the office to the pictures to the cinema to the theatre*

Notice the difference between

He was sent *to prison* for five years. (=he is a prisoner)
and She went *to the prison* to visit him. (=she went into the building)

c BY+NOUN *(means of travel)*

The pattern BY+NOUN is used to express the method of travelling:

to go by bus, by car, by train, by air (by plane), by bicycle (by bike), by coach, by sea (by ship), by taxi, by Tube (= the London Underground).

The pattern ON+NOUN is used in the expressions: *on foot* and *on horseback*.

Notice the difference between:

I'm going to London tomorrow. I shall *go by car*.
and I'll have to *go in my wife's car*, because my car is too small.

2.3.4 Deliberate omission of articles

The articles are left out whenever you want to save space, time or money, as in:

Headlines: POLICE QUESTION YOUTH AFTER BRITISH MUSEUM EXPLOSION
i.e. *The* police are questioning (or have questioned) *a* youth following *an* explosion which took place in or near *the* British Museum.

Telegrams: REGRET MEETING CANCELLED STOP SUGGEST DATE BEFORE NEXT AGM STOP LETTER FOLLOWS
i.e. We regret that *the* meeting has been cancelled. We suggest that *a* date should be chosen before *the* next AGM. We will send you *a* letter about this matter right away.

Notices and labels: DO NOT LEAN OUT OF WINDOW
(See left.) RING BELL AND WAIT

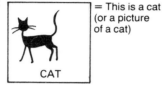

= This is a cat
(or a picture
of a cat)

CAT

2.3.5 Names of public buildings and institutions

Names of buildings, monuments and institutions in towns and cities vary, and there are few useful rules.
Perhaps the sphere of interest of Londoners (← Section 2.2.3) accounts for the definite article in the following:
    the Strand the Mall the British Museum the Monument the City.
On the other hand, names ending with these words are without **the:**
Bridge, Gate, House, Palace, Square, Cross, Road, Abbey, Park.
e.g. London Bridge Lancaster Gate Wellington House
    Buckingham Palace Grosvenor Square Charing Cross
    King's Road Westminster Abbey Hyde Park
The is always used in the pattern THE A OF B,
e.g. the Houses of Parliament the Palace of Westminster the Tower of London

Note
There are sometimes alternative ways of saying the same name. For example, we can talk about *Oxford University* or *The University of Oxford*. The pattern THE A OF B is used in more formal situations such as documents:
    Several of my friends are studying at *Bristol University*.
    This is to certify that it appears by the Register of *the University of Oxford* that Michael Jackson, St John's College, satisfied the examiners . . .

B   Demonstratives

The Two Squirrels

A grey squirrel and a red squirrel lived next to each other in an old oak tree. They got on well together until, one day, the grey squirrel found a beautiful coconut lying at the base of the tree.

He was just about to pick it up when the red squirrel jumped out and said:

'Put that coconut down! It doesn't belong to you.'

The grey squirrel calmly picked up the coconut, and replied, 'You are mistaken. This coconut belongs to me.'

'Prove it!' said the red squirrel in a reasonable tone of voice.

'That's easy,' retorted the grey squirrel. 'I found it, I picked it up, and I am holding it. This coconut is, therefore, legally mine.'

As he said this, the grey squirrel lifted the coconut and brought it down on the red squirrel's head, killing him instantly.

Moral: The way to get justice is this: don't argue, go and get a policeman.

2.4   Form of the demonstratives

2.4.1   Singular and plural forms

Singular	*Plural*
this	**these**
that	**those**

2.4.2   THIS etc. + NOUN

This house   These houses
That day   Those days

2.4.3   THIS/THAT + ONE

e.g. 'Which piece do you want?' 'I want *this one*.' 'I want *that one*.'
In the plural, we use **these/those** without 'ones':
e.g. 'Which pieces do you want?' '*These* look nicer than *those*.'

2.4.4   *This* etc. as pronoun (→ Section 5.12)

This etc. can stand alone instead of or without an accompanying noun:
What is the meaning of *this*?
Who said *that*?
These are my books; *those* must belong to someone else.

2.4.5   THIS etc. + ADJECTIVE + NOUN

(For the order of adjectives before nouns, → Section 4.4). The order is DEMONSTRATIVE + ADJECTIVE(S) + NOUN:
e.g. *this* old house   *that* certain feeling   *these* treasured possessions   *those* wonderful days
When the adjective is a possessive (my, your, his, her, our, their → Section 5.5), the pattern changes to
THIS etc. + NOUN + OF mine/yours/his/hers/ours/theirs
e.g. *this* country of ours   *that* old car of yours
these things of mine   *those* friends of his

2.5 Meaning of the demonstratives

This identifies something *near to* the speaker; it is associated with **here**.

That identifies something *farther from* the speaker; it is associated with **there**.

2.5.1 Physical location

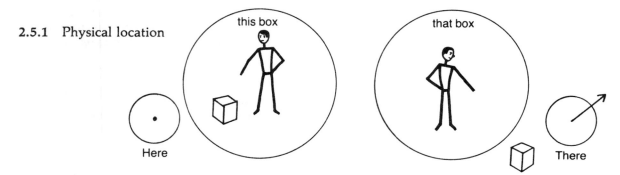

2.5.2 Sphere of interest

This/these and **that/those** are often used not simply to describe things which are physically located near or farther from the speaker, but to identify things which are inside or outside the speaker's personal universe or 'sphere of interest' (← Section 2.2.3 b).

The diagrams in Section 2.5.2 can be understood as follows: everything inside the circle is **this – here**; everything outside the circle is **that – there**. You can relate this idea to other pairs of words:

	this		that
⊙	here	♂	there
	← to (towards)		→ from (away from)
	come		go
	near to		far from
	bring		take
	I – my – mine		you – your – yours
	we – our – ours		you – your – yours
	now		then
	at this moment		at that moment
	I am doing this		I was doing that
	up ↑		down ↓

a

'I can't stand this weather

'What is that object in the sky?'

b

'Hm, this looks interesting!'
(He is holding the object up
towards him)

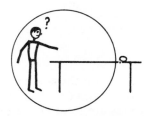

'Hm, that looks interesting!'
(He is pointing down at the object)

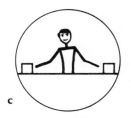

c

'Do you want this one,
or this one?'

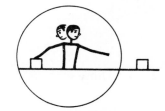

'Do you want this one,
or that one?'

d 'Just listen to this!'   'Just listen to that!'   VROOM!!!

Remember: it is not always the physical location of the object but the
speaker's attitude to it (whether it is inside or outside his sphere of interest)
that causes him to use **this** or **that**.

2.6 Other uses of the demonstratives

2.6.1 This = a(n) (→ Section 2.2.2)

People sometimes use **this** instead of **a(n)** in the sense of *known
but not yet specified* (→ Section 2.2.2), when they are telling you
about an experience they have had:

e.g. We met this marvellous man when we were in Bristol. He
took us to this fantastic restaurant in this funny old
house . . .

The purpose of using **this** is probably to make the experience
sound more exciting than it really was. If it is used too much, it
becomes irritating: we advise you to recognize it but not to
imitate it.

2.6.2 Referring forward and referring backward

This is used to refer to something which has already been said,
or is about to be said:

Forward The way to get justice is this: go and get a policeman.
Backward The grey squirrel wanted to keep the coconut. The red squirrel thought this was not fair.

That can only refer backward:
'Prove it!'   'That's easy.'

2.6.3   *That/those* in comparative statements (...er than that/those...)

We can use **that/those** in sentences of the pattern

THE X OF A	is / are	...ER THAN	THAT / THOSE	of B.

e.g. The feathers of owls are softer than those of other birds.

2.6.4   Those who...

The expression **those who**...is used for *those people who*...:
e.g. I don't agree with those who believe that we should...
Politicians are fond of the expression *Those of us who*...which suggests that they are part of a very special group:
e.g. Those of us who were alive during the war will never forget...

2.6.5   *This* in time expressions

This occurs in a number of time expressions:

Parts of today	*Others*
this morning	this Thursday (etc.)
this afternoon	this week
this evening	this month
(but *tonight*)	this September (etc.)
	this year

2.6.6   Emphatic use of *that*

a The following dialogue shows how **that** can be used in an emphatic way – the stress falls heavily on the demonstrative:
A 'Uncle George is coming to stay with us.'
B 'Which Uncle George?'
A 'You know, the one with the parrot and the wooden leg.'
B 'Oh *that* Uncle George!'

b **That** is also used emphatically in place of *so* in such sentences as:
WIFE   'Do you realize we are £75.00 overdrawn at the bank?'
HUSBAND 'I knew we were short of money, but I didn't **realize** we were *that* short!'

In other words, '...I didn't realize we were **so** short!' or '...I didn't realize we were as short as that!'

**2.7 Appendix III:
Expressions using the pattern
VERB+NOUN**

Where appropriate, we have given the preposition which is used with the expression.

to catch cold
     sight (of)
to declare war (on)
to do business (with)
to feel sympathy (for)
to find fault (with)
     time (for)
to get pleasure (from)
to give birth (to)
     way
     rise (to)
to have breakfast
     lunch
     tea
     dinner
     supper
     faith (in)
     pleasure (in)
     occasion (to)
     (good) reason (to)
     confidence (in)
     fun
to lose track (of)
     touch (with)
     sight (of)
to make contact (with)
     fun (of)
     love (to)
     money

to make progress
     way (for)
to pay attention (to)
to play football*
     tennis
     (+other sports)
to set fire (to)
to shed light (on)
to show mercy
to take care (of)
     exception (to)
     offence
     part (in)
     pity (on)
     place
     pleasure (in)
     pride (in)
     shelter
to wage war (on)
to change jobs
     places (with)
     sides
to go halves (with)
to make friends (with)
to play tricks (on)
to shake hands (with)
to take sides
to make arrangements
     eyes (at)

Note: to play football (and other sports), but *to play the piano* (and other) musical instruments.

2.8 Appendix IV: Expressions using the pattern PREPOSITION+NOUN

by accident	in difficulties	in luck	in respect of
on account of	on duty	by mail	in response to
in addition to	off duty	by means of	at rest
in advance	at ease	(call) to mind	in return for
by agreement with	on edge	by mistake	at risk
in answer to	in effect	in motion	for sale
by appointment	in exchange for	by word of mouth	(start) from scratch
on approval	as a matter of fact	by name	in search of
by arrangement	in fact	by nature	in season
on arrival	in fashion	in need of	in secret
by association	in favour of	by night	in sight
under attack	for fear that	at night	on sight
in attendance	on file	at short notice	by sight
on average	on fire	on occasion	at (great) speed
on balance	on foot	on offer	in spite of
on behalf of	in future	in operation	on stage
out of breath	in gear	by order	in step
in bulk	in general	in order (to)	out of step
on business	under guarantee	out of order	in stock
in case	on guard	in pain	out of stock
out of character	for good	in particular	in store
in charge of	out of mind	on paper	on strike
in common with	in half	at peace	in style
in company with	by hand	in person	by surprise
in comparison with	in hand	by phone	in tears
in competition with	in harmony	out of place	in theory
on condition that	by heart	in place	on time
in connection with	on heat	in possession of	in time
under consideration	for hire	in practice	at times
out of control	on holiday	out of practice	in town
under control	at home	at present	out of town
under cover	in honour of	in private	on trial
in credit	for instance	in principle	on top of
by chance	by invitation	in progress	in touch with
by choice	on land	under protest	on tour
in danger of	at last	in public	on trust
out of danger	by law	on purpose	in turn(s)
out of date	at length	within reason	in use
up to date	at liberty	on receipt of	on vacation
by day	for life	in receipt of	in vain
in debt	in line with	with reference to	in view
without delay	on loan	with regard to	by virtue of
on demand	not for long	in relation to	at war
by design	in love	in reply to	out of work

[See also → Section 6.8 for a list of common fixed expressions with prepositions]

3 Contents

3 Quantifiers (*some, any,* etc.) and distributives (*each, every, all,* etc.)

The Serious Rabbit and the Beautiful Widow
(*Part 1*)

There was once a very serious rabbit. He was not handsome or clever, but he worked hard and saved all his money. After a number of years, he decided to get married. There was a beautiful lady rabbit who lived near him. She was a widow, and she had a lot of admirers, but he knew that few of them were as rich as he was.

The widow had several children, so every time he visited her, he brought a different present for each child. He loved the widow and her children. For her part, she liked the way he treated her little ones, and she soon grew very fond of him.

One day, a handsome stranger came to town. He had long silky ears, and a great deal of charm. Soon every female rabbit in the place was in love with him. But he, like so many others, had eyes only for the beautiful widow; and to tell the truth, she found him very attractive too. Everyone agreed that this was the start of a fine romance.

A Quantity

3.1 Quantifiers with mass and count nouns

(See also Section ← 2.3.1a). The table on p. 53 shows adjectives or adjectival phrases (→ Chapter 4) which describe quantity. Notice that the expressions in the left hand column can only go with **mass nouns** – they answer the question *how much?* The expressions in the right hand column can only go with **count nouns** in the plural – they answer the question *how many?* The expressions in the central column can be used with both mass and count nouns.

You can say:

no snow	*no* snowballs
a little snow	*a few* snowballs
a bit of snow	*a number of* snowballs
some snow	*some* snowballs
—	*several* snowballs
a lot of snow	*a lot of* snowballs
{*a great deal of* snow	*a* {*great*} *number of* snowballs
{*a large amount of* snow	{*large*}
plenty of snow	*plenty of* snowballs
lots of snow	*lots of* snowballs
tons of snow	*tons of* snowballs

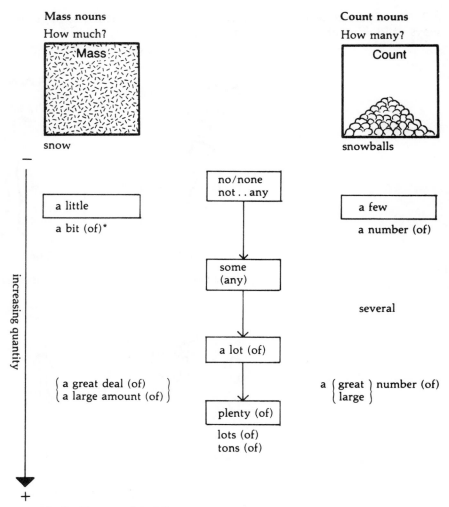

Mass nouns

How much?

snow

Count nouns

How many?

snowballs

− increasing quantity +

Mass nouns		Count nouns
	no/none not . . any	
a little a bit (of)*		a few a number (of)
	some (any)	
		several
	a lot (of)	
{ a great deal (of) { a large amount (of) }		a { great } number (of) { large }
	plenty (of) lots (of) tons (of)	

*for liquids, use *a drop (of)*

Notes

1 Although the quantifier may be singular (e.g. *a lot of*) or plural (e.g. *lots of*), the verb agrees with the noun, i.e., use a singular verb with a mass noun, and a plural verb with a count noun:

Quantifier	*Noun*	*Verb*	
A lot of	towns	are	celebrating the centenary. (i.e. *towns are*)
Lots of	time	is	wasted in teabreaks. (i.e. *time is*)

2 Expressions like *plenty of*, *lots of* and *tons of* are informal spoken forms. In writing or more formal speaking, use *a great deal of*, *a large amount of* and *a large/great number of*.

3.2 Positive and negative ways of looking at things

Two people can look at the same thing and see it quite differently:

'The bottle is half full!'

'There's *some* wine left.'

'The bottle is half empty!'

'There *isn't much* wine left.'

'I have *a few* friends.'

'I have *few* friends.'

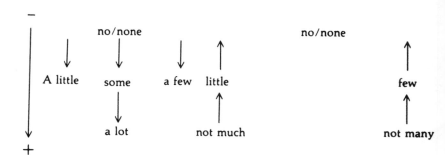

Other examples are:
I have got *a little* money: it should be enough to live on. (=some)
There is *little* point in going on now: it is too late. (=hardly any)
There are *a few* things that I want to see you about. (=several)
He knew that *few* of them were as rich as he was. (=almost none of them)

3.3 Meanings of *some*

The word **some** has two main uses.

a When you are interested in the quantity, especially in contrast with other words expressing quantity, you use **some** with the pronunciation [sʌm].

e.g. I have *some* good friends but *not many*.
Some people say he is a genius; *others* say that he is mad.
Sometimes the contrast is not expressed:
Some people do not know how to behave properly. (i.e., some do not, but others do.)
Some of my best friends are accountants. (i.e., some, but not all)

b The word **some** is also used as a sort of *indefinite article*. In this case, you are interested in the object itself rather than in the quantity. The pronunciation of **some** is unstressed [səm]:

e.g. There's some cheese.

This could be the response to a question like 'Is there any food in the house?' or a statement like 'I am very hungry.' In other words the important thing is that there is *cheese*, not that there is a certain quantity of cheese.

e.g. She bought me some records for my birthday, but I would have preferred books.

The interest is in *records* rather than the number of records. Note that you could say *books* or *some books* without any important change of meaning.

Notes

1 some, prounounced [sʌm], is also used to mean *a particular one but I do not know which one*, and is often said when you are impatient or have a poor opinion of someone or something. Notice particularly that **some** in this meaning is followed by a **count noun** *in the singular*:

a *Some* man called this morning, but he refused to give his name.
(=I do not know who he was, but I did not like the look of him!)

b There must be *some* shop in this town where you can buy dog food!
(=I cannot believe that it is impossible to buy dog food in a town as big as this.)

2 There is a difference between **sometimes**, which means *occasionally*; and (**at**) **some time**, which means *at an unspecified time*:
I would like to see you (at) *some time* next week. (=**one day** next week)
I'll be there (at) *some time* this evening. (=I am not sure exactly when I will be there).

3.4   *Some* and *any*

The opposite of **some** is **no** or **not . . . any**

3.4.1   In statements

some apples

There are *some apples*
in this picture.

no apples

There are *no apples*
in this picture.
There are *not any* apples . . .

The normal unemphatic way of talking about the absence of things is to use the construction **not . . . any**:
e.g. I bought some cigarettes, but I could *not* get *any* matches.
You cannot have a drink of milk because there is*n't any* left.
I could *not* think of *anything* to say.

Use **any** instead of **some** after other negative words like *without, seldom, hardly, scarcely, rarely* and *never*:
e.g. They *never* tell you *anything*.
I did it *without any* help from *anyone*.
There is *hardly any* food left in the house.
We *rarely* go *anywhere* nowadays.

Notes

1 The difference between **not . . . any** and **no** is largely one of emphasis:
A   I *don't* know *anything* about car mechanics.
B   I know *nothing* about car mechanics.

Sentence A is a normal unemphatic statement of a simple fact. Sentence B is more likely to be said emphatically or defensively (e.g. you might say it if someone asked you to help him to repair his car).

2 Beware of the *double negative*. The opposite of *I can give you something* is *I cannot give you **anything***. The sentence *I cannot give you nothing* means *I must give you **something**, it would be unfair not to give you a present.* Unfortunately, you will often hear the combination *not . . . no* when people really mean *not . . . any*, especially in popular songs and other careless or dialect situations. For example:

Pop song title (incorrect English)		*Correct English would be:*
I can't get no satisfaction	→	I can't get any satisfaction
She don't love me no more	→	She doesn't love me any more
I ain't got nobody	→	I haven't got anybody

3.4.2   In questions

Some changes to **any** in normal unemphatic questions, that is, in questions which you ask in order to find out if something exists. You are making a simple inquiry and you do not have any idea what the answer will be:
e.g. Are there *any* good theatres in Birmingham?
Did you buy *any* presents when you were in Spain?
Has *anyone* called while I have been out?
Is there *anything* good on television tonight?

When you have an idea what the answer will be, for **example**, when you are *checking* to make sure that your idea is correct, use **some** in the question:

Did he give you *some* money? (=I am sure that he gave you some money, and I want to confirm that he did.)
Is there *some*where quiet where we can talk? (= there must be somewhere)

3.4.3 In requests, invitations, etc.

We often use the question *form* not to ask for information, but as a means of *making a request, giving an invitation* or *encouraging*. Because these are not true questions, we use **some**:

A *making a request:* Could I have some more tea please?

B *inviting:* Would you like some more toast?

C *encouraging:* Why don't you do some revision for your exams?

Sentence A means the same as *I would like some more tea.*
Sentence B means the same as *Have some more toast if you want some.*
Sentence C means the same as *You should do some revision...*

3.4.4 Any=*it does not matter which one*

Any means **no** in the negative constructions *not...any, without...any,* etc.

It also has another meaning, *one, but it does not matter which one,* as in the sentences:
Anybody who votes for the yellow party must be mad!
Give me a pen: *any* pen will do.
Come and see me *any* time you are in Zurich.
The parcel should arrive *any* day now.

Consider the difference between these sentences:
A Nobody can do it.   =It cannot be done.
B Everybody can do it.   =It can be done.
C Anybody can do it.   =It can be done, and it does not
                            matter who does it.
                            or
                            It is very easy and requires no
                            special skill or practice.

Other examples are:
Nobody can foretell the future.
Everybody knows that Paris is the capital of France.
She is lazy and dishonest. Ask *anybody* about her.
Anyone can be brave as long as he is not in danger himself.

(See also→Section 3.6)

3.5 Quantifiers as pronouns

3.5.1 Some

When **some** is used as an adjective (i.e. SOME+NOUN), it is pronounced [səm] or [sʌm] (◄ Section 3.3).

When **some** is used as a pronoun (i.e. on its own), it is pronounced [sʌm]

[səm]	[sʌm]
e.g. I want some bread.	Please give me some.
Make some cakes for tea.	Make some.

3.5.2 *No* and *none*

No is an adjective (i.e. NO+NOUN); **none** is a pronoun (i.e. it is used on its own):

Adjective

There is *no* bread left.

I have *no* suggestions to make.

Pronoun

There is *none*.

I have *none*.

Note

In theory, **none** expresses a singular idea (i.e., *not one*). In practice we are influenced by the noun which it replaces:

A Give me some cheese.   There *is* none. (=no cheese)

B Give me some apples.   There *are* none. (=no apples)

C She made several suggestions, but *none of them* were any good.

We advise you to use the verb in the plural after **none** in cases such as examples B and C, i.e., where it replaces a plural noun.

3.5.3 Other quantifiers

All the other quantifiers given in the table on page 53 can be used without a following noun. The expressions with **of** (e.g. *a lot of*) drop the **of** when they are used alone.

e.g. They say there are *a lot of deer* around here, but I have never seen *any*.

Well, there used to be *a lot*.

I don't need any paper; I've already got *plenty*.

3.6 Compounds with *-one,* *-body, -thing* **and** *-where*

Useful words are formed by combining **some, any, no** and **every** with **-one, -body, -thing** and **-where**.

	Some	Any	No	Every
-one	someone	anyone	no-one	everyone
-body	somebody	anybody	nobody	everybody
-thing	something	anything	nothing	everything
-where	somewhere	anywhere	nowhere	everywhere

Notes

1 There is no difference in meaning between **-one and -body** words. Notice that they all refer to people, not to things. Notice the difference between the following sentences:

Go to the stockroom. *Anyone* will tell you where it is. (=any person)

Get me a newspaper. *Any one* will do. (*Any one* written as two words = any newspaper)

When I arrived at the party, *everyone* had left. (= every person)
I wanted to buy a Cup Final ticket, but *every one* had been sold. (*every one* written separately = every ticket)

(See also ← Section 3.4.4)

2 In those cases where **some** changes to **any** (←Section 3.4), the compounds with **some-** also change to **any-**:
Go and buy some potatoes. You should be able to get *some* from *somewhere*.
I couldn't find *any anywhere*.

3.7 Uses of *much/many*

Much and **many** are mostly used in combination with other words. The commonest combinations are with:

how	to form the question words	*how much?* and *how many?*
not	to form the negatives	*not much* and *not many*
too	to state how much/many	*too much* *too many*
(not) so		*so much* *so many*
(not) as		*as much* *as many*

They are also used before **more** and **less** to state how much more or less: *much more   much less   many more*
The form *many less* is often used instead of the correct form *many fewer)**. In all these cases, you could use *a lot* instead of *much/more* without any change of meaning.

*You can think of **less** as the comparative form of **little**, and **fewer** as the comparative form of **few**
e.g. I have *little* time to spare, but you have even *less*. (time)
    I have *few* friends, but you have even *fewer*. (friends)

Much and **many** are only used alone in positive statements which are formal, i.e., when you want the statement to sound important:
e.g.   There is *much to be said* for your point of view.
    I know many who would not agree with you.

In everyday speech, use *a lot of*:
e.g.   There's still *a lot of* work to do before we leave.
    I know *a lot of* people who would like to emigrate.

Much as an adverb (→ Section 12.9.3) occurs only with words like, *how,   not,   very,   too* and *so*.
e.g.   I love you *very much*.
    He smokes *too much*.
    I wish you wouldn't drink *so much*!

In other cases, use *a lot*:
>You talk *a lot*, but you don't do much.

Note

There is a construction beginning with the words *much as*, as in the sentence
>*Much as* I would like to go with you, I'm afraid I cannot leave.

It means almost the same as *although*:
>Although I would like to go with you very much, I'm afraid . . .

B   Distribution

3.8   Words which describe distribution

These words are concerned with the group of things or people, and the individual members of the group. The words **each**, **every** and **all** describe the group but in different ways:

Yes, *each* one of you

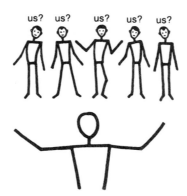

Yes, *every* one of you

Yes, *all* of you

The same number of individuals is involved, but the way of looking at them is different:

 all = the group seen as one thing

 **every** = the group seen as a series of X members

 each = the members of the group seen individually

e.g. He worked hard and saved *all* his money.
Every female rabbit in the place was in love with him.
He always brought a different present for *each* child.

3.8.1 All

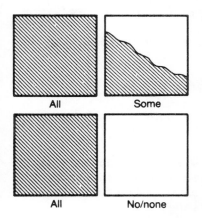

All Some

All No/none

a Meaning of **all**

The word **all** contrasts with **some** and with **no/none** (see illustration on left).

b The word **all** occurs in these combinations.

	1	Ø*	MASS NOUN
	2	THE	or
ALL +	**3**	MY, etc.	COUNT NOUN in the plural
	4a	THIS, THAT	MASS NOUN
	4b	THESE, THOSE	COUNT NOUN in the plural

*Reminder: the symbol Ø means that nothing appears in this space.

Examples

1 Give up *all hope* of seeing them again.
All passengers are requested to remain seated.

2 Have you been here *all the time*? I didn't notice you before.
You can tell *all the people* without tickets to wait outside.
Where have *all the flowers gone*? (title of popular song)

3 Where have you been *all my life*?
All my friends have gone away for Christmas.

4a Who has made *all this mess*?
You will never get *all that luggage* into the car.

4b *All these books* belong to me.
You will never get *all those suitcases* into the car.

Note

The only other words which can be combined in the same way as **all** are the words **both** and **half**.

	1	Ø	
BOTH +	**2**	THE	COUNT NOUN in the plural
	3	MY, etc	
	4	THESE, THOSE	

	1	Ø	
	2	THE	MASS NOUN
HALF +			or
	3	MY, etc	COUNT NOUN
	4	THIS, THAT THESE, THOSE	

Examples

He liked Bach so much that he went to *both concerts*. (or *both the concerts* → Section 3.8.1d)

Both my children are still at school. (or *Both of my children . . .* →Section 3.8.1c)

It was so bad that *half the audience* left after the interval.

Half these apples are bad. (or *Half of these apples . . .* →Section 3.8.1c)

For the patterns and uses of **either**, see→Section 3.10).

c all+of

You must use **all of** with a following pronoun:

*all of you, all of us, all of them**

(Similarly, *both of you, both of us, both of them**, half of you, half of us, half of them* and *half of it*)

You can use **all of** instead of **all** when it is in contrast to **some**:

e.g. I do all (of) the work and you get all (of) the credit.

He worked hard and saved all (of) his money.

You could not use **all of** in such sentences as

All passengers are requested to remain seated.

Who has made all this mess?

because there is no contrast with **some** (It would make no sense to talk about *some of (the) passengers* or *some of this mess*).

For this reason we advise you to use **all of** only when there is a following pronoun (e.g. *all of them*), and to use **all** in all other cases.

*This form emphasizes the pronoun **all** or **both**; the emphatic form is **you all, you both**, etc. Compare *'I like them both'* (=they are both nice) and *I like both of them* (=I like one just as much as I like the other).

d ALL+NOUN without the

Use ALL+Ø+NOUN when you want to make a general statement (← Section 2.3.1):

e.g. All passengers are requested to keep their seatbelts fastened.

Not all snakes are poisonous.

The can be left out in time expressions:

all day, all afternoon, all evening, all night, all week, all year, etc.

(To give the idea of a repeated action, use **every**: *every day*, etc.)

The exception is the expression *all the time*.

e All *or* the whole?

We prefer to use **the whole** with count nouns in the singular:

e.g. I read *the whole book* in one evening.

The whole can also be more emphatic than **all**, i.e., it draws the listener's attention to what you have done:

e.g. I've spent *the whole day* washing and cleaning!

In this sentence, *all day* would not sound so dramatic.

Notes

1 A WHOLE+NOUN,

e.g. I was so thirsty that I drank *a whole bottle* of milk in **one** go.

contrasts with *(a) part of, half of, some of* etc.

2 THE WHOLE+OF can be used as well:

I read *the whole of* the book . . .

I searched *the whole of* the building . . .

The form *the whole of* is used especially with names of particular people, places and things (◄ Section **1.1**):

The whole of Westminster Abbey was lit up for the occasion.

I know *the whole of 'Hamlet'* by heart.

f All *or* **everything?**

We generally prefer not to use **all** on its own without a noun. Instead we use **everything** for things, and **everybody/everyone** for people:

e.g. *Everything* I've told you is true.

Everybody in the office knows about them.

Give *everyone* a copy.

Note

All occurs on its own, i.e. without a following noun, in expressions where it means *the only thing* as in *All I want is a quiet life*; and in a few expressions such as *That will be all, thank you.* , *Is that all?* and *not . . . at all*

3.8.2 Every

a *Meaning of* **every**

Think of **every** as a word to describe a series consisting of three or more people or things.

The series may be *a complete one* (i.e., a set):

Every player in the team is a first-class footballer.

Manchester United football team

In this case, *every player* compares with *all the players*.

Or the series may be *an incomplete one*:

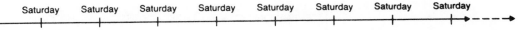

| | Saturday | Saturday | Saturday | Saturday | Saturday | Saturday | Saturday | Saturday |

I go shopping *every Saturday*.

In this case, you cannot use **all**.

b *The word* **every** *occurs in the following combinations:*

EVERY +	COUNT NOUN in the singular
	ONE (pronoun)

This means that **every** is an adjective (→ Chapter 4) and must always be followed by a noun or the pronoun *one*.
e.g. I've read *every book* in this library.
Every cloud has a silver lining.
'Have you checked all the invoices?' 'Yes, I've checked *every one*.'

For the difference between **every one** (for things) and **everyone** (for people) see ← Section 3.6.

c Every *in frequency expressions*
We use *every* in expressions which describe the *frequency* with which something happens, i.e., *how often* it happens:
i) With plural nouns, as in *every three days*, *every twenty minutes*
ii) With the word **other** or with ordinals (→ Section 4.6).

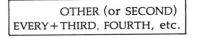

identify points in a series:

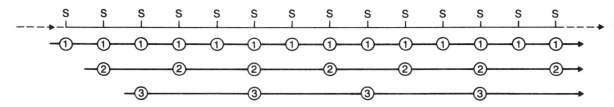

① We go shopping *every Saturday.*
② We go to the pictures *every other Saturday* (or *every second Saturday*)
③ My mother visits us *every third Saturday.*

d Every one of
When you are talking about a complete series (a set), you can use the combination:

EVERY ONE OF +	THE	
	THESE/THOSE +	COUNT NOUN in the plural
	MY, etc.	
	US, YOU, THEM	

I've read *every book* in this library
or   I've read *every one of the books* in this library.

This construction is particularly useful with **possessives** (*my, your*, etc., and *John's, the children's*, etc.):
e.g.   I seem to have lost every one of my pens.
I can remember every one of the children's birthday parties.

Sentences with *every one of* sound more emphatic, especially if you add the word *single* – *every single one of them.*

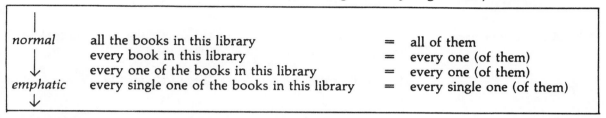

normal	all the books in this library	= all of them
	every book in this library	= every one (of them)
	every one of the books in this library	= every one (of them)
emphatic	every single one of the books in this library	= every single one (of them)

3.8.3   Each

a *Meaning of* **each**
The word **each** is used to point to the individuals in a group of two or more, and to consider them one by one:
e.g.   I've checked every book on the subject, and I find that *each one* says something different.
He kissed all the children, and then gave *each child* a little present.

b **Each** is used in the following combinations

EACH	+ **1**	COUNT NOUN in the singular
	+ **2**	ONE
	+ **3**	Ø

Examples:
1 He gave *each child* a present.
2 He picked up the letters and examined *each one* carefully.
3 See next section.

c **Each** *on its own*
You can use **each** on its own without *one*, as in the sentence *I like all of Mozart's symphonies:* **each** *has its special charm*, but we advise you to use **each one** because it is more common.
In the following cases, you can only use **each** on its own:

Prices: How much are the apples? Sixty pence a kilo, or *15p each.*
With pronouns: He kissed the children and gave *them each* a present.
Plural noun + each: The *children each* received something different.
Reciprocal each other: They love *each other* very much.

d Each of

Just as you can say *every one of the books* instead of *every book* you can say *each (one) of the children* instead of *each child*. The difference in emphasis is not very big.

You must use *each of* before a pronoun:

each (one) of you
each (one) of them
each (one) of us

e.g. The meeting had begun. *Each (one) of us* stood up in turn and made a short speech.

3.9   *All, every* or *each*?

You choose the word which best describes the way you look at things. Notice especially the contrast:

Seen collectively   **Seen individually**

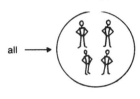
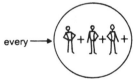
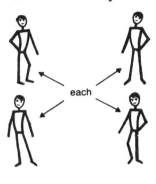

They're all very good students and I'm proud of *every one of them.*

Every student must take the written examination, and *each one* will be interviewed personally.

3.10   *Either* and *neither*

We can describe distribution between two things by using the word **either** or its negative form **neither** (= not either). These words, which can be used as adjectives or as pronouns, are used to describe alternatives:

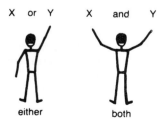

X or Y – either will do
not X and not Y – neither will do

The difference between **either** and **both** is that **either** *separates*, whereas **both** *combines*:

Examples

a *Both* roads lead to the city centre. You can take *either/either* road/*either* one/*either* of them.

b There is a big one and a little one. You can have *either* (of them).

If you are really hungry, you can have *both* (of them).

Notice the slight difference of emphasis, and the difference of the combinations between
You can have *one* but not *two*. (or both)
You can have *either* but not *both*.

Notes

1 (N)either may be pronounced ['(n) aɪðə] or ['(n) iːðə].

2 The same contrast that exists between the emphatic **no . . .** and the unemphatic **not . . . any** (← 3.4.1) is true also for **neither** and **not . . . either**. Compare these two sentences:
A They are both ugly. I do*n't* like *either* of them. (normal, unemphatic)
B They are both ugly. I like *neither* of them. (emphatic, special effect)

3 **Either** and **neither** express a singular idea, i.e. (not) this one and/or (not) that one. When they are used as adjectives, i.e. in the pattern (N)EITHER + SINGULAR NOUN, the following verb is in the singular form:
e.g. Either *road* takes you to the city centre.
   Neither *dress* really *suits* you.
When they occur as pronouns, i.e. alone, or in the patterns (N)EITHER OF + PLURAL NOUN, or (N)EITHER OF US/YOU/THEM, **we** are influenced by the plural noun or pronoun, and tend to put the rest of the sentence into the plural:

   Either of these roads take(s) you to the city centre.
   Neither of these dresses really suit(s) you.

   Neither of the boys {*wants* to leave *his* friends behind *him*.
                        {*want* to leave *their* friends behind *them*.

   Has }
   Have} either of you seen my glasses?

For the use of (n)**either** as a conjunction, see → Section 14.11.

4 Contents

4 Adjectives

The Serious Rabbit and the Beautiful Widow
(Part 2)

When the serious rabbit found out about the handsome stranger
with the long silky ears, he became even more serious than
usual. He went round to the widow's house, and entered without
knocking.

'Marry me at once, and forget this young stranger,' he said
boldly.

'But he is young and handsome and romantic,' she replied
calmly. 'You are old and serious and not at all romantic.'

'True,' said the serious rabbit after some thought, 'but he is
poor and I am rich. I have plenty of money for you and your
little ones.'

'That is true,' said the widow, smiling.

They got married shortly afterwards. The handsome stranger,
his ears drooping sadly, left town and never came back.

Moral: Romance is not dead, but it needs all the help it can get.

4.1 Types of adjective

There are a number of kinds of words that can describe or
qualify a noun:
determiners, including the articles and the demonstratives, and
the words *both*, *all* and *half*; and the possessives (→ Section 5.5);
quantifiers, such as *some* and *any*.

We generally use the word **adjective** to describe words which tell
us about the *quality* of a noun or pronoun:
the *last* post   *green* ones   a *useful* book

These adjectives of quality answer a question like
what is it like?   or   *what is he like?*

The **cardinal numbers** (one, two, three, etc.) and the **ordinal
numbers** (first, second, third, etc.) may be regarded as adjectives
which refer to quantity and distribution respectively. See
Appendix V for a full list and description of cardinal and ordinal
numbers.

The **interrogative** (question) words **which? what?** and **whose?**
may also function as adjectives as in *which book do you mean?*,
what clothes are you taking with you? and *whose pen is this?*
(see also → Section 5.7).

Note
Adjectives are invariable, i.e. they do not change their form

whether the noun they qualify is singular or plural:

an		boy
an		girl
–	*intelligent*	boys
–		girls

4.2   Formation of adjectives

Most of the commonest adjectives have no particular form or ending (i.e. there is nothing which makes them look like an adjective);

right, wrong, big, small, nice, little, tall, thin, black, etc.

4.2.1   Suffixes

There are, however, a number of **suffixes** (endings which are attached to words) which can help you to understand the meaning of the adjectives. The commonest are:

-y
This suffix is often added to nouns to form adjectives with the meaning *having the look or quality of*:

air→airy cloud→cloudy dirt→dirty ease→easy
fog→foggy fun→funny grease→greasy hair→hairy
health→healthy hunger→hungry luck→lucky
mist→misty noise→noisy rubber→rubbery silk→silky
thirst→thirsty water→watery
Note also: busy, lazy, pretty, tidy, tiny

-ly
This suffix is added to nouns denoting some kinds of people to form adjectives with the meaning *having the qualities of*:

brother→brotherly coward→cowardly father→fatherly
friend→friendly man→manly woman→womanly
mother→motherly
Note also: home→homely leisure→leisurely life→lively
shape→shapely earth→(un) earthly (See also→Section 12.6.11).

The suffix **-ly** is also used to form words which describe periods of time:

hour→hourly day→daily night→nightly week→weekly
fortnight→fortnightly month→monthly year→yearly
(These words can be used as adjectives or as adverbs, →Section 12.6).

-like
This suffix is added to some nouns to form adjectives with the meaning *looking or behaving like*:

business→businesslike child→childlike god→godlike
life→lifelike workman→workmanlike

-ish
This suffix has several uses:
a added to nouns denoting some kinds of people to form adjectives with the meaning *looking or behaving as badly as*:
child→childish fool→foolish man→mannish
snob→snobbish; *also* selfish
b added to the names of nationalities to describe the people or their language:

Britain→British Denmark→Danish Spain→Spanish
(Appendix VI)

c added to adjectives, especially those which describe *colour*, to
form other adjectives with the meaning *having this quality
more or less*:
red→reddish green→greenish white→whitish fat→fattish
young→youngish

-ful

This suffix is added to nouns, usually abstract nouns, to form
adjectives with the meaning *having the quality of* or *full of*:
beauty→beautiful care→careful doubt→doubtful
faith→faithful hope→hopeful play→playful
shame→shameful skill→skilful truth→truthful
use→useful wonder→wonderful
Also: grateful

-less*

This suffix is added to nouns to form adjectives with the meaning
not having the quality of:
aim→aimless care→careless hope→hopeless life→lifeless
meaning→meaningless point→pointless speech→speechless
tact→tactless use→useless
Note also: listless, reckless, ruthless

*The suffix **-less** is dynamic, that is, it is still used to form new adjectives; the suffix
-ful is not.

-able/-ible

These suffixes form adjectives with the meaning *which is able to
do this or have this quality*. Although there are no useful rules to
tell you whether the ending will be **-able** or **ible**, note that **-able**
is much more common, and you can usually take off the **-able**
suffix to leave a recognizable noun or verb. Words in **-ible** have
been introduced directly from Latin, and you cannot usually
separate the root from the suffix.

Common words in **-able**

accept	⟶ acceptable[1]	eat	⟶ eatable[1]
adapt	⟶ adaptable	laugh	⟶ laughable
admire	⟶ admirable	love	⟶ lovable[1]
answer	⟶ answerable[1]	memory	⟶ memorable
avoid	⟶ avoidable[1]	read	⟶ readable[1]
bear	⟶ bearable[1]	reason	⟶ reasonable[1]
believe	⟶ believable[1]	recognize	⟶ recognizable[1]
change	⟶ changeable[1]	regret	⟶ regrettable
consider	⟶ considerable[2]	rely	⟶ reliable[1]
debate	⟶ debatable	respect	⟶ respectable
deny	⟶ deniable[1]	sale	⟶ saleable[1]
depend	⟶ dependable[1]	tax	⟶ taxable
desire	⟶ desirable[1]	value	⟶ valuable[2]
despise	⟶ despicable	vary	⟶ variable[2]
drink	⟶ drinkable[1]	wash	⟶ washable

These six adjectives in **-able** cannot be reduced to a corresponding noun or verb:

capable[2], formidable, irritable, probable[2], viable, vulnerable[2].

Common words in **-ible**

contemptible	gullible
convertible	horrible
divisible[2]	intelligible[1]
edible[2]	legible[2]
eligible[2]	possible[2]
fallible[2]	responsible[2]
feasible	tangible[2]
flexible[2]	terrible
	visible[2]

Note

To form the opposite of these adjectives, i.e., to make them into words with the meaning *not being able to do this or have this quality*, use the **prefix -un** with words marked 1; and the **prefix -in** (modified to **-il** before the letter l, **-im** before p and **-ir** before r) with words marked 2. Use *not* in other cases (e.g. taxable – not taxable).

e.g.   believable→unbelievable   reliable→unreliable
       legible→illegible   visible→invisible

Most of the words in **-able** take the prefix **-un**; most of the words in **-ible** take the prefix **-in**.

-ed

This suffix is added to some nouns to form adjectives with the meaning *having or possessing*. Many of these compound adjectives are compounds which describe people:

bad-tempered, blue-eyed, bow-legged, cross-eyed, flat-chested, good-natured, knock-kneed, left-handed, long-haired, open-hearted, open-minded, pale-skinned

-ese

This suffix is added to the names of countries to form adjectives which describe the people or their language:

China→Chinese   Japan→Japanese   Vietnam→Vietnamese
(→Section 4.7, Appendix VI)

-(i)an

This suffix is added to the names of countries to form adjectives which describe nationalities or their language:

Africa→African   Brazil→Brazilian (→Section 4.7, Appendix VI)

It is also used to form adjectives from the names of kings and queens, and to describe religious and political movements.

George→Georgian   Elizabeth→Elizabethan
Victoria→Victorian   Republic→Republican
Parliament→Parliamentarian   Francis→Franciscan

-ive
This suffix is used to make adjectives from verbs. The resulting adjective usually means *which performs the action of the verb*. For example *something impressive* is *something which impresses you*.
Common adjectives of this type are:

administer	⟶ administrative	explode	⟶	explosive
attract	⟶ attractive	impress	⟶	impressive
construct	⟶ constructive	intend	⟶	intensive
destroy	⟶ destructive	possess	⟶	possessive
digest	⟶ digestive	progress	⟶	progressive
exceed	⟶ excessive	respond	⟶	responsive
extend	⟶ extensive	succeed	⟶	successive

Notes on suffixes

1 Most of the other suffixes which you will meet form **adjectives** to describe things in the world of intellectual activity, science, technology and medicine:
   -ist, e.g. socialism → socialist; **-al**, e.g. crime → criminal; **-ic**, e.g. science → scientific; **-ary**, e.g. revolution → revolutionary; **-ory**, e.g. satisfy → satisfactory; **-ical**, e.g. geography → geographical; **-ate**, e.g. affection → affectionate; **-ent**, e.g., depend → dependent.
   Note also the suffix **-ous**, as in *enormous*, *previous* and *serious*.

2 There are a number of cases where a common everyday noun (of Germanic origin) has a corresponding scientific adjective (of Latin or Greek origin). For example, the word *sun* has an ordinary everyday adjective *sunny* (as in *a sunny day*), and also a scientific adjective *solar* (as in *solar energy*). Common examples are:

body	bodily	physical	*moon*	moon('s)	lunar
country	country	rural	*mouth*	mouth	oral
cat	cat('s)	feline	*night*	nightly	nocturnal
day	daily	diurnal	*salt*	salty	saline
dog	dog('s)	canine	*sea*	sea	marine/maritime
eye	eye	optical	*star*	starry	stellar
hand	hand	manual	*time*	timely	temporal
home	homely	domestic	*tooth*	tooth	dental
law	law	legal	*town*	town	urban
mind	mind	mental	*year*	yearly	annual

4.2.2 Participles

A number of participles (→ Section 7.2.3) in **-ing** and **-ed** are frequently used as adjectives. The commonest are:

-ing:			
amazing	daring	frightening	shocking
amusing	embarrassing	interesting	surprising
boring	entertaining	pleasing	thrilling
charming	exciting	promising	tiring
confusing	fascinating	satisfying	worrying

-ed			
amazed	conceited	excited	reserved
amused	disappointed	fascinated	satisfied
badly-behaved	distinguished	frightened	shocked
well-behaved	well-dressed	interested	surprised
bored	well-educated	pleased	tired
well-built	embarrassed	relaxed	unexpected
			worried

Notice also such compounds as *fast-moving; long-suffering; time-consuming; time-saving; air-conditioned; dry-cleaned; deep-frozen.*

Note
The difference in meaning between such pairs as *interesting/interested, boring/bored* and *exciting/excited* is:
The thing that excites you is *exciting* (i.e., the **active** participle).
The result is that *you* become *excited* (i.e., the **passive** participle).
e.g. *The film* was *boring. I* was so *bored* that I fell asleep.

4.2.3   Adjectives describing measurement

Adjectives which describe the measurement of *size, weight, value, time* can be made on the pattern:

CARDINAL NUMBER   + UNIT OF MEASUREMENT

For example, a conference which lasts *three days* could be described as a *three-day* conference. Notice that the unit (*day*) is in the singular.

Other examples are:
a ten-ton lorry a half-hour programme a twelve-inch ruler a 300 mm lens (a three-hundred-millimetre lens) a five-day week a six-mile walk a five-hour drive a three-litre engine a fifteen-storey building a five-star hotel a two-piece suit a three-course meal a sixteen-year-old schoolgirl

There is a similar construction using ordinal numbers, as in a first-class restaurant a third-rate (=poor) production a second-year student a seventeenth-century painting a third-floor flat.

4.3   Position of adjectives: attributive and predicative uses

Adjectives may be used **attributively**, i.e. they (usually) come before the noun or the pronoun *one(s)*; or **predicatively**, i.e. they are separated from the noun, usually following a verb like *be, seem, appear, look,* or in constructions like the ones given in Section 4.3.2.

4.3.1 Attributive

Examples:

a The *serious* rabbit and the *handsome* stranger.
I have enough money for you and your *little* ones.

b The adjective comes immediately after the pronouns *someone*, *somebody*, *something*, *somewhere*, and the corresponding forms with *any-*, *no-* and *every-*:
I feel that *something terrible* is about to happen.
Are you going *anywhere interesting* tonight?
'Who called?' '*Nobody important*.'
Everything useful has been kept; the rest has been thrown away.

c The adjective follows the noun in a few fixed expressions, mostly to do with important positions or the law:
a court martial   the Prince Regent   the Attorney General   the heir apparent   the President elect   the Postmaster General.

Note also the use of the word *proper* in such expressions as *the town proper*, i.e. the town itself, excluding the outskirts or the surrounding countryside.

d The adjectives *involved*, *concerned* and *present*

After the noun
I want to speak to the students *involved*.
(the students who have something to do with the matter)

The people *concerned* are waiting outside.
(the people who have something to do with the matter)

He will talk to the people *present*.
(the people who are in the building at the time)

Before the noun
an *involved* explanation = a *complicated* explanation
a *concerned* expression on her face = a *worried* expression
the *present* situation = the *current* situation

4.3.2 Predicative

a He *is poor* and I *am rich*.
The serious rabbit *became* even more *serious* than usual.
She soon *grew fond* of him.
You *look tired*.
The milk *turned sour* in the hot weather. (See also → Section 13.2.3).

b In constructions on the pattern MAKE ME ANGRY:
You *make* me very *angry*.
I *consider* her *brilliant*.
I *found* it quite *exciting*.
Please don't *think* me *rude*, but . . .

c In constructions on the pattern ACTION VERB + ADJECTIVE
DESCRIBING RESULT:
Please don't *tie* the knot too *tight*.
Would you *hold* the door *open* for me please?
He tried to escape so they *shot* him *dead*.

d In constructions on the pattern DRINK IT COLD:
The sentences *I always drink milk cold* and *I prefer to buy my
clothes second-hand* could be regarded as other ways of saying
I always drink milk when it is cold or *I prefer to buy clothes
which are second-hand*.

Other examples are:
I eat some vegetables *raw*, but I always eat cabbage *cooked*.
Most people drink coffee *black*, but I prefer mine *white*.
Some like it *hot*. (*film title*)
This car may look second-hand, but in fact I bought it *new*.

**4.3.3 Adjectives which can
be used only predicatively**

These adjectives are usually in the pattern

NOUN or PRONOUN	+	LOOK, FEEL, BE APPEAR, SEEM, etc.	+	PREDICATIVE ADJECTIVE

A number of these adjectives refer to temporary conditions, i.e.,
to something which is true only for a short time, such as states
of health:
ill well unwell faint.
You don't look very well. Have you been ill? I feel faint.

Other predicative adjectives are:
glad, content, upset, far (except in fixed expressions such as
the *Far East*) near (except in fixed expressions such as *the Near
East*)
and the set of adjectives with the prefix **a-**:
afraid, alert, alike, alive, alone, ashamed, asleep, awake,
aware (of).
e.g.   I'm so *glad* you were able to come.
       She's *upset* because she can't go out tonight.
       Who's *afraid* of Virginia Woolf? (*title of a play*)
       Which is my briefcase? They all look *alike* to me.
       Thank God you're still *alive*!
       I prefer to live *alone*.
       You ought to be *ashamed* of yourself!
       I fell *asleep* on the sofa.
       'Did I disturb you?' 'No, I was already *awake*.'

Many adjectives, when used predicatively, are followed by a
particular preposition, *afraid of, amazed at, worried about, good
at*, etc. A list of adjectives with their corresponding prepositions
is given in Appendix VII.

4.3.4 Adjectives which can be used only attributively

a inner outer latter former late (=dead)

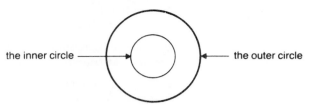

the inner circle ⟶ ⟵ the outer circle

e.g. the former Principal of the College
the late President Kennedy
The problem of unemployment and the problem of
inflation: the latter problem is more serious. (Note that
the latter=the last one mentioned, i.e., the problem of
inflation.)

The former and *the latter* often occur on their own:
Some people believe strongly in private enterprise, while
others think that state ownership is preferable. *The former*
usually support the Conservative Party, while most of *the
latter* are Labour supporters.

b mere sheer utter
All these words suggest that the noun they describe have the
maximum (*sheer, utter*) or the minimum (*mere*) quantity of the
qualities usually associated with the noun:
e.g. You're a *mere* child!=You are far too young to
understand.
It's a *sheer* waste of time and money!
What *utter* nonsense!

They are all used in an emphatic way. If you wanted to say
these things without special emphasis, you might say:
You're just a child or You're very young;
It's a complete (or *total*) waste of time and money,
What (a lot of) nonsense.

Mere often occurs with figures to suggest that they should be
higher:
e.g. Wages have increased 300 per cent in three years;
productivity has increased by *a mere 15 per cent* in the
same period.

c *Adjectives which have an adverbial meaning*
(adverbials → Chapter 12)
a *heavy* smoker=someone who smokes *a lot*
(i.e. *heavy* here does not refer to weight.)

an *old* friend=someone I have known *for a long time*
(i.e. *old* here does not refer to age.)

a *hard* worker=someone who works *well*
(i.e. *hard* here does not refer to the person's character.)

the *present* MP for Chester＝the MP who represents Chester *at the moment*
(i.e. *present* here is not the opposite of *absent*.)

our *new* neighbours＝the neighbours who have *just* moved in
(cf. *an old friend*).

d   certain   particular   chief   main   principal   sole   only
These words are used to identify which one you are talking about or which one is important or special in some way:
e.g.   She has a *certain* charm.＝a *particular kind* of charm
Certain people in this office are not working as hard as they should.＝I'm sure you know which people I mean, so I won't name them
a *particular* reason for wanting to know
the *chief* aim of the plan
the *main* argument against building a new supermarket
the *principal* reason
the *sole* survivor of the crash
the *only* time I go out

4.4   Order of adjectives

4.4.1   Position of adjectives in relation to determiners, etc.

determiners		ordinals	quantifiers	adjectives	np
BOTH ALL HALF	THE THIS/THESE THAT/THOSE MY etc.	LAST NEXT OTHER FIRST SECOND etc.	FEW LOT OF LITTLE 1,2,3, etc	ADJECTIVES★	NOUN PHRASE
A	B	C	D	E	F

4.4.2   Order of adjectives★   If you have more than one adjective in column E, the usual order is:

Value	Size	Age/ Temperature	Shape	Colour	Origin	Material
oeautiful	small	old	round	red	French	iron
nice	little	young	square	blue	Victorian	wooden
famous	enormous	new	triangular	black	London	cotton
important	heavy	original	circular	white	domestic	woollen
dirty	light	cold	L-shaped	light blue	urban	plastic
tall		hot		dark green	rural	metal

★To help you remember the order of these eight kinds of adjective, learn the sentence *Very soon a train should come* in which the bold letters stand for **v** value, **s** size. **a** age, t temperature, sh shape, c colour, o origin, m material.

Of course, you would not normally use so many adjectives before a noun. Here are some examples using four or five adjectives:

a beautiful old red London bus

all those enormous circular wooden tables

the last few original Victorian iron bridges

Notes:

1 Column **F**—**noun phrase**—includes **compound nouns** (◄ Section 1.7.8) such as frying pan, alarm clock, office block, law school, science block.

It also includes those cases where the first element is a noun used as an adjective such as:

gold coin, woman driver, government buildings, the city centre.

These compounds are never separated by other adjectives.

e.g. a famous old Georgian *city centre*

2 Certain verb forms may be put in immediately before adjectives which describe origin or material

i.e. **v s a t sh c** verb form **o m**

a *painted* ceramic tile   a *growing* French problem

$\underbrace{\text{verb form}}\ \underbrace{\text{material}}$ $\underbrace{\text{verb form}}\ \underbrace{\text{origin}}$

3 *Little* is often used as a sort of diminutive (◄ Section 1.7.2) in such combinations as:

a *pretty little* house   a *tiny little* man   a *sweet little* girl
a *beautiful little* pub

Big is sometimes used as an augmentative (◄ Section 1.7.2) in combination with *great* as in: a *great big* dog. Generally it comes *before* **value** adjectives:

a *big bad* wolf   a *big handsome* policeman   a *big tall* building   a *big fat* man

4 When you have two **value** adjectives coming together, the order usually does not matter. The difference between

a *beautiful, intelligent* woman and
an *intelligent, beautiful* woman

is very slight. The comma (,) suggests that the two adjectives are equally important (→ Appendix XV). There are a number of pairs of **value** adjectives which have fixed order, and may almost be regarded as single adjectives:

a *good honest* meal   a *good plain* steak   a *sweet old-fashioned* girl

5 The word *pretty* is both an adjective and an adverb (→ Chapter 12) meaning *quite* or *rather*. A sentence like *She's a pretty clever student* would be taken to mean *She's quite a clever student*. If you want to say that she is (a) pretty and (b) clever, you would use:

pause or comma   She's *a pretty, clever* student.
(In speaking, the comma would become a slight pause)

and   She's *a pretty and (a) clever* student.

change of order   She's a *clever, pretty* student.

6 We also use the comma (,) and the conjunction *and* in the following cases:
  a with **colour** adjectives:
    a *blue and red* striped tie
    a *brown, yellow and green* background

  b with adjectives used predicatively:
    I'm *tired and hungry*.
    I found the film *silly, vulgar and boring*.

  c as a special effect to give equal importance to each adjective:
    He is *young and handsome and romantic*.
    instead of the normal
    He is *young, handsome and romantic*.

4.5 Comparison of adjectives

4.5.1 We can compare

a *Two objects or sets**

$\boxed{A} = \boxed{B}$ A is *as big as* B.

$\boxed{A} > \boxed{\text{B}}$ A is *bigger than* B.

$\boxed{A} > \boxed{\text{B}}\ \boxed{\text{C}}$ A is *bigger than* $\begin{cases} \text{the rest.} \\ \text{any of the other letters.} \end{cases}$
     $\boxed{\text{D}}$

b *More than two objects or sets*

$\boxed{A}\ \boxed{\text{B}}\ \boxed{\text{C}}\ \boxed{\text{D}}$ A is *the biggest* $\begin{cases} \text{of all the letters} \\ \text{in the group.} \end{cases}$

*When they are asking or talking about preferences, people usually say 'Which do you like *best*?' even if there are only two objects.

4.5.2 The patterns in which adjectives appear when you are making comparisons are usually:

AS ADJ. AS	ADJ.-ER THAN
NOT AS ADJ. AS $\big\}$	THE ADJ.-EST $\big\}$ OF / IN
NOT SO ADJ. AS $\big\}$	

4.5.3 Form

We form the **comparative** (two objects compared) **and the superlative** (more than two objects compared) **in one of two** ways:
a Add **-er** or **-est** to the adjective.
b Put **more** or **most** before the adjective.

a *With -er and -est*

The following kinds of adjective form the comparative and superlative by adding **-er** and **-est**:

Monosyllables (i.e., having one syllable)

small–smaller–smallest   dry–drier–driest
green–greener–greenest   brave–braver–bravest
gay–gayer–gayest   near–nearer–nearest

Notes

1 Adjectives with spelling CONSONANT/SINGLE VOWEL/CONSONANT double the last consonant:
sad–sadder–saddest   thin–thinner–thinnest   fat–fatter–fattest

2 The irregular adjectives are:
good–better–best   much–more–most
bad–worse–worst   little–less–least
far { farther–farthest
    { further–furthest

Better is used as the comparative form of *well*, and *worse* as the comparative form of *ill* when we are talking about people's health:

She has been ill but she is getting better.
She is not well, and in fact she is getting worse.

Disyllables (i.e., having two syllables)
   i) ending in an unstressed vowel -y*, -ly and -ow
      e.g. happy → happier → happiest   lively → livelier → liveliest
      yellow → yellower → yellowest
  ii) ending in **-le -er** or **-ure**
      e.g. simple → simpler → simplest
      clever → cleverer → cleverest   mature → maturer → maturest
 iii) some other common adjectives:
      common, handsome, polite, pleasant, quiet

Notes

1 All these disyllabic adjectives can also form the comparative with *more* and *most*, and there are several which normally do, e.g. *eager* → *more eager*. If you are not sure, form the comparative with *more* and *most*.

2 The comparative of *little* meaning *small* is sometimes given as *littler* but we advise you to say *smaller* if you need a comparative form.

3 Adding the negative prefix **un-** does not affect the formation of the comparative. For example, we say *unhappy–unhappier* just as we say *happy–happier*.

---

*Note that -y becomes -i- after a consonant. 'gay → gayer' but 'happy → happier'.

b *With* **more** *and* **most**

The following kinds of adjective form the comparative and superlative with **more** and **most**:

i)   Adjectives with other endings such as **-ful, -less, -al, -ic, -ate, -ish, -ed, -ing, -ous, -ive, -ent, -ory/-ary, -(i)an, -ist, -able/-ible**
useful–more useful–most useful
vital–more vital–most vital
private–more private–most private
amused–more amused–most amused
serious–more serious–most serious
recent–more recent–most recent
hopeless–more hopeless–most hopeless
public–more public–most public
foolish–more foolish–most foolish
boring–more boring–most boring
pensive–more pensive–most pensive

ii)   other common disyllabic adjectives such as foreign, solemn

iii)   all adjectives of more than two syllables
peculiar–more peculiar–most peculiar
cowardly–more cowardly–most cowardly
horrible–more horrible–most horrible

4.5.4   Uses of the comparative and superlative forms

a To say that one object has more of a quality than another object:
e.g.   Pluto is more distant than Mars.
Tokyo is a bigger city than Kyoto.
It is more interesting to visit a place than simply to read about it.

If you want to say $\boxed{B} \langle \boxed{A}$ instead of $\boxed{A} \rangle \boxed{B}$, you can do it in one of three ways:

i)   with the construction NOT SO/AS...AS:
B is not as big as A *or* B is not so big as A.
Mars is not so/as distant as Pluto.

ii)   with an adjective of opposite meaning:
B is smaller than A.
Kyoto is smaller than Tokyo.

iii)   with the words **less** and **least**, which are the opposite of **more** and **most**:

Restaurant A is less crowded than restaurant B.

Item A is the least expensive of all the items.

Only use this form with **less/least** when you want to say *all the objects are X, but some are less X than others.* In the example above, both restaurants are crowded, but A is less crowded than B; all the items are expensive, but A is the least expensive.

b *To describe something which is increasing* (**more and more**) *or decreasing* (**less and less**):

People are getting *more and more worried* about the economic situation.

In spite of my diet, I seem to be getting *fatter and fatter!*

As I get older, I find I am getting *less and less interested* in politics.

c To describe how one thing increases or decreases in relation to another. The pattern for this is:

```
          LESS              LESS
THE   MORE   A   ,   THE   MORE   B
      -ER               -ER
```

e.g. *The bigger* your income, *the more* you spend.

This construction is used with adverbs (→ Chapter 12) as much as with adjectives.

e.g. *The sooner* you finish, *the sooner* you can go home.

4.6 Appendix V
Cardinal and Ordinal Numbers

The numbers in bold type are either unique (e.g., the numbers 1 to 12, 100, 1000) or they differ slightly from the regular pattern (e.g. 14, **four**+**teen**, is regular, *fourteen*, 15, **five**+**teen** is irregular, *fifteen*.

0	**zero**		30	**thirty**	thirtieth
1	**one**	first	40	**forty**	fortieth
2	**two**	second	50	**fifty**	fiftieth
3	**three**	third	60	sixty	sixtieth
4	**four**	fourth	70	seventy	seventieth
5	**five**	fifth	80	**eighty**	eightieth
6	**six**	sixth	90	ninety	ninetieth
7	**seven**	seventh	100	**one hundred**	(the) hundredth
8	**eight**	eighth	101	one hundred and one	(the) hundred and first
9	**nine**	ninth	102	one hundred and two	(the) hundred and second
10	**ten**	tenth	etc.	etc.	etc.
11	**eleven**	eleventh	200	two hundred	(the) two hundredth
12	**twelve**	twelfth	201	two hundred and one	(the) two hundred and first
13	**thirteen**	thirteenth	etc.	etc.	etc.
14	fourteen	fourteenth	1000	one thousand	(the) thousandth
15	**fifteen**	fifteenth	1001	one thousand and one	(the) thousand and first
16	sixteen	sixteenth	etc.	etc.	etc.
17	seventeen	seventeenth	2000	two thousand	(the) two thousandth
18	**eighteen**	eighteenth	2001	two thousand and one	(the) two thousand and first
19	nineteen	nineteenth	etc.	etc.	etc.
20	**twenty**	twentieth	10 000	ten thousand	(the) ten thousandth
21	twenty-one	twenty-first	100 000	one hundred thousand	(the) hundred thousandth
22	twenty-two	twenty-second	1 000 000	one million etc.	(the) millionth
23	twenty-three etc.	twenty-third etc.			

Notes

1 The difference in pronunciation between the **-teen** and the **-ty** numbers is small, and English people often mishear them. You can make your pronunciation a little clearer by stressing the **-teen** ending, but not the -ty ending:
thir*teen* ← but *thir*ty, four*teen* but *for*ty, fif*teen* but *fif*ty, etc.

2 The numbers 100–199 and 1000–1099 may be said with *a* instead of *one*: 123 = *one hundred and twenty-three* or *a hundred and twenty-three*.

3 There are various ways of writing and saying dates. In speaking, we suggest you use the commonest pattern, which is:

THE **-st / -nd / -rd / -th** OF (MONTH), NINETEEN EIGHTY-NINE

The corresponding way of writing this date would be:
xth month, 1989   e.g. 24th February, 1989
or x month, 1989   e.g. 24 February, 1989

4 Notice that the cardinal number ending **-ty** (as in *twenty*) changes to the ordinal number ending **-tieth** (as in *twentieth*).

5 The spoken forms of 0

a **nought** ([nɔːt])   used in mathematics –
0.7 = nought point seven
.07 = point nought seven

b **zero** [zɪːrou]   used in science, for example, in temperatures –
−15°C = minus fifteen degrees *or* fifteen degrees below zero

c **o** ([ou])   used in telephone numbers –
01–500–3026 = o one – five double o – three o two six

d **nil** or **nothing**   used in scores in such games as football –
2–0 = the score was two nothing *or* two-nil

6 Books use various numbering systems, including Roman numerals: I, II, III, IV, V, VI, VII, VIII, IX, X, etc. for 1–10. Dates on monuments are also sometimes written in Roman, e.g. 1985 would be MCMLXXXV, where M = 1000 (CM = 1000−100 = 900), L = 50, XXX = 30 (i.e. 3 × 10), and V = 5.

4.7 Appendix VI:
Nationality adjectives

The usual pattern to form the adjective is

NAME OF COUNTRY +
- -ESE
- -(I)AN (or -N)
- -ISH (or SH, or CH)
- -I

-ese		-(i)an (-n)					
China	Chinese	Africa	African	Hungary	Hungarian		
Japan	Japanese	America	American	India	Indian		
Lebanon	Lebanese	Asia	Asian	Iran	Iranian		
Malta	Maltese	Argentina	Argentinian	Italy	Italian		
Portugal	Portuguese	Australia	Australian	Libya	Libyan		
Sudan	Sudanese	Belgium	Belgian	Mexico	Mexican		
Vietnam	Vietnamese	Brazil	Brazilian	Norway	Norwegian		
		Canada	Canadian	Romania	Romanian		
		Egypt	Egpytian	Russia	Russian		
		Europe	European	Scandinavia	Scandinavian		
		Germany	German	Venezuela	Venezuelan		

Note

-ese: you refer to all the people of, for example, China as *the Chinese* or *the Chinese people*

-(i)an: you refer to all the people of, for example, Canada as *the Canadians* or *the Canadian people*

-ese: one man from, for example, Portugal is *a Portuguese.*

-(i)an: one man from, for example, Egypt is *an Egyptian.*

-ish(-sh, -ch)			
Country	*Adjective*	*One citizen*	*All the people*
Britain	British	a Briton	the British
Denmark	Danish	a Dane	the Danes or the Danish
England	English	an Englishman	Englishmen or the English
Finland	Finnish	a Finn	the Finns or the Finnish
Ireland	Irish	an Irishman	Irishmen or the Irish
Poland	Polish	a Pole	the Poles or the Polish people
Scotland	Scottish*	a Scot or a Scotsman	Scotsmen or the Scots**
Spain	Spanish	a Spaniard	the Spanish (people)
Sweden	Swedish	a Swede	the Swedes or the Swedish
Turkey	Turkish	a Turk	the Turks or the Turkish people
Wales	Welsh	a Welshman	Welshmen or the Welsh
France	French	a Frenchman	Frenchmen or the French
Holland	Dutch	a Dutchman	Dutchmen or the Dutch

*also *Scots*. The adjective *Scotch* is best used to describe certain traditional Scottish drinks and types of food such as *Scotch whisky* and *Scotch eggs*.
**or *the Scottish people*.

-i *and* **various**			
Country	*Adjective*	*Citizen*	*all the People*
Czechoslovakia	Czech	a Czech	the Czechs
Greece	Greek	a Greek	the Greeks
Iraq	Iraqi	an Iraqi	the Iraqis
Israel	Israeli	an Israeli	the Israelis
Kuwait	Kuwaiti	a Kuwaiti	the Kuwaitis
Oman	Omani	an Omani	the Omanis
Pakistan	Pakistani	a Pakistani	the Pakistanis
Qatar	Qatari	a Qatari	the Qataris
Switzerland	Swiss	a Swiss	the Swiss
Thailand	Thai	a Thai	the Thais
Saudi Arabia	Saudi	a Saudi	the Saudis

Some special cases

Arab One person of this race is *an Arab*. The people are *the Arabs*.
The adjective is also *Arab* as in *Arab customs*.
Their language is *Arabic*.
The adjective *Arabian* is now little used, except in the title *Arabian Nights* and occasionally in the expression *Saudi Arabian* (we advise you to use the adjective *Saudi* on its own).

Jew One person of this race is *a Jew*. The people are *the Jews* or *the Jewish people*.
The adjective is *Jewish*, as in *Jewish customs*.
Their language (originally and in present-day Israel) is *Hebrew*.

4.8 Appendix VII: Adjectives + Prepositions

at
amazed
amused
astonished
shocked
surprised
bad
brilliant
clever
expert
good
hopeless
quick
weak

against
prejudiced

for
answerable
bad
bound
convenient
due (=ready)

eager
famous
fit
good
grateful
late
prepared
qualified
ready
sorry
suitable
useful
responsible
eligible

to
accustomed
allergic
answerable
attentive
averse
blind
close
contrary

due
faithful
harmful
inferior
married
new
peculiar
sensitive
similar
superior
thankful
used (=accustomed)

about
angry
annoyed
anxious
certain
clear
concerned
(=worried)
crazy
curious
doubtful
excited
glad
happy

hesitant
honest
mad
mistaken
positive
puzzled
sad
selfish
sensible
sensitive
serious
sincere
sorry
sure
suspicious
thrilled
uneasy
worried
wrong

of
afraid
ahead
ashamed
aware
capable
certain

confident
conscious
critical
envious
fond
full
guilty
independent
jealous
proud
sick
sure
suspicious
tired

with
angry with
    someone
annoyed with
    someone
busy
concerned
contented
delighted
disappointed
disgusted
familiar

level
patient
pleased
satisfied

from
absent
different
safe
separate

on
dependent
intent
keen

in
(in)experienced
interested

Notes

1 **Adjectives in -ed** are often followed by **by**, especially when the -ed word may be regarded as a verb past participle.

2 The construction ADJ.+AT, as in *good at* refers to how well you can do something.
The construction ADJ.+FOR, as in *good for* refers to what something is worth.

5 Contents

5 Pronouns

The Kind Duck and the Poor Frog

One beautiful summer's day, a duck decided to go to the river for a picnic. She took a lot of food with her, and was really looking forward to eating it. She sat down on the river bank and spread the food out in front of her.

'You're not going to eat all that food yourself, are you?' said a small voice.

She looked up and saw a frog sitting at the water's edge.

'Please give me some of it. I am very poor and very hungry,' pleaded the frog, wiping a tear from his eye.

She gave him a sandwich. To her surprise he did not eat it, but simply put it on the ground beside him.

'Won't you give me something else? After all, my need is greater than yours.'

Bit by bit, the kind-hearted duck handed over most of her food: cakes and biscuits, apples and sweets. Soon, the frog had a huge pile of food next to him. With an effort he picked it all up, put it on his back, and started to swim away across the river. But the food was so heavy that he sank like a stone, and the duck never saw him again.

Moral: When it is really hard to say 'no', say '*no*'.

A Personal pronouns

5.1 Summary of forms

Subject	Object	Separate	Possessive adjective	Possessive pronoun	Reflexive/ Emphatic
I	me	me!	my	mine	myself
you*	you	you!	your	yours	yourself/ves
we	us	us!	our	ours	ourselves
he	him	him!	his	his	himself
she	her	her!	her	hers	herself
it	it	it!	its	(its)	itself
they	them	them!	their	theirs	themselves

*The old singular form *thou-thee-thy-thine-thyself* is no longer in use except in dialect. You might see it in poetry and religious writings.

5.2   Meaning and use of personal pronouns

Pronouns *are used to replace a noun already referred to,* that is, we use them instead of repeating the noun:

e.g. *The duck* decided to go to the river. *She* took a lot of food with *her*.

   . . . *the frog* had *a huge pile of food. He* picked *it* all up . . .

   This house will go to *the children. It* will be *theirs* after my death.

The pronoun it is used in some impersonal expressions (→ 5.3.2)

e.g. *It* was a beautiful summer's day,

   It is raining.

We distinguish three persons to which pronouns refer

The person or people speaking:	**I**	and	**we**	**(first person)**
The person or people spoken to:	**you**			**(second person)**
The person or people spoken about:	**he/she**	and	**they**	
The thing or things spoken about:	**it**	and	**they**	**(third person)**

He is used for male human beings, and for some animals, such as house pets, horses and favourite farm animals.

She is used for female human beings, and for female pets. Ships and other naval vessels are traditionally referred to as *she*.

It is used for all other inanimate objects and for animals where the sex is not known or not important.

They is used as the plural of **he**, **she** and **it**.

The parts of the third person plural pronoun (**them**, **their**, **theirs** and **themselves**) are also used in the following cases:

a After the indefinite pronouns *everybody*, *somebody*, etc. (← Section 3.6)

   e.g. *Everybody* should have *their* books with *them*.

   Somebody has parked *their* car in front of my drive.

   You could also say, more correctly,

   Everybody should have *his* books with him.

   Somebody has parked *his* car in front of my drive.

   (But see section **b** below.)

b **They** etc., is used to mean **he** or **she**, especially now that many women do not like the use of **he** to refer to an unspecified person who could be male or female. For example, an advertisement might read:

   WE ARE LOOKING FOR SOMEONE TO HELP IN THE SHOP. *THEY* MUST BE SMART AND HAVE *THEIR* OWN CAR

The alternative, which is rather clumsy, is to say:

   . . . IN THE SHOP. *HE OR SHE* MUST BE SMART AND HAVE *HIS OR HER* OWN CAR

5.3 Subject pronouns

Singular	Plural
I	we
you	you
he she it	they

5.3.1 Subject of verbs

a The **subject pronouns** are used with verbs:
e.g. *I am* very poor.
Won't you give me something else?
She sat down on the river bank.
They went around the world together.

b They cannot be left out except in very informal conversation:
e.g. Looks like rain.   *for* It looks like rain.
Saw John last night.   *for* I saw John last night.
Been anywhere interesting? *for* Have you been anywhere interesting?

c In modern English, they are always followed by a verb. In the case of *short answers*, the verb is a modal or an auxiliary (→ Section 7.2.2):

Question   *Short answer*
'Who wants a drink?'   'I do.'
'Who is going to the party?' 'We are.'
'Who made that noise?'   'She did.'

Here, you can use the *separate* forms, which are the same as the **object pronouns** (**me, him, her, us, them**):
e.g. 'Who's there?   'Me.' (or 'It's me.')* *for* 'I am.'
'Who broke this window?   'Not me.'   *for*
'I didn't.'

*The 'correct' form *it is I* is no longer used, unless the pronoun is followed by more information about it:
e.g. *It's them* but *It is they who must pay for the damage.*

5.3.2 *It* in impersonal expressions

The pronoun **it** is used in a wide range of expressions where there is no obvious subject (→ Section 13).
e.g. It's raining/snowing/freezing/windy/cloudy/cold/hot etc.
It is half past six./It's my birthday today./It's June the fifth.
It is a nice day for walking.
It's me, sir.
It is time to go.
It seems/looks as if/appears etc.

Notes

1 The word **there** is used in a similar way as a kind of 'empty' subject. In such cases it is unstressed and usually takes the verb **is** or **was** i.e., in the singular, regardless of what follows:
  e.g. There's someone to see you.
  There's some people waiting to see you.
  There was very little left to eat.

2 In sentence patterns like IT IS/ADJECTIVE/TO . . .
  it stands for the part of the sentence which follows the adjective.
  e.g. It is important to drive carefully in built-up areas.
  This is the usual way to say *X is important* when X is a long phrase or group of words. (In this case X = *to drive carefully in built-up areas.*) It would be very unusual to say
  To drive carefully in built-up areas is important.

5.3.3 Impersonal use of *they, you* and *we*

They
They is used to refer to unknown people who have power, authority or expertise which we do not have. At its simplest, **they** have knowledge or information:
e.g. *They say* we're going to have a long, hot summer.
This is the usual way to express this idea, rather than the very formal *It is said that we're . . .'*
At its most political, **they** are the people who rule our lives but who do not understand us:
e.g. Even if you earn a bit of money, *they* always find a way to take it off you.
  I hear *they*'ve invented a bomb that kills people without damaging property.
It is this use of the disliked and mistrusted **they** which gives rise to the expression *them and us* to describe those who have the power (*them*) and the ordinary people (*us*) who suffer.

You
You is frequently used, often with a very weak stress([jə]), in statements and descriptions when the speaker is not thinking of anyone in particular, i.e., when he or she is generalizing:
e.g. How to make an omelette. First *you* beat three eggs in a bowl, then *you* add a little salt and pepper.
  (a recipe, i.e., instructions about how to do something)
  You never know what will happen next, do *you*? (general comment on the situation)
  You can never find a taxi when you want one, can *you*?
  (i.e., this describes the situation that confronts everybody. It is based upon the speaker's personal experience (*I* can never find a taxi when *I* want one), and asks for the listener's agreement and understanding.)

We
We is used to mean *all of us*, i.e., the speaker, his listener(s) and

other people in the same situation. It can be a simple observation, as in the sentence

We're going to have some rain by the look of it.

or it can be political, calling for the solidarity of *us* against *them*, as in the sentence:

They can tell *us* what to do but they can't tell *us* what to think.

Compare **we** and **you** in these situations:
(*see illustration left*)

Notes

1 There is a pronoun **one – one – one's – oneself** which is impersonal, but it is not often used except in formal speech. The sentence *one can never find a taxi when one wants one*, is possible, but we advise you to use the impersonal **you** in such cases.

e.g. You can never find a taxi when you want one.

2 The passive (→ Section 8.9) is used in impersonal expressions such as ENGLISH SPOKEN instead of WE SPEAK ENGLISH. These passive constructions are much more usual in formal situations, e.g. in official notices.

5.3.4 Order of the subject pronouns

The accepted patterns are:

a X AND I

You and I can go together.

Anna and I are just good friends.

b HE/SHE/IT/THEY/AND X

She and her husband never go out together.

He and several other people have expressed their interest.

c X AND YOU or YOU AND X

Either pattern is possible, but YOU AND X is more frequent in speaking.

You and your friends are welcome to come any time.

5.4 Object pronouns

Singular	Plural
me	us
you	you
him her it	them

5.4.1   Uses of object pronouns

a Their commonest use is as the object of verbs (→ Section 13) and prepositions (→ Chapter 6):

After verbs
I still love *him*.
Take *me* to your leader.
Where have you put *them*?

After prepositions
Look *at me*!
I want to go *with them*.
Between you and me, I think she's mad.

b As we have seen (← Section 5.3.1 c), the object form of the pronoun is used when we want to use the pronoun alone or after *It's* . . . . It is more emphatic than the form SUBJECT PRONOUN + AUXILIARY VERB.

	Emphatic	*Normal*
'Who wants an ice-cream?'	'Me!'	'I do.'
'Who broke the window?'	'Not me!'	'I didn't.'

5.4.2   Indirect object pronouns

The same pronouns are used as **indirect objects**. The pattern is

VERB	INDIRECT OBJECT	DIRECT OBJECT
give	me, us	
tell	him, her	something
show	them	
etc.		

e.g. Can you *tell me* the time, please?
      I'd like to *show you* something.
      Ask him what he's doing.
      Don't *give them* any more sweets.
      They've *offered us* a flat in the town centre.
Common verbs on this pattern are:
   ask, bring, buy, fetch, give, hand, lend, pass, send, show, teach, tell

A similar pattern occurs in the following cases:
Get me a drink!
Can you *find us* a table near the window, please?
Why don't you *make him* an offer for his house?
Sing me a love song!
Write me a letter.

Note
There is a construction using the passive voice (→ Section 8.8 ff)

with these verbs, where the **indirect object** becomes the **subject pronoun**:

e.g. They gave me a present.
I was given a present.

It is used especially when the subject *they* in the active sentence is impersonal, i.e., does not refer to anyone in particular. For example, the sentence *They've offered us a flat* becomes *We've been offered a flat*.

5.4.3 Order of the object pronouns

a In general, the order is less important than it is for the subject pronouns, but we advise you to keep to the same order i.e.,
X AND ME   HIM, etc. AND X   YOU AND X
He spoke to *my father and me*. (→ Section 5.6.1 d)
I visited *them and their family* in Chatham.
I'd like to have a word with *you and John* this afternoon.

b Where there are two objects, one direct and one indirect, the possible patterns are:

VERB	INDIRECT OBJECT	DIRECT OBJECT
Pass	me	(it)
	John	the salt

VERB	DIRECT OBJECT	INDIRECT OBJECT
Pass	it	to me
	the salt	to John

The combinations *pass John it* and *pass me it* are possible but unusual.

5.4.4 Subject or object? The problem of . . . *more than him/more than he*

The sentence *John likes Anne more than Mary* is ambiguous, i.e., it can have two meanings:
A John likes Anne more than he likes Mary.
B John likes Anne more than Mary likes Anne.

Using pronouns, we avoid the ambiguity in the following way:
A (Talking about Mary) He likes Anne *more than her*. (i.e., more than he likes her)
B (Talking about Mary) He likes Anne *more than she does*.

The same applies to *as . . . as*:
e.g. He can speak French as well as me/I can.

5.5 Possessive adjectives and possessive pronouns

Singular	Plural
my–mine	our–ours
you–yours	you–yours
his–his ⎱ her–hers ⎰ its–(its) ⎰	their–theirs

5.5.1 Possessive adjectives

a The **possessive adjectives** are used before nouns to say who is the possessor* of the noun. They are invariable, i.e., they do not change:

my book – my books   our child – our children
his friends   her brother and sister   their house

*For the meaning of *possessor*, (◄— Section 1.8.1).

b We use the possessive adjective even when it is quite clear who the possessor is, especially with *parts of the body*:

Have *you* hurt *your* arm?
She is going to wash *her* hair.
They decided to keep *their* hats on *their* heads.
I must get *my* teeth seen to.

Notes

1 We use **the** instead of the possessive in the pattern
VERB+OBJECT+PREPOSITION+part of the body
I tapped *him on the shoulder*. (not *on his shoulder*)
He shook *me by the hand*. (not *by my hand*)
The same is true with passive constructions:
I was bitten *on the ankle*.

2 People sometimes use **the** instead of the possessive when they are talking about a particular possession in their 'sphere of interest' (◄—2.2.3 b), e.g., *the car   the house   the dog*
Clean the car, paint the house, take the dog for a walk.

c Double possession, as in *my and my brother's business* can lead to difficult constructions, and sometimes to ambiguities (more than one meaning). The sentence *These are John's and my books* might mean *These books belong to both of us* or *Some of these books are mine, and the rest of them belong to John.*

d My *and* **my own**
The word **own** in the pattern POSSESSIVE ADJECTIVE+OWN +NOUN, is used to emphasize that the object or the action is *yours and not someone else's.*

Compare:
⎰ Wash *your* hair!   =Your hair is dirty, so wash it.
⎱ Wash *your own* hair!   =Wash it yourself, don't expect
                                                someone else to do it for you.

{ This is John's room. = John uses this room.

{ John has *his own* room. = He doesn't share it with anyone else.

Other examples:

We grow *all our own* vegetables.

'Would you like a cigarette?' 'No thanks, I'll smoke *my own*.'

They live with their parents but one day they hope to have a home *of their own*.

Note also the expression *on my own* meaning *alone* or *by myself*.*

*REMEMBER! own is *never* used without a possessive. We say *He lives in his own flat* or *He has a flat of his own*.

5.5.2 Possessive pronouns

The **possessive pronouns** *mine* etc., are used when the noun is understood:

'Is this John's book?' 'No, it's mine.' (= my book.)

They have the same meaning as the possessive form for nouns using -'s or -s':

'Is this your book?' 'If it isn't *mine*, it must be *John's*.'

That is, they answer the question *Whose is it?*

They are also commonly used in the following situations:

a Comparisons

Our car is bigger than *yours*.

b In the pattern A(N) X OF MINE

A friend of mine has just bought a house in Esher.

The expression *a friend of mine* is much commoner than *my friend*:

John is a friend of mine = I regard him as a friend, but he is only one of a number of friends.

John is my friend = he is someone special (or John is the only or best friend I have).

The pattern A(N) X OF MINE also occurs with nouns, as in:

He is a friend of my father's, with the meaning *one friend from my father's circle of friends. It is an obsession of Joe's* means *one obsession amongst the many obsessions which Joe has*. You can also say *He is one of my father's friends* and *It is one of Joe's obsessions* with no important change of meaning.

5.6 Reflexive emphatic pronouns

Singular	Plural
my + self = **myself**	our + selves = **ourselves**
your + self = **yourself**	your + selves = **yourselves**
her + self = **herself** him + self = **himself** it + self = **itself**	them + selves = **themselves**

5.6.1 Reflexives

a There are a number of verbs where the subject and the object of the action are the same:

Look at yourself in the mirror!
We *enjoyed ourselves* very much in London.
Have you *hurt yourself*?
I've left my purse on the bus. I could *kick myself*!
Did the children *behave themselves*?
We *washed ourselves* in cold water.

In each case, the stress is on the verb. In the sentence *He's old enough now to be able to dress himself*, the stress falls on the pronoun *himself*, because the sentence means *He is old enough to dress himself, he doesn't need anyone else to do it for him*.

VERB + ... SELF/VES + OBJECT

The **reflexive pronoun** is also used in sentences on the same pattern as *Make me a sandwich* (← Section 2.1 c):
e.g. I'll just *get myself something to eat* before we go out.
Find yourself somewhere to sit.
She *made herself* (or *fixed herself*) a drink.
I've just *bought myself* a new hi-fi.

b PREPOSITION + ... SELF/SELVES
There are a few cases where prepositions are followed by the **reflexive pronoun** (e.g., *myself*) instead of the ordinary **object pronoun** (e.g., *me*):

i) where the preposition is part of a **phrasal verb** (→ Chapter 11).
Look after yourself.
Take care of yourself.

ii) after *for* in such sentences as
Don't do it *for him*, let him do it *for himself*.

iii) after *by* in the expression BY ... SELF/VES meaning *alone*:
She lives by herself. = alone
He's old enough to go to London by himself. = on his own
I did it all by myself! = nobody helped me

iv) some people use **myself** instead of **me** in the pattern
PREPOSITION + SOMEONE/AND ME/MYSELF
The quarrel is between him and myself   *for* him and me
They wrote to John and myself   *for* John and me

Reflexive

X and Y are very proud of themselves

Reciprocal

X and Y are very proud of each other

c Reflexive or reciprocal? **themselves** or **each other**?

Note the difference between these two statements about a brother and sister:

A They are old enough now to look after themselves.
B They are very close: they always look after each other.

Sentence A means that *he* looks after *himself*, and *she* looks after *herself*. Sentence B means that *he* looks after *her*, and *she* looks after *him*.

The difference in meaning is sometimes very slight. Referring to the Freemasons' Society, one man said:

'They look after each other.' = They are good to each other in times of difficulty, and this is a good thing.

The other man said:

'They look after themselves.' = They only care about themselves, they are not interested in other people.

5.6.2 Emphatic use of ... *self/ves*

a The ... **self/ves pronouns** are used to emphasize that *the person concerned and not someone else* did something:

'What a pretty dress.' 'Do you like it? *I* made it *myself*.'
'Would you carry this for me?' 'Carry it *yourself*!'

The usual position of the **emphatic pronoun** is at the end of the phrase, after the *object* or *complement*, but it can come immediately after the *subject* in more formal style:

e.g. Most people prefer sunshine, but *I myself* prefer rain.
The company is losing money – *the boss himself* told me.

b The ... **self/ves** form is also used in the pattern NOUN + ... SELF/VES to contrast the difference between two parts of something:

They have a beautiful home. *The house itself* is quite small, but the garden is enormous.
Some towns in the north are not very nice, but *the people themselves* are very friendly.

B Other pronouns

5.7 Interrogatives: *who? what? which? whose?*

Who?
The pronoun **who**, can be subject or object*:

*The object form of the interrogative pronoun **whom?** is now rarely used except in formal style, especially in the pattern PREPOSITION + WHOM?, e.g., *To whom should I address my complaint?* for *Who should I complain to?*

Who loves her?
(Perhaps they all love her!)

Who does she love?
(Perhaps she loves them all!)

Whose?
Whose can be either an adjective or a pronoun:
Whose car is that? (adjective)
Whose is that car? (pronoun)
There is no important difference of meaning between the two sentences.

What? *and* **which?**
What is used when you wish to identify something:
e.g. *What's* that?'   'It's a screwdriver.'
    '*What* are you doing?'   'I'm making a kitchen table.'
It can be used as an adjective or a pronoun with the meaning *what kind of*?:
e.g. '*What* are you going to wear for the dance tonight?'
    '*What clothes* are you taking with you on holiday?'

What books do we need?

Which is used when you wish to identify one or more things or people from a group of things or people. It can be used as an adjective or as a pronoun.
e.g. She has four boyfriends. *Which* does she like best? (Or *Which one* does . . . ?)
    Which is heavier, a kilo of feathers or a kilo of gold? (*children's joke*)

The difference between **what?** and **which?** is sometimes very slight:

What books do we need for the course?	=you are not thinking of any particular books.
Which books do we need for the course?	=which particular ones from a particular list of books.

Which books do we need?

5.8 Relatives: *who(m),*
which, whose, that

The relative pronouns are used to join ideas, often on the pattern
NOUN + INFORMATION ABOUT THE NOUN (also ➞ Chapter 14)

e.g. John is a man.   *John* understands machines.

John is *a man who* understands machines.

John is a man.   *His* work takes him abroad a lot.

John is *a man whose work* takes him abroad a lot.

Mathematics is a subject.   I find *it* difficult.

Mathematics is *a subject which* I find difficult.

or Mathematics is *a subject that* I find difficult.

When the pronoun is the object of the verb, as in the sentence
Mathematics is a subject that/which I find difficult
the pronoun is usually omitted:
Mathematics is a subject I find difficult.
Similarly,
John is someone I have known for a long time.
(For the rules concerning the omission of the relative pronoun,
see →14.9.3).

5.9 Quantitative and distributive pronouns: *some, each, all*, etc.

(← also Chapter 3).
Quantitative and **distributive pronouns** can combine with **personal object pronouns** as follows:

Quantitative distributive		*Personal object*	*Quantitative distributive*		*Object*
some			some		
(not) any		us	(not any)		
several			a little		
few			much		
a few	of	you	most	of	it
most			none		
none		them	all		
all*					
both					
either					
each (one)					

Reminder: **every** is only an adjective and must be followed by the pronoun **one**:
e.g. every one of you.

Both and *all* can also follow the pronoun: *She loves them both, We have all eaten.* The difference in meaning is slight. See note on p. 62.

5.10 Indefinite pronouns (*somebody, anybody*, etc.)

Note: For the change from **some-** to **any-**, see ← Section 3.4. For the difference between not . . . any- and no-, see ← Section 3.4.1.

5.10.1 With *else*

The indefinite pronouns, and also the adverbs with **-where**, can be followed by the word **else**. The meaning is similar to *more another* or *different*:
I did not take the message. *Someone else* must have taken it. (i.e., another person, not me.)

Do you want *anything else*?
(i.e. you have had several things. Do you need any more?)
We always go to Don Giovanni's. Can't we go *somewhere else*
for a change?
(i.e. to another, different restaurant.)
Why can't I go to the party? *Everyone else* is going.
(i.e. all the others, but not me.)
Won't you give me *something else*?
(i.e. something more.)

5.10.2 Possessive form

These pronouns form their possessive with -'s:
somebody's anybody's nobody's everybody's
someone's anyone's no-one's everyone's

Examples
It's *nobody's business* if I do.
It is *anybody's guess* how long the strike will last.
She has taken *everyone's clothes* to the laundrette.

When the word **else** follows the pronoun, add the -'s to **else**:
e.g. My car has broken down. Can I borrow *someone else's*?
Must I do *everyone else's work* as well as my own?
If she was *anyone else's* sister, I would tell her exactly what
I think of her. (i.e., If she was not your sister . . .)

5.11 *One(s), other, another*

5.11.1 One(s)

We use **one(s)** as a pronoun to replace a count noun already
referred to. The most frequent patterns are:

a ADJECTIVE + ONE(S)
'Do you want a blue pen or a black *one*?'   (i.e. a black
                                                   pen)

'Give me a blue *one*.'   (i.e. a blue
                                                   pen)

'Which dress shall I wear?'
'Why don't you wear your nice black *one*?'   (i.e. your
                                                   black dress)

'What do you think of these new desks?'
'I preferred the old *ones*.'   (i.e. the old
                                                   desks)

Notes

1 Although it is not always necessary to add **one(s)** after an
   adjective (e.g. 'Shall I wear my striped shirt or my check
   shirt?' 'I prefer the striped (one).'), we advise you to use **one(s)**
   to avoid confusion with expressions like **the old**, which means
   old people (← Section 2.2.3 e).

2 A mass noun is not replaced:
   Some people like English mustard, others **prefer French**.

b THE ONE(S)+ADJECTIVAL PHRASE/CLAUSE
(For adjectival phrases and clauses, see→Section 14.9.1).
'Which are your favourite chocolates?'
'I like *the ones with soft centres*.' (i.e., the chocolates with . . .)
'Which dress shall I wear?'
'Why don't you wear *the one you bought for Penny's wedding*?' (i.e., the dress which you . . .)

Note
One, used as a cardinal number, occurs in the expression: ONE OF THE+PLURAL COUNT NOUN, as in
Roy is *one of the finest jazz pianists* I have ever heard.

5.11.2 Other/another

a The word **other** is an adjective (e.g., *the other day*, *in other words*). When it is used with the indefinite article, the two words are joined: AN+OTHER=ANOTHER (e.g., another story). Notice that **another** has two meanings:
Would you like another drink? (i.e., one more of the same)
Would you like another drink? (i.e., a different drink)
To avoid the ambiguity (the danger that you will be misunderstood), use *different*:
I don't like this beer. Can I try another (or a *different*) kind?

b The words **other** and **another** are used as pronouns, and occur most often in these patterns:

i) *In contrast to* **this, one, some**
e.g. *This* is the only C60 cassette I have. All *the others* are C90 cassettes.
Anna bought two folders. She kept *one* for herself, and gave *the other* to Michael.
Some people like English mustard, *others* prefer French.

ii) **Each other/one another**
The expressions really mean the same, but we tend to use **each other** for two people or things, and **one another** for more than two.

Joe and Anna *looked at each other* for a moment.
We must all try to help *one another*.

For the difference between **each other/one another** and reflexives with **self/ves**, see ◄ Section 5.6.1 c.

5.12 Demonstrative pronouns

The demonstratives **this/these** and **that/those** (◄2.4.4) can also be used as pronouns:
e.g. Listen to *this*!
Look at *that*!
These aren't mine.
Those belong to Janet.

6 Contents

6 Prepositions

Farmer Jones and the One-eared Dog
(*Part One*)

Farmer Jones was very lonely and very bored. He lived by himself in an old house on the edge of the village, and rarely talked to anyone. The villagers thought that he ought to have a pet for company, but the only animal they could find was a dog which had only one ear.

When Farmer Jones saw this peculiar-looking animal, he shouted: 'Get out of my house!'

The dog, to his surprise, responded by doing exactly the opposite. It wagged its tail and went *into* the house.

The farmer stared at the funny dog for a while and then said finally, 'Ah, well, you might as well stay, I suppose. Come and sit next to me.'

The dog wagged its tail, but walked *away from* the man, and went to sit on the other side of the room.

'Sit on the chair,' said the farmer. The one-eared dog promptly sat *under* it.

The farmer took the dog outside and pointed *up* the road: the dog immediately turned round and went *down* the road. The farmer was absolutely fascinated.

'Why do you always do exactly the opposite of what I tell you to do?' he asked. The dog just looked up at him with his head on one side, and his solitary ear sticking up like a radio aerial.

6.1 The meaning and use of prepositions

Prepositions are words which show the relationship between things, people or events.
They express relationships in *space*:
  He lived by himself *in* an old house *on* the edge of the village.
They express relationships in *time*:
  He stared at the dog *for* a while . . .

They also express many other kinds of relationship. For example:
Purpose   He ought to have a pet *for* company.
Possession It went to sit on the other side *of* the room.
Result   death *from* drowning

6.2 Patterns with prepositions

6.2.1 PREPOSITION+NOUN/ PRONOUN

Prepositions are followed by a *noun, pronoun* or *noun phrase*.
(→13.4.1).

Examples
Followed by noun   Sit on *the chair*.
Followed by pronoun   The dog sat under *it*.
Followed by noun phrase   Why do you always do the opposite
                            of *what I tell you to do?*

6.2.2   PREPOSITION + -ING
VERB FORM (GERUND)

e.g. The dog responded by *doing* exactly the opposite.
      I am no good at *typing*.
      He went home without *saying* goodnight.
      She is not used to *eating* so much.

Note
It is important to distinguish between **to** when it is part of the
infinitive (→ 13.4) as in *I want to go home*, and **to** as a
preposition as in *I'm not used to eating so much*. You can decide
which it is by trying to put *it* after **to**: if it still makes sense, then
to is a preposition:
e.g. I'm not used to | it.   This makes sense, so **to** is a
                      | eating.   preposition.

I want to ✗   This doesn't make sense, so **to** is
I want | to go.   part of the infinitive.

Other common constructions where **to** is a true preposition and
has to be followed by the **-ing** form of the verb are:
to be used
to be accustomed
to be reduced
to be resigned
to look forward   **to**   doing . . .
to resign oneself
to restrict oneself
to confine oneself

6.2.3   Prepositions at the
end of the sentence

There are a number of cases in everyday English where the
preposition comes at the end of the sentence, that is, it is
separated from its noun or pronoun. In most cases, a **phrasal
verb** (→ Chapter 11) of the type VERB + PREPOSITION* is
involved, and the pronoun is either
a **relative** – who, which, that or Ø; or
an **interrogative** – what?, who?, which (one)? where?

*We use the expression **phrasal verb** for any verb on the pattern
VERB + PREPOSITION/ADVERBIAL

Relatives: I was talking *about* a book + Here is the book =
Here is the book (that) I was talking about.

Other examples
I have the money (that) you asked for.
That is something (that) I have been wondering about.
She is a girl (who(m)) I work with.

Interrogatives: He is looking *at* something+ What?=
What is he looking at?

Other examples:
What were they talking about?
Who did you give it to?
Where do you come from?

The pattern is also common in reported speech
(→ Chapter 14 B.):
Tell me what you are thinking about.
Ask him where he got it from.

6.3 Prepositions which express relationships in space

The most important are:

above	across	against	along	among	around
at	behind	below	beneath	beside	between
beyond	by	down	from	in	in front of	inside	into
near	next to	off	on	on to	opposite	out of	outside
over	past	round	through	to	towards	under
underneath	up				

6.3.1 At, in to(wards), (away) from, by, (a)round, up and down

In these diagrams, the dot ● is a place.

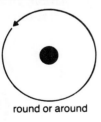

round or around

round or around

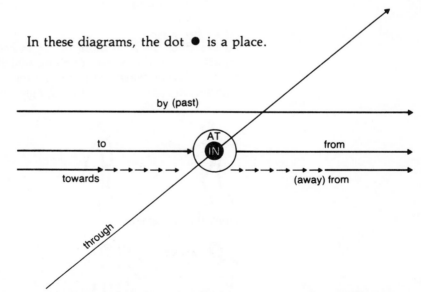

In many cases, prepositions can be used with verbs referring to either *movement* or *rest*.

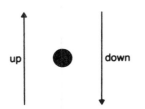

Examples

Movement	*Rest*
Move *away* from the fire.	She lives *away from* home.
He pointed *up* the road.	Stay *up* the ladder.
The dog ran *down* the road.	My house is just *down* the road.
The car went *round* the corner.	Meet me *round* the corner.

At *or* in?

At is used to describe where you are in a general way without defining exactly whether you are in, on, under, behind, etc., the space:

e.g. I'm sitting at my desk.
  I'm at home.
  My children are at school.
  My sister is at University.
  We stayed at the Heathrow Hotel.
  At the bottom of page 125 . . .

In, like *on, under, behind,* etc., is more specific (definite):

e.g. I keep my pens in my desk.
  You're welcome any time in my home.
  There were some policemen in (the) school today.
  Is there a restaurant in the Heathrow Hotel?

With the names of villages, towns and cities, especially with the verb *arrive,* the choice of **at** or **in** can be a little difficult. We advise you to choose:

arrive at when you are thinking of the station, airport or seaport,
arrive in when you are thinking of the place itself.

e.g. arrive at London (at the airport)
  arrive in London (in the city)

At *or* to?

At describes the final point of the movement, seen as something separate from the person or thing which moves. **To** suggests a relationship between the person/thing and the destination. In a transferred sense, **at** can suggest aggression, **to** co-operation:

Don't throw it *at* me!   Throw it *to* me!

you fool   HELLO!

Shouting *at* him   Shouting *to* him

Similarly, *to point at/to*. The meaning of **at** is suggested in *to laugh at someone*, which is unkind, *to shoot at* and *to aim at*, which treat the final point of the movement as a target. Even *to look at* suggests a similar idea:

6.3.2 In(to), inside, out of, outside, behind, in front of

In, into or inside?
Both **in** and **inside** can be used for movement or rest; **into** refers

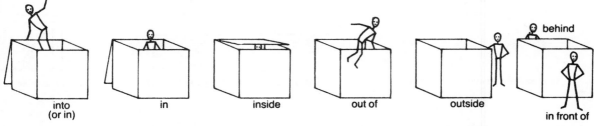

only to movement. Think of **in** as the more general word, and of **into/inside** as more specific (definite), emphasizing the movement (**into**) and the location (**inside**):

e.g. *A in B*: Don't put all your eggs in one basket. (proverb)
 A into B: We drove into Spain (=clearly from one country into another. We drove *in* Spain=When we were in Spain, we travelled by car.)*

*The difference is clear when you think of a sentence like 'The police burst *into* the room.' The sentence *The police burst in the room* produces a picture of exploding policemen!

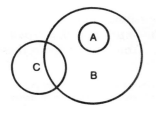

A inside B: Circle A is inside circle B; circle C is partly inside and partly outside circle B.*

*There is a preposition *within* with a similar meaning, but emphasizing *not more than* e.g. *We must work within the budget.*

6.3.3 Above and below, over and under

The meaning of these pairs of prepositions is very similar, and in some cases you can use one or the other. The difference between them is:

Over and **under** describe a vertical relationship: (*see below left*)

Above and **below** describe the relative position of two things when one is higher/lower than another:

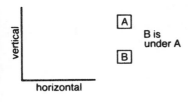

House B
is below house A

Further examples:

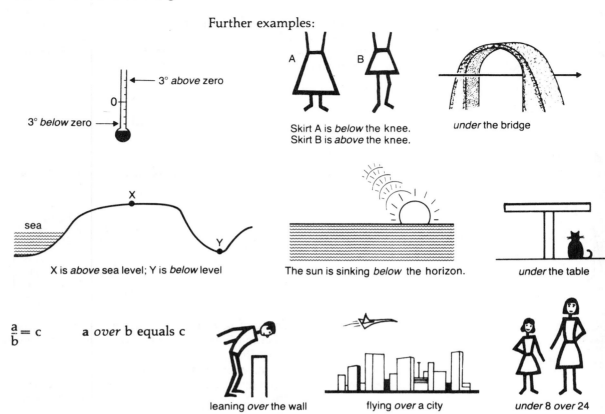

Skirt A is *below* the knee.
Skirt B is *above* the knee.

under the bridge

X is *above* sea level; Y is *below* level

The sun is sinking *below* the horizon.

under the table

$$\frac{a}{b} = c$$ **a** *over* b equals c

leaning *over* the wall   flying *over* a city   *under* 8 *over* 24

They are also used in certain fixed expressions: *under the circumstances below average under the impression that road under repair under £10.00* (=less than). You have to learn these expressions individually.*

*The preposition *beneath* can be used instead of *below*, but it is best used in fixed expressions, e.g., *beneath contempt. Underneath* is a less common form of under.

6.3.4   On, on to, off, across

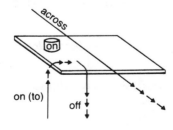

These prepositions describe movement or rest in relation to a surface (see diagram on left).

On to (written as two words, cf. *into*) is used like *into* to make it clear or to emphasize that movement is from one place to another:

The cat jumped *on* the table could mean

or

To make it clear, you could say
   The cat jumped *on to* the table.

Note the use of **on** in these expressions:
a calendar on the wall a fly on the ceiling the news on **page 4**
a programme on television on the left/right on the one hand/on
the other hand

6.3.5 Near, next to, by, beside

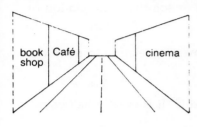

Near is the most general preposition with the meaning *close to*: it
tells us that things or people are in the same general area.
Next to tells us that the things or people are side by side in the
same line.

| The cinema is | across the road from / opposite | the cafe. |
| The cafe is | *next to* / next door to | the bookshop. |

All these places are quite **near** one another. The street itself is
near (=not far from) the town centre.

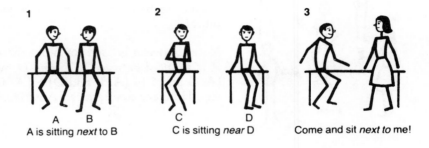

A is sitting *next* to B   C is sitting *near* D   Come and sit *next to* me!

1 suggests that A and B are together, that they know each other.
2 suggests that C and D are not together, that they just happen
to be sitting in the same room.
3 is a friendly invitation. You could use **by** or **beside** here, or in
sentence 1 without any important change of meaning.

Note these other expressions with **by**
    to live by the sea
    The road runs right by (or *past*) our house.

6.3.6 Against

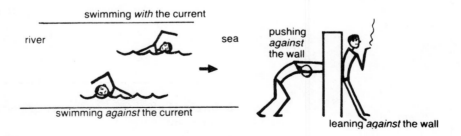

swimming *with* the current
river   sea
swimming *against* the current
pushing *against* the wall
leaning *against* the wall

From the idea of opposition illustrated by *swimming against the current*, we can get the idea of being **against** a suggestion, a policy, etc.

I'm in favour of NATO, but I'm *against* the use of nuclear weapons.

6.3.7   Between and among

Between (which is connected with the word *two*) refers to position or movement of something or somebody in relation to *two* objects.

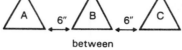

between

Among describes position or movement in relation to more than two objects.

Triangle B is situated *between* A and C. It is exactly halfway *between* them.
What is the difference *between* a boat and a ship?

It's nice to be *among* friends. (the word after *among* is always plural.)

among

Note: **Between** is used for more than two objects in a pattern like *A is situated between B, C and D*, which can be interpreted as [A: B and C]+[A: B and D]+ [A: C and D]
e.g. Hungary lies *between* Austria, Romania, Czechoslovakia and the USSR.

6.4   Prepositions which express relationships in time

The most important are:

after	at	before	between	by	during
for	from	in	on	past	since	through(out)
to	towards	until (*or* till)	within		

6.4.1   Before and after

In the following diagrams X is *a point in time*; X Y is *a period of time*, i.e. the distance between two events.

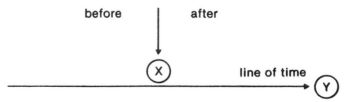

Before and **after** refer to points or periods of time on **either side** of an event.
e.g. before the war after dinner before the **game** and **after** it
     before Thursday after the weekend

They are followed by the **-ing** form of the verb, as in the notice:
> Please adjust your dress *before leaving* (notice in public lavatories).
> *After thinking* (or *having thought*) about it for a while, I decided to choose the dark blue suit.

We advise you, however, to use the construction CONJUNCTION+CLAUSE (→Chapter 14 A), as in the sentences:
> Have a drink *before you go.*
> We'll go out *after we've had* something to eat.

The construction PREPOSITION+ . . . ING would seem very formal or unusual (*before going;* . . . *after having* or *after having had*).

6.4.2 Since, for, during, by, until

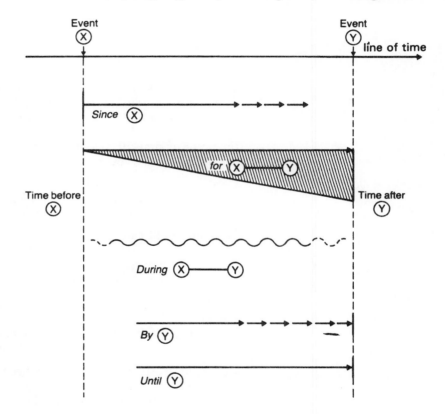

Read the diagrams in this way:

Since a point of time, i.e., starting from that point (→Section 8.4.5)

For a period of time, i.e., starting at Ⓧ and finishing at Ⓨ

During a period of time, but not necessarily for the whole period.

By a point of time, i.e., *not later than* Ⓨ , and perhaps before.

Until a point of time, i.e., stopping only when that point is reached.

Examples

since　since 1982　since breakfast　since the beginning of May
　　　　since the third of May.

for　for a week　for several years　for a long time
　　　　for ages　for the last three weeks

during　during the concert　during the night　during my stay in
　　　　France　during August

by　*Time*: 8 o'clock　*Place*: Manchester　*Travelling time to
　　　　Liverpool*: 1–2 hours, depending on traffic.

If we leave now we should be in Liverpool | *by* nine if the roads are quiet
by nine-thirty if there's not too much traffic.
by ten o'clock at the latest.

The meaning is *not later than*: you are making an *estimate of
probability* (=you are trying to say what might or should
happen. See→10.2). *If we leave now we should be in Liverpool
at ten o'clock* is slightly different because you are thinking about
the point of time *10 o'clock* rather than the period of time before
ten during which you have to make your journey.

Until　until Friday　until the end of the lesson　until tomorrow
　　　　We're staying here *until Friday*. (i.e., then we will leave)
　　　　He's not coming *until Friday*. (i.e., then he will come)

Since and **until** can be used as conjunctions (→Chapter 14 A):
　　　　e.g. We've had nothing but trouble ever *since she
　　　　　arrived*.
　　　　Don't hurry. I'll wait *until you have finished*.

During is only a preposition; the corresponding conjunction is
while:
　　　　e.g. I fell asleep | during the concert.
　　　　　　　　| while the concert was going on.

By, in the sense of *not later than*, becomes BY THE TIME + VERB:
　　　　e.g. *By the time you receive* this letter, I shall be on the
　　　　　other side of the world.

6.4.3 In, at, on, within, past, to, from, between

AT　POINT OF TIME　　ⓧ
ON　A DAY OR A DATE　ⓧ
IN　PERIOD OF TIME　ⓧ — ⓨ

Examples

at　at 10 o'clock　at midnight　at Easter　at Christmas
　　　also, at night　at the weekend,　at present

on　on Monday　on Mondays　on Tuesday morning/
　　　afternoon/evening　on the first of the month　on my birthday
　　　on Christmas Day　on holiday

in　in 1983　in July　in the first/last/next three months　in the past
　　　in the future　in our lifetime　in the twentieth century

In these examples, in is similar in meaning to *during*. It can also be used to mean *not more than*:

e.g. I'll be back *in a minute.*

I'll be with you *in just a moment.*

Can you come back *in an hour?* or . . . *in an hour's time?*).

The preposition **within** can be regarded as a more formal word for **in** (=not more than), e.g. The goods must be paid for *within* thirty days.

Note

All three prepositions can be used with the word *time*, but with different meanings:

On time: Try to arrive *on time*=be punctual, come when you should come.

In time: If you hurry, you should be (just) *in time* to catch the train=you will not be too late.

At the time: Fred called. I was in the bath *at the time.* =at the moment when he called.

At one time: *At one time* you could get a hotel room for £5.00 a night. =there was a time when this was true.

and,

At times: He behaves a little strangely *at times.* =sometimes.

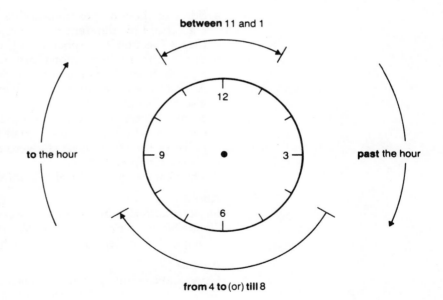

TO, FROM, PAST	A POINT OF TIME X
BETWEEN	TWO TIMES, X and Y

Examples

past	5, 10, (a) quarter, 20, 25, half *past* 4
to	25, 20, (a) quarter, 10, 5 *to* 5
	(with other numbers, add the word *minutes*:
	2.23 = twenty-three minutes past two.)
from ... to	from July to September from now to the end of the
	month (i.e., the whole period)
between ...	between July and September between now and the
and	end of the month (i.e., within the period).

Note the useful extension of **from** in these expressions:

from | the time
the moment | + clause ...
the minute

e.g. *From the moment I saw you*, I knew that you were the one for me.

6.5 Prepositions to express other relationships

6.5.1 Simple prepositions

about	against	at	besides	by	but	despite
except	for	from	in	like	of	on	out of
than	to	unlike	with	without		

a Some of these prepositions are used with adjectives:
  e.g. afraid of different from angry with amazed at
  (See ← Section 4.8 Appendix VII for a list.)
b Some of these prepositions form fixed expressions with nouns:
  e.g. by heart from memory on leave without fail
  A list of the most common is given in Appendix IX: (See
  also ← Section 2.7.)
c Some of these prepositions are used with verbs:
  e.g. depend on go without wait for prevent from
  A list of the commonest is given in Appendix VIII. (See
  also → Chapter 11.)
d They express a variety of relationships:

About
Subject matter: a book about insects
Concerning: She is worried about her exams.
                 Tell us about your holiday.

Against
Opposition: I am against the idea.
              Some MPs voted against the proposal.

At
Reaction (especially emotional): I am amazed at your suggestion.
              At my request, he has resigned from the party.
Level of ability: good at games   bad at remembering faces

Besides
It means the same as *apart from* or *in addition to*.
The sentence
> *I know you have oranges*, but do you have anything else?
can be simply expressed using **besides**:
> Do you have anything else *besides oranges*?

But
Similar to *except*:
> She said hello to everyone but me.
The compound **but for** is useful. For example, the sentence
> *If it had not been for me*, you would all have been killed.
can be simply expressed using *but for*:
> *But for me*, you would all have been killed.

By
Means or method: go by car (→ Section 12.16.2)
> He entered by the window and left by the side door.
> We got the car started by pushing it down the road.

The creator: a novel by Charles Dickens = a novel *which was written* by Charles Dickens.
> A painting by Turner = a painting *which was done* by Turner.
If you use **of**, you would say *one of Turner's paintings* or *a painting of Turner's* (← also Section 1.8.4 b).

Despite
Similar to and slightly less used than *in spite of*:
> Despite their political differences, the two countries do a lot of trade with each other.

Except
Commoner than *but* (see above):
> She said hello to everyone except me.

For
Purpose: I only did it for the money.
> We're only here for the beer. (advertisement)

The one who receives: I bought it for you.
> A new stylus for the record player.

Destination: Where are you heading for?
> They set off for Paris at dawn.

Support: I am (all) for the idea.
> Some MPs voted for the proposal.
> (i.e., **for** is the opposite of **against**)

A kind of comparison: He is a bit too old for you.
> She is very advanced for her age.

From
Origin: I come from Barcelona.
This lamp was made from (or *out of*) an old wine bottle.
He borrowed the money from his sister.

Separation/distinction: Can't you tell butter from margarine?
It was stolen from the office safe.

In
Manner: Tell me in a few words what happened next.
She replied in a most offensive manner/way.

Like
Manner: He smokes like a chimney.
He plays football like his brother.
=he plays football in the way (as well as) his brother
plays football.

Comparison: Like his brother, he plays football.
=he is like his brother in one respect, i.e., they
both play football. The opposite is *unlike*
Unlike Czech and Polish, Bulgarian uses the
Cyrillic alphabet.

Of
This preposition expresses many kinds of relationships, including:
Possession: the symphonies of Mozart a man of few words a
friend of my father's the University of Edinburgh

Material: made of gold a door of solid steel

Quantity/contents: a piece of paper a glass of water
full of hatred

Result: to die of old age

On
Subject matter: He spoke on *The Birds of Christchurch Harbour.*
You could also use **about** instead of **on** to refer to subject matter
(e.g. *a book about birds*). The preposition **on** suggests a formal
situation, **about** suggests an informal unprepared one. Thus, you
would say *to lecture on a subject* but *to have a chat about
something.*

Out of
No longer possessing: out of stock run out of food out of breath

Material/origin: He made a table out of old orange boxes.
(see also **from**). The similarity of material and origin gives rise to
a children's joke: He made a table out of his own head. (i.e., the
idea originated in his head).

Motive/cause: She acted out of spite.

Than
Using in making comparisons: Half a loaf is better than none.
(*proverb*)

To
Comparison/ratio: We won by two goals to nil.
                            Odds of 10 to 1.
Also, when comparing two amounts, as in an *exchange rate of
1000 zloty to the £, a petrol consumption of 25 miles to the
gallon.*

Cause (emotional reaction): To my surprise, nobody replied to
                            the advertisement.

It replaces **of** *or* **for**: in some expressions like *secretary to the
                            managing director, financial advisor to the
                            board*, where **to** means *who works for.*

With
Manner: with a smile   with pleasure

Instrument: He cut it with a knife.
Note There is a difference between the use of **by** and **with** to
express the means/instrument: **with** tells us what someone used
in order to do something, but there is not necessarily a person
with an *intention* when we use **by**. For this reason, you could
say *He was killed with a sword* but you could not use **with** in
sentences like *He was killed by a train* or *by a lion*. The test is
this: if you can substitute the word **using**, the preposition should
be **with**. (For the use of **by** to express the personal agent in
passive constructions, e.g. *The money was stolen by the chief
clerk,* (see ➔ Section 8.11)

Accompaniment: Come with me. I'd like a steak with a green
                            salad.

Support: We are with you. (see also **for**)

Possession: a man with a long black beard a dog with only one
                            ear

Ingredients/contents: filled with walnuts

Without
The preposition **without** usually expresses the opposite of **with**:
Manner: without hesitation
Instrument: he cut it without a knife.
Accompaniment: You must go without me
Possession: A beard without a moustache is like a violin without
a bow (proverb which has given rise to humorous variations like
the feminist slogan *A woman without a man is like a fish
without a bicycle!*)

6.5.2 Compound prepositions

There are a lot of **compound prepositions** in English to express relationships other than space and time relationships. They often have the pattern PREPOSITION + NOUN + PREPOSITION:
e.g. in spite of   by means of   on behalf of

				But these refer to time/space:		
in	addition	to		at the bottom		of
on	behalf	of		in the centre		of
in	favour	of		in	front	of
by	means	of		in the middle		of
in	spite	of		at the side		of
in	view	of		on	top	of
as	well	as				

Other useful compound prepositions:

according	to
ahead	of
apart	from
because	of
instead	of
other	than
owing	to

Notes

1 There are many (too many!) compound prepositions which are used by people, especially in writing, in order to make what they write seem more important and 'educated'.

We wish to talk to you	with respect to with reference to in respect of in connection with	your proposal

All of these long-winded compounds can – and should – be replaced by the simple word *about*.

2 The expression **due to** is often used as a preposition with the same meaning as *because of* or *owing to*, but they are different in construction: say X is due to Y   or Because of Y, X   (or Owing to Y, X)
e.g. *Because of* bad weather, the match has been cancelled.
The cancellation *is due* to bad weather.

6.5.3 Prepositions in **-ing**

Apart from the useful preposition **according to**, there are a number of words derived from verbs which may be regarded as prepositions expressing relationships. They are mostly used in formal situations such as written English, and can sometimes be replaced by a simpler word (see ← Section 6.5.2 Note 2). The commonest are:
concerning and **regarding**, which both mean *about* (subject matter, Section 6.5.1)
including and its opposite **excluding**.

6.6 The pattern
VERB + PREPOSITION

6.6.1 Meaning

In this Grammar, we use the term **phrasal verb** to describe compound verbs which are on the pattern VERB + PREPOSITION or VERB + ADVERBIAL (Adverbials→Chapter 12; Phrasal verbs, →Chapter 11). The meaning of the phrasal verbs with prepositions is usually obvious once you have become familiar with the meaning of the prepositions. In some cases, the meaning of the phrasal verb cannot be guessed so easily: *to look up* a word in a dictionary means *to find its meaning.* To *come across* something is to *find something by chance.*

You can learn a lot about the meaning of prepositions by comparing pairs of verbs like the following:

A I'm *thinking of* going to Greece for my holidays this year.
B I'm *thinking about* going to Greece for my holidays this year.
A is almost a decision but not quite definite; B shows that the speaker has a lot of thinking to do before he makes a decision. *Think about* is more complex than *think of.*

The same distinction occurs with pairs like *hear of/hear about dream of/dream about, talk of/talk about.*

Agree with/agree to
I *agree with* you, and I *agree with* what you say. = I have the same opinions as you
I have listened to your plan, and *I agree to* it. = I consent or give my permission.

Ask for/ask about
To *ask someone for money or advice* is to say *'Please give me some money or advice.'*
To *ask about something* is to try to get information about it.

6.6.2 Which preposition?

The pattern VERB + PREPOSITION + OBJECT (→Section 13.4) is very common in English. In some cases it is easy to remember which preposition, because of the meaning of the preposition, e.g. *look into* = *investigate* (*The police are looking into the matter*). In other cases, you could not predict the preposition, e.g. *look after* = *take care of* or *nurse.* There is a list of common verbs with their prepositions in Appendix VIII. See also→Chapter 11 on phrasal verbs.
In general, we advise you to get into the habit of recording verbs *together with the pattern in which they occur.*
e.g. Learn *depend on*, and not simply *depend.*
   Learn *prevent someone from doing something*, and not simply *prevent.*

Note: Many common prepositions are also adverbs.
See→Section 12.4).

6.7 Appendix VIII: Verbs with following prepositions

on
act on
take revenge on
be based on
comment on
concentrate on
congratulate someone on
    something
count on (=rely)
experiment on
decide on
depend on
embark on
impress on someone that
intrude on
live on (food)
operate on someone
play something on an
    instrument
pride oneself on
reckon on
rely on
make war on
work on (a project)

at
arrive at
guess at
hint at
marvel at
play at (=pretend)
wonder at
work at
look at
stare at
peep at
peer at

against
be prejudiced against
insure against
protest against (or to)
react against (or to)
rebel against
warn against (or about)

about
joke about
laugh about
sing about
speak about
talk about
think about
worry about
be/get upset about
tell someone about
    something

in
believe in
delight in
be engaged in
be included in
indulge in
take a pride in
be interested in
invest in
get involved in
persist in

from
abstain from
borrow from
demand something from
    someone
differ from
discourage someone from
distinguish A from B
draw money from
emerge from
escape from
exclude from
hinder from
prevent someone from
prohibit from
recover from (illness)
refrain from
separate A from B
suffer from

for
account for
act for someone
apologize for
ask for something
blame someone for
beg for
call for (=require)
charge for
exchange A for B
be intended for
long for
hope for
pay for something
prepare for
provide for
search for
substitute A for B
thank someone for
wait for
vote for

of
accuse someone of
approve of

beware of
consist of
be convicted of (a crime)
convince someone of
cure someone of (an
    illness)
despair of
disapprove of
dream of
repent of
get rid of
smell of
taste of
suspect of
think of
tire of
get tired of
warn someone of

to
accustom oneself to
get accustomed to
amount to
appeal to
apply to
be attached to
attend to
attribute A to B
belong to
challenge someone to
compare to (or with)
be condemned to
be confined to
consent to
be converted to
be entitled to
entrust something to
    someone
invite someone to
listen to
look forward to
object to
react to
be reduced to
resort to
respond to
reply to
be subjected to
submit to
succumb to
surrender to
subscribe to
be/get used to
talk to
turn to
yield to

with
acquaint someone with
be afflicted with
agree with someone
help someone with
be charged with (crime)
communicate with
compare A with B
compete with (or against)
comply with
conflict with
confuse A with B
A contrasts with B
cope with
correspond with someone
begin with something
be infected with
interfere with
be threatened with
A doesn't mix with B
part with
quarrel with
fight with (or against)
reason with someone
be satisfied with

6.8 Appendix IX: Common fixed expressions with prepositions

out of
out of bounds
out of breath
out of control
out of danger
out of date
out of doors
out of fashion
out of interest
out of luck
out of order
out of the ordinary
out of place
out of practice
out of all proportion
out of the question
out of sight
out of stock
out of turn
out of use

on
on (the) average
on board (ship)
on business
on the contrary
on fire
on foot
on holiday
on horseback
on the job
on leave
on the level
on the other hand
on purpose
on second thoughts
on time
on the way
on the whole

in
in the circumstances
in church
in doors (indoors)
in difficulty
in difficulties
in fact
in fashion
in haste
in hospital
in a hurry
in love
in order
in pain
in part
in the post

in practice
in prison
in any case
in particular
in bed
in trouble
in reply
in school
in stock
in style
in tears
in theory
in time
in turn(s)
in use
in vain
in common
in public
in private
in a way
in half
in general
in the long run

by
by accident
by air
by all means
by car (+other vehicles)
by chance
by coincidence
by default
by degrees
by design
(play) by ear
by force
by heart
by no/any means
by mistake
by name (know someone
  by name)
by myself (etc.)
by order
by sight (know someone
  by sight)
by surprise
by the way

at
at dinner (+other meals)
at ease
at first
at first sight
at home
at last
at least

at short/a moment's
  notice
at the office
at once
at present
at any rate
at school
at sea
at the theatre
at one time
one at a time
at the time(=then)
at times
at the same time
at war
at work

for
for ever (forever)
for example
for good (=for ever)
for instance
for the record
for my sake (etc.)
for Heaven's sake
for sale
for the time being

to
go, etc., to church
          to court
          to prison
          to hospital (*or*
             into hospital)
          to school
          to sea
          to war

Miscellaneous
beside the point   *within* reason
from memory   *without* doubt
         now on   fail
off the cuff
        the record
        (=unofficially)
under the/no circumstances
             protest
             repair
             suspicion
             way
             the weather
up to date
       to now
with interest
        luck

7 Contents

7 Verb forms

The Farmer and the One-eared Dog
(*Part 2*)

'Perhaps it is because the poor thing has only one ear,' he
thought to himself. Anyway, he began to spend all his spare time
training the dog, until eventually it would do everything he
ordered – as long as he said the opposite of what he wanted.

A horse, which had been watching these strange events, finally
asked the dog: 'Why do you always do the opposite of what he
tells you to do? Is it because you have only one ear?'

'Of course not,' replied the dog. 'I started to do it because I
don't think he would have been interested in an ordinary dog, do
you?'

And, indeed, the farmer was no longer lonely or bored: he
now had very interesting company.

Moral: There is nothing peculiar about being peculiar.

7.1 Introduction

Verbs are words which refer to actions, e.g. *go, talk, move,* or
to states, e.g. *be, seem, appear*. (See also Chapter 13,
introduction.) Chapter 7 deals with the forms and the formation
of verbs; the meanings and uses of these verb forms are dealt
with in Chapters 8, 9 and 10.

Note
In the explanations which follow, we use the symbol Ø to
indicate an empty category, i.e., it means that no letter or word
is needed in this space. Compare, for example:

I+Ø+go	⟶	I go
I+don't+go	⟶	I don't go
I+go+Ø	⟶	I go
he+go+es	⟶	He goes

7.2 The 'building blocks' of the verb

7.2.1 Any verb in English is made from two elements or 'building blocks':

First element		*Second element*
a	Ø	
or **b**	part of **to be**	
or **c**	part of **to have**	+**e** part of the **main verb**
and/or **d**	a modal	

Examples:

she+	**a** Ø	+ **e** moves	She moves.
she+	**b** is	+ **e** moving	She is moving.
she+	**c** has	+ **e** moved	She has moved.
she+	**d** must	+ **e** move	She must move.

The first element may consist of more than one word,
e.g. She has been moved.   She will be moving.

7.2.2. Parts of the first element

a *The empty category:* Ø
The empty category only occurs in the **present simple** and the **past simple** tenses (→ Chapter 8, preface), e.g.:
Present simple   she moves   we live   I like
Past simple   she moved   we lived   I liked

The verb **to be**
b The parts of the verb **to be** are:

	Person	Present	Past
	1 I	am	was
Singular	2 you	are*	were
	3 he/she/it	is	was
	1 we	are	were
Plural	2 you	are	were
	3 they	are	were
Participles		*being*	*been*

*The form is, of course, the same whether *you* refers to one or to more than one person. You will only meet the old forms with *thou* (← Section 5.3, footnote) such as *thou art* and *thou hast* in old writing, such as the Authorized Version of the Bible.

c *The verb* **to have**
The parts of the verb **to have** are:

	Person	Present	Past
	1 I	have	had
Singular	2 you	have*	had
	3 he/she/it	has	had
	1 we/you/they	have	had
Plural	2 you	have	had
	3 they	have	had
Participles		*having*	*had*

d *The modals*
The modal verbs are:

will	would	must	have to
shall	should	need	be able to
can	could	used to	dare
may	might	ought to	

The modals **will/shall** are used to form the future (→ Chapter 9). The other modals are fully dealt with in Chapter 10.

In the tables which follow, **have to** and **be able to** are dealt with separately (→ 7.3 notes 1 and 2). The modal **dare** is not a common verb and has not been included in the tables.

Need and **dare** are also regular verbs (→ Section 7.4.3).

7.2.3   Parts of the second element

e *The main verb*
The main verb (**e**) is the part of the verb phrase which carries the meaning:

e.g. I can *go*. You have been *cheating*. He should *know*.
   Whereas *can, have been* and *should* express *time* and *attitude* (→ Section 8.1).

The parts of the main verb are:
   base + Ø
   base + (e)s
   base + ing
   base + ed

The base form + Ø or the endings is used to form the following:

infinitive	without *to*		move
	with *to*		to move
present tense	move + Ø	I/we/you/they	move
	move + s	he/she/it	moves
present participle	move + ing		moving
past tense	move + d	I/we/you/they	moved
		he/she/it	
past participle	move + d		moved

7.3   **Active and passive, simple and continuous**

The verb forms in English fit into one of these four categories*: **active**, simple or continuous; **passive**, simple or continuous. For example:

	Active	*Passive*
Simple	it moves	it is moved
	it moved	it was moved
Continuous	it is moving	it is being moved
	it was moving	it was being moved

*This does not mean, of course, that *all* verbs can fit these four **categories**. **Verbs** which do not take an object (**intransitive verbs**), → Chapter 13A) do not occur in the passive, and a number of them do not normally occur in the continuous form (→ Section 8.2.1 and Section 8.2.3).

The following table contains every verb form you **are ever likely** to meet. What they mean and how they are used is dealt with in Chapters 8, 9 and 10.

	Active			Passive			

Simple

	Active			Passive		
I we / you they	Ø	move	I / he she it / we you they		am/was is/was are/were	
		moves				
I we / you they	do not	move	I we / you they / he she it	have has		
he she it	does not	move			been	moved
I we / you they / he she it	Ø	moved	I we / you they / he she it	had		
I we / you they / he she it	did not	move	I we / you they / he she it	will/would shall/should can/could may/might must/need used to/ought to	be	moved
I we / you they	have	moved			have been	
he she it	has					
I we / you they / he she it	will/would shall/should can/could may/might must/need used to/ought to	move / have moved				

Continuous

	Active		Passive			
I / he she it / we you they	am/was/have been is/was/has been are/were/have been	moving	I / he she it / we you they		am/was is/was are/were	being moved
I we / you they / he she it	had been					
I we / you they / he she it	will/would shall/should can/could may/might must/need used to/ought to	be moving / have been	*Note:* (Other continuous passive forms, using **have** or modals are possible in theory, e.g., it might have been being moved, but we never need them in practice)			

Notes

1 Other parts of the modal **can** are supplied by **be able to**:

Part of *to be*	Modal	Able to	Main verb
am/is/are was/were			
has/have had	been		
used to	be	able to	move
will/would shall/should	be		
may/might must ought to	have been		

For the difference between **can** and **is able to** and **could** and **was able to**, see →Section 10.7.

Forms not shown in this table are either very unusual (e.g., *might have been able to have moved*) or meaningless (e.g., *could have been able to have been moving*).

2 Other parts of the modal **must** are supplied by **have to**:

has/have had				
has/have had	had			
used to	have			
will/would shall/should may/might	have		to	move
will/would should may/might	have had			

For the difference between **must** and **have to**, see →Section 10.4.
Unusual or meaningless forms are not shown in this table.

3 The base form is used as the **imperative**, i.e., when you tell someone directly to do something:

    Go!   Don't go!
    Help me!   Don't leave me!

Other ways of expressing the imperative, e.g., *Do go!*, *Let's go* and *You go!*, are dealt with in →Sections 8.6 and 8.7.

4 The participles **moving** and **moved** can be combined with **having (been)** to form the following:

	Active	*Passive*
Present	moving	being moved
Past	having moved	having been moved

As the table on page 128 shows, the forms **moving** and **being moved** are used in making compound verb forms, e.g., *it is being moved, we are moving.*

All the forms can also be used alone as participles or as gerunds (→Chapter 13A):

Participle
He began to spend all his time *training* the dog.

Participle
Having said goodbye, he left the party. (=After he had said goodbye . . .)

Gerund
I did not like *being told* what to do.

Gerund
There is nothing peculiar about *being* peculiar.

(See also → Section 13.2.4 and → Section 13.7.2).

7.4   The parts of the main verb

7.4.1   Spelling and pronunciation of the -(e)s ending

The third person singular of the present simple tense is formed by adding the ending -(e)s to the base;
e.g. *sit* → he sits   *love* → she loves   *catch* → it catches
The rules for both spelling and pronunciation are the same as the rules for the plural ending -(e)s (← Section **1.3.1**).

Examples

	[s]	[z]	[ɪz]
Pronunciation	takes	digs	alleges
	keeps	rubs	catches
	hits	hides	misses
		tries	judges

Spelling   **+s**   sit → sits   keep → keeps   play → plays
know → knows   take → takes   move → moves
+es   catch → catches   miss → misses   fix → fixes

Note: go → goes   do → does (pronounced [dʌz]
-y → **ies**   try → tries   hurry → hurries   deny → denies

*Remember that this rule only applies when the verb ends in a CONSONANT+Y, e.g., fly → flies. After VOWEL+Y, simply add an s, e.g. buy → buys

7.4.2   Spelling of the -*ing* form

The present participle or gerund is formed by adding **-ing** to the base form of the verb:
want → wanting   kiss → kissing   match → matching

Slight changes of spelling are needed in the following cases:

a Verbs ending in single -e—remove the e:
e.g. move → moving   take → taking   write → writing
(but agree → agreeing   free → freeing
guarantee → guaranteeing)

b Verbs ending in *single vowel+single consonant*—double the consonant:
e.g. rub → rubbing   slip → slipping   bar → barring
The exceptions are **-y**, **-x** and **-w**:
e.g. play → playing   fix → fixing   allow → allowing (Note too that the **-y** does not change even after a consonant: fly → flying. Compare → Section 7.4.3b)
Verbs with the last syllable in **-er** only double the consonant if the **-er** is stressed:

Syllable unstressed	*Syllable stressed*
'differ→'differing	pre'fer→pre'ferring
'offer→'offering	in'fer→in'ferring
'suffer→'suffering	trans'fer→trans'ferring
'cater→'catering	

The same applies to other verbs where the last syllable is stressed or unstressed:

Syllable unstressed	*Syllable stressed*
de'velop→de'veloping	ad'mit→ad'mitting
'gossip→'gossiping	trans'mit→trans'mitting
'benefit→'benefiting	
in'habit→in'habiting	
'visit→'visiting	

Note   panic→panicking   picnic→picnicking
In spite of the rule, you will often see **-ing** forms of *benefit* and *focus* (stress 'focus) written as *benefitting* and *focussing*.

7.4.3 Spelling and pronunciation of the *-(e)d* ending

a *Spelling*
The simple past tense and the past participle is formed by adding **-ed** to the base:
e.g. want→wanted   kiss→kissed   match→matched
     play→played   renew→renewed   video→videoed

Slight changes of spelling are needed in the following cases:

i)   Verbs ending in **-e** – simply add **-d**:
     love→loved   agree→agreed   die→died   lie→lied

ii) Verbs ending in *consonant + y* – change the **y** to **i**:
     try→tried   hurry→hurried

iii) Verbs ending in *single vowel + single consonant* – follow the same rules as for adding **-ing** (See→ Section 7.4.2):
     rub→rubbed   slip→slipped   bar→barred
     Similarly (See notes to 7.4.2b):
     fix→fixed   allow→allowed
     'differ→'differed (but pre'fer→pre'ferred);
     develop→developed   visit→visited   benefit→benefited
     focus→focused (also *benefitted* and *focussed* ← Section 7.4.2 Note) picnic→picnicked   panic→panicked

b *Pronunciation*
The ending **-ed** is pronounced in one of three ways:

After unvoiced consonants (← Section 1.3.2)	[t]
After voiced consonants and vowel sounds (← Section 1.3.2)	[d]
After the consonants [t] and [d]	[ɪd]

Examples

	[t]		[d]		[ɪd]
[pt]	helped	[bd]	rubbed	[ɪd]	needed
[kt]	picked	[gd]	longed	[ɪd]	handed
[ft]	laughed	[vd]	lived	[ɪd]	delighted
[st]	kissed	[zd]	raised	[ɪd]	wanted
[ʃt]	washed	[ʒd]	garaged		
[tʃt]	scratched	[dʒd]	judged		
		[θt]	berthed		
		[ld]	filled		
		[nd]	explained		
		[ðd]	bathed		
		[md]	combed		
		[eɪd]	stayed		
		[jud]	reviewed		
		[ə:d]	murdered		

Note: A few verbs ending in -l, -m and -n have alternative past forms:

burn → burned	[bɜːnd]	*or*	burnt	[bɜːnt]
dream → dreamed	[driːmd]	*or*	dreamt	[dremt]
lean → leaned	[liːnd]	*or*	leant	[lent]
smell → smelled	[smeld]	*or*	smelt	[smelt]
spell → spelled	[speld]	*or*	spelt	[spelt]
spill → spilled	[spɪld]	*or*	spilt	[spɪlt]
spoil → spoiled	[spɔɪld]	*or*	spoilt	[spɔɪlt]
(Also leap → leaped	[liːpt]	*or*	leapt	[lept]

7.4.4   Irregular verbs

The **regular** verb, as we have seen, has four parts:
e.g. *move   moves   moving   moved*
There are about 100 verbs in English which are **irregular** in the sense that they form the past tense and past participle in a different way from adding -(e)d to the base.
To describe the various combinations or types, we indicate the **base** by the letter A, change the letter to **B** if the **past tense** changes, and then to C if the **past participle** is different from the past tense. There are five types:

Type	Base	Past tense	Past participle	
a A B B	find	found	found	about 55 verbs
b A B C	speak	spoke	spoken	about 55 verbs
c A A A	put	put	put	about 25 verbs
d A B A	come	came	come	3 verbs
e A A B	beat	beat	beaten	this is the only one

a *Type A B B – ending in* **-d**

(i)		(ii)	(iii)
have–had–had	say–said–said	bleed–bled–bled	bind–bound–bound
hear–heard–heard	sell–sold–sold	breed–bred–bred	find–found–found
hold–held–held	slide–slid–slid	feed–fed–fed	grind–ground–ground
lay–laid–laid	stand–stood–stood	flee–fled–fled	wind–wound–wound
make–made–made	tell–told–told	lead–led–led	
pay–paid–paid		read–read–read*	

*Note that the pronunciation changes from **base** [ri:d] to **past** and **past participle** [red]

Type A B B – ending in -t

(i)		(ii)
bend–bent–bent	sleep–slept–slept	bring–brought–brought
build–built–built	spend–spent–spent	buy–bought–bought
creep–crept–crept	sweep–swept–swept	catch–caught–caught
deal–dealt–dealt	weep–wept–wept	fight–fought–fought
dwell–dwelt–dwelt		seek–sought–sought
feel–felt–felt	*The following can also be regular:*	teach–taught–taught
keep–kept–kept	burn–burnt–burnt (or burned)	think–thought–thought
kneel–knelt–knelt	dream–dreamt–dreamt (or dreamed)	
leave–left–left	lean–leant–leant (or leaned)	**(iii)**
lend–lent–lent	leap–leapt–leapt (or leaped)	get–got–got
lose–lost–lost	learn–learnt–learnt (or learned)	light–lit–lit
mean–meant–meant	smell–smelt–smelt (or smelled)	shoot–shot–shot
meet–met–met	spell–spelt–spelt (or spelled)	sit–sat–sat
send–sent–sent	spill–spilt–spilt (or spilled)	spit–spat–spat
	spoil–spoilt–spoilt (or spoiled)	

Type A B B – -i- *to* -u- *(or* -o-*)*

-u-

cling–clung–clung	sting–stung–stung
dig–dug–dug	strike–struck–struck
fling–flung–flung	string–strung–strung
hang–hung–hung	swing–swung–swung
shrink–shrunk–shrunk*	wring–wrung–wrung
sling–slung–slung	**-o-**
spin–spun–spun	shine–shone–shone (pronounced [ʃɔn])
stick–stuck–stuck	win–won–won

*This can also be an ABC type: shrink–shrank–shrunk

b *Type A B C – ending in* -n

Base	Vowel in past	Participle
	– o –	
	– e –	
- - - - -	– i –	- - - - - - n
	– a –	
	– oo –	

-o-

arise–arose–arisen
awake–awoke–awoken
bear–bore–borne
break–broke–broken
choose–chose–chosen
drive–drove–driven
forget–forgot–forgotten
freeze–froze–frozen
ride–rode–ridden
rise–rose–risen
speak–spoke–spoken
steal–stole–stolen
stride–strode–(stridden)
strive–strove–striven
swear–swore–sworn
tear–tore–torn
tread–trod–trodden
wake–woke–woken
wear–wore–worn
weave–wove–woven
write–wrote–written

-oo-

forsake–forsook–forsaken
mistake–mistook–mistaken
shake–shook–shaken
take–took–taken

-e-

blow–blew–blown
draw–drew–drawn
fall–fell–fallen
fly–flew–flown
grow–grew–grown
know–knew–known
throw–threw–thrown
withdraw–withdrew–**withdrawn**
also, go–went–gone

-i-

bite–bit–bitten
hide–hid–hidden
also, do–did–done

-a-

be–was–been
eat–ate–eaten
forbid–forbade–forbidden
forgive–forgave–forgiven
give–gave–given
lie–lay–lain
see–saw–seen

Type A B C: having the vowel pattern **i -a -u**

begin–began–begun	sink–sank–sunk
drink–drank–drunk	spring–sprang–sprung
ring–rang–rung	stink–stank–stunk
sing–sang–sung	swim–swam–swum

Type A B C: having the vowel pattern BASE **-ed   -n**

mow–mowed–mown	show–showed–shown
saw–sawed–sawn	sow–sowed–sown
sew–sewed–sewn	

It will not surprise you to hear that English-speakers often treat these verbs as regular verbs, i.e., they used the **-ed** form also for the past participle.

c *Type A A A*

bet–bet–bet	forecast–forecast–forecast	quit–quit–quit
bid–bid–bid	hit–hit–hit	rid–rid–rid
broadcast–broadcast–broadcast	hurt–hurt–hurt	set–set–set
burst–burst–burst	knit–knit–knit	shed–shed–shed
cast–cast–cast	let–let–let	split–split–split
cost–cost–cost	outbid–outbid–outbid	spread–spread–**spread**
cut–cut–cut	put–put–put	shut–shut–shut

Note: one or two of these, especially *bet, knit* and *quit*, may also be treated as regular verbs.

d *Type A B A*
become–became–become
come–came–come
run–ran–run

e *Type A A B*
beat–beat–beaten

Appendix X gives an alphabetical list of all the irregular verbs in current use. It does not include archaic or little-used verbs. We have also left out verbs derived from the simple irregular verbs using such prefixes as **for(e)-, re-, over-, mis-, un-, under-** and **with-** (e.g., foresee, overtake, understand, withdraw).

Note
The following verbs have an alternative past participle in **-en**, which is only used adjectivally (← Chapter **4**):

Verb	*Usual past participle*	*Adjectival past participle*
melt	melted	molten
prove	proved	proven
shave	shaved	shaven
shear	sheared	shorn
shrink	shrunk	shrunken
sink	sunk	sunken
strike	struck	stricken
Also,		
work	worked	wrought

These adjectival past participles usually appear in fixed expressions:
e.g. molten iron
    a clean-shaven face
    a shorn lamb
    a shrunken head
    an unproven assertion
    a sunken treasure-ship
    a grief-stricken widow
    a wrought-iron gate

7.5 The formation of the negative: *not/n't*

7.5.1 The basic pattern

The basic pattern is

```
                BE
SUBJECT  +   HAVE   +    NOT  +  MAIN VERB
             MODAL
```

Notice the position of *not* in compound tenses, i.e., verb forms of more than two elements:

am/is/are was/were		moving { moved { being moved
has/have had		{ moved { been moving { been moved
will/would shall/should can/could may/might must/need	not	{ move { be moving { have moved { have been moving { be moved { have been moved
ought	not to	

In the simple tenses (**present** I move, he moves; **past** I moved), when there is no modal/auxiliary present the Ø category (◄ Section 7.1) is replaced by **do/does/did** before *not*, and the main verb reduces to the base form BASE+Ø:

he		move [+s]	=	he		moves
he do [+es]	not	move [+Ø]	=	he does not	move
he		move [+d]	=	he		moved
he do [+d]	not	move [+Ø]	=	he did not	move

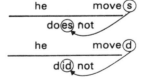

Or you can look at it like this (see left):

Notes

1 Strictly, the negative form of **used to** is **used not to** (or **usedn't to**), but you will often hear *didn't use to*. (The negative with *used* is often the adverb *never* (I never used to . . .) which avoids the problem.)

2 **Need** becomes either **need not** or **do not need to**, but with a change of meaning (→ Section 10.6).

3 **Have to** becomes either **have not to** or **do not have to**, but with a change of meaning (→ Section 10.4).

4 **Do/does/did** is also used in the positive form, strongly stressed, to contradict negative questions/statements, or to make statements and imperatives which are polite but forceful (see also → Section 8.6) e.g.
'Why didn't you finish it? 'But I '*did* finish it!')
'It's a pity John doesn't like school.' 'But he '*does* like school.'
'I '*do* think you ought to tell her the truth.' (=I really think . . .)
'*Do* come and see us any time you are in town.' (=Please come . . .)

7.5.2 Abbreviated forms

In speaking and in informal writing, we abbreviate (shorten) either the **modal/be/have** or the word **not**:

Full form	Be/have/modal shortened	Not shortened
am not	I'm not	–
is not	he's not	isn't
are not	they're not	aren't
was not	–	wasn't
were not	–	weren't
has not	he's not	hasn't
have not	they've not	haven't
had not	he'd not	hadn't
will not	he'll not	won't
would not	he'd not	wouldn't
shall not	I'll not	shan't
should not	I'd not	shouldn't
cannot	–	can't
could not	–	couldn't
may not	–	(mayn't)
might not	–	mightn't
must not	–	mustn't
need not	–	needn't
ought not to	–	oughtn't to
used not to	–	usedn't to
do not	–	don't
does not	–	doesn't
did not	–	didn't

Note that *cannot* is written as one word. *Mayn't* is uncommon. For the uses of *shall* and *should* with persons other than *I/we*, see →9.5 (note).

Take care with the pronunciation of these short forms:

mustn't = [mʌsnt], i.e. the *t* of *must* is not pronounced
can't = [kɑːnt], with a long [aː] to distinguish *can't* from *can* [kæn] or [kən]
won't = [w ou nt], with a well-rounded [ou] to distinguish *won't* from *want* [wɒnt]
shan't = [ʃɑːnt]
usedn't = [jˈusənt], i.e. the *d* of *used* is not pronounced (compare used to = [juˈstuː], where the d is also silent.)

General advice: We recommend that you use the shortened forms where *not* is abbreviated to *n't*: they are clearer, and, except for *I'm not*, there is a short form for every modal and part of *be/have*.

7.6 The formation of questions

There are two kinds of questions:

Simple questions: You ask simple questions when you need information, that is, when you don't know what the answer will be.

'*Coloured' questions*: Sometimes you seem to be asking a question when in fact you are not seeking information, but when you wish to express an attitude, such as surprise, hope etc.

7.6.1 Form of simple questions

Invert the **subject** and the **modal/be/have**:

he is coming   ———→   is he coming?

he isn't coming   ———→   isn't he coming?

(he is not coming ———→   is he not coming) – this form is not a common spoken form

Invert also after a question word:
e.g. Where *are you* going?
      Whereabouts *do you* live in London?
      Why *hasn't she* replied to our letter?

Notice that in the simple tenses (I go/he goes, he went), the empty category Ø is replaced by **do/don't**, **does/doesn't** or **did/didn't**:

It Ø moves   ———→   Does it move?
It Ø moved   ———→   Did it move?
It doesn't move   ———→   Doesn't it move?
It didn't move   ———→   Didn't it move?

You can think of it like this:

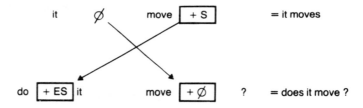

7.6.2 Coloured questions

The commonest forms of these *question+attitude* utterances (spoken forms) are:

a	⊕ ⊖ It will work, won't it?	Expecting or hoping for a *yes* answer
b	⊕ ⊖ It won't work, will it?	Expecting or hoping for a *no* answer
c	⊕ (So,) you're coming with us, ⊕ are you?	Expressing interest, surprise etc., about something which you already know (or at least believe) to be true.

Notice that the **be/have/modal** is repeated in the question tag (or 'tail'):

will ..., *won't it? can* ..., *can't you? haven't* ..., *have they?*

Do/does/did (+**n't**) are used with simple tenses:

e.g. *He plays* football, *doesn't he?*

  So *you went* out with John again, *did you?*

A special case is:

  Let's go and have a meal, *shall we?*

These coloured questions using 'question tags' are very common, but their exact meaning depends on the *intonation* used.

7.7 Formation of verbs

7.7.1 Verb or noun?

Many common words are both verbs and nouns.

e.g. I *travel* a lot in my job. *Travel* here is a verb

  Travel broadens the mind. *Travel* here is a noun

For a list of common words of this kind, see ← Section 1.7.7

Note

A number of words make a change of pronunciation (and sometimes a slight change of spelling) between noun and verb:

Noun	*Verb*	*Noun*	*Verb*
[s]	[z]	[θ]	[ð]
abuse	abuse	bath	bathe
advice	advise	breath	breathe
device	devise	mouth	mouth
house	house	sheath	sheathe
use	use	teeth	teethe
		wreath	wreathe
[f]	[v]		
belief	believe	*Other changes*	
grief	grieve	blood	bleed
half	halve	choice	choose
relief	relieve	food	feed
shelf	shelve	loss	lose

7.7.2 Verbs which express small or repeated actions

(See also ← Section 1.7.3). Some endings suggest small or repeated actions, especially movements of the body (shudder, stumble, etc) and various qualities of light and sound (glitter, twinkle, tinkle, etc.). For example:

-ckle, -ggle, -ngle, -kle   tickle, trickle, cackle, giggle, wriggle, tingle, twinkle, tinkle, sparkle

-tter   flutter, glitter, stutter, titter, totter, twitter

-mmer   glimmer (*from* gleam), shimmer, stammer

-mble, -bble   amble, mumble, ramble, stumble, tremble, tumble; bubble, dribble

Also, *shudder, shiver* and *whimper*. Some words with these endings do not carry the idea of small repeated actions, e.g., *gamble, single, tackle.*

7.7.3 Verbs in -en

There are about 30 useful verbs, mostly formed on the pattern ADJECTIVE+-EN, with the meaning *to make or to become the quality expressed by the adjective*:

Adjective	Verb	Adjective	Verb
black	blacken	red	redden
bright	brighten	sad	sadden
broad	broaden	sick	sicken
cheap	cheapen	short	shorten
coarse	coarsen	soft	soften
damp	dampen	straight	straighten
dark	darken	thick	thicken
deep	deepen	tough	toughen
fast	fasten	weak	weaken
fat	fatten	white	whiten
glad	gladden	wide	widen
hard	harden		
light	lighten		
mad	madden		
moist	moisten		

Also: heighten, lengthen, strengthen, hearten and dishearten.

Note:
Other adjectives can be used as verbs in this sense without adding **-en**:
e.g. *warm*   She warmed up some milk.
     dry   Dry your clothes.

7.7.4 Verbs ending in -*ify*, -*ize* (-*ise*) and -*ate*

-ify
This suffix expresses the idea *to cause or to make*:
e.g. to electrify a railway   = to convert it from steam or diesel to electric power.
      to falsify a statement   = to add or change something in such a way that it becomes false (invalid).

The suffix is stressed, [i'faɪ], and in most cases forms abstract nouns by changing to -*ification*, pronounced [ɪfɪk'eɪʃn] (*satisfy* → *satisfaction* is an important exception). A list of the commonest verbs in **-ify** is given in Section 7.9 Appendix XI.

-ize
This suffix expresses the idea *to cause or to make* or *to change or convert to*:
e.g. to legalize marijuana   = to make it legal
      to modernize a railway   = to make improvements, by, for example, converting it from steam to electric power.

The suffix is unstressed [aɪz] and generally forms abstract nouns by changing to -*ization*, pronounced [aɪzˈeɪʃn]. The spelling of this ending is a matter of argument, because it is often spelled **-ise**, also pronounced [aɪz]. We advise you to use the spelling **-ize** (but see note below).

This suffix is widely used (some would say overused) and **new** verbs are being invented constantly. A list of the most useful is given in Section 7.9 Appendix XI.

Note

There are a number of verbs which must be spelled **-ise** because these letters are not a suffix but part of the word itself:
e.g. advise is ad-+-vise   surprise is sur-+-prise

The commonest verbs ending in the letters **-ise** are:
advertise   advise   comprise   compromise   despise   devise   disguise   exercise   improvise   promise   revise   supervise   surprise   televise.

-ate

The ending **-ate** also expresses the idea of making or causing in many cases. The ending, pronounced [eɪt], is unstressed. It forms abstract nouns by changing to -*ation*, pronounced [ˈeɪʃn]. A few are related to simple nouns or adjectives,
e.g. origin → originate   alien → alienate
but most of them cannot be derived in this way.
A list of the most useful is given in Section 7.9 Appendix XI.

Note:

Notice the following cases where there is a corresponding noun or adjective which is pronounced with final [ət]:

[eɪt]	[ət]	[ət]	[eɪt]	[ət]	[ət]
Verb	*Adjective*	*Noun*	*Verb*	*Adjective*	*Noun*
advocate		an advocate	degenerate	degenerate	a degenerate
alternate	alternate		delegate	delegate	a delegate
appropriate	appropriate		deliberate	deliberate	
approximate	approximate		elaborate	elaborate	
articulate	articulate		estimate		an estimate
associate	associate	an associate	intimate	intimate	an intimate
co-ordinate		a co-ordinate	moderate	moderate	a moderate

7.7.5 Prefixes

a The following prefixes are added to existing verbs to make new verbs with a modified meaning (consult a dictionary to find out which prefixes can be used with any particular verb.)

Prefix	Meaning	Examples
re-	again, a second time	rebuild, re-elect, reopen, reorder
fore-	happening before	foresee, foretell, forewarn
co-	accompanying, together	co-exist, co-operate
out-	more than	outgrow, outlive, outweigh
over-	too much	overcharge, overeat, overindulge
under-	too little	underachieve, undercook, underpay
un-	removing, reversing	undo, unpack, untie, unwrap
de-	removing, reversing	defrost (a refrigerator), decode
dis-	removing, reversing	disconnect, discourage, disinfect
mis-	using wrongly, badly	miscalculate, mislead, misuse

b The prefix **en-** (em-) is used to make transitive verbs (→13.6–10).
The most useful are:

embitter	endear
embody	enforce
empower	enlarge
enable	enlighten
enact	enliven
enchant	enrich
encircle	ensure
enclose	entangle
encourage	entitle
endanger	entrust

c *Prefixes attached to Latin roots*

A great many useful verbs in English are on the pattern LATIN PREFIX+LATIN VERBAL ROOT. For example.*

trans-	(=across)	+	**-mit**	(=send)	transmit
pre-	(=before)	+	**-fer**	(=carry)	prefer
ex-	(=out)	+	**-clude**	(=close)	exclude
ob-	(=against)	+	**-ject**	(=throw)	object
in-	(=in)	+	**-pel**	(=push)	impel
inter-	(=between)	+	**-rupt**	(=break)	interrupt
de-	(=about)	+	**-scribe**	(=write)	describe
sub-	(=under)	+	**port**	(=carry)	support
ad-	(=towards)	+	**-tain**	(=hold)	attain

A matrix of common prefixes and verb roots is given in →7.10, Appendix XII.

*The examples are a guide only. Unfortunately, because words change their meaning over a long period of time, you cannot always see the relationship between the original prefix+root and the present meaning of the word.

7.8 Appendix X: Alphabetical list of irregular verbs

Infinitive	Past tense	Past participle	Infinitive	Past tense	Past participle
arise	arose	arisen	get	got	got
awake	awoke	awoken	give	gave	given
be	was	been	go	went	gone
bear	bore	borne	grind	ground	ground
beat	beat	beaten	grow	grew	grown
become	became	become	hang	hung, hanged	hung, hanged
begin	began	begun	have	had	had
bend	bent	bent	hear	heard	heard
bet	bet, betted	bet, betted	hide	hid	hidden
bid	bade, bid	bid	hit	hit	hit
bind	bound	bound	hold	held	held
bite	bit	bitten	hurt	hurt	hurt
bleed	bled	bled	keep	kept	kept
blend	blended; blent	blended	kneel	knelt	knelt
blow	blew	blown	knit	knitted, knit	knitted, knit
break	broke	broken	know	knew	known
breed	bred	bred	lade	laded	laden
bring	brought	brought	lay	laid	laid
broadcast	broadcast	broadcast	lead	led	led
build	built	built	lean	leant, leaned	leant, leaned
burn	burnt, burned	burnt, burned	leap	leapt, leaped	leapt, leaped
burst	burst	burst	learn	learnt, learned	learnt, learned
buy	bought	bought	leave	left	left
cast	cast	cast	lend	lent	lent
catch	caught	caught	let	let	let
choose	chose	chosen	lie	lay	lain
cling	clung	clung	light	lit	lit
clothe	clothed, clad	clothed	lose	lost	lost
come	came	come	make	made	made
cost	cost	cost	mean	meant	meant
creep	crept	crept	meet	met	met
cut	cut	cut	mistake	mistook	mistaken
dare	dared	dared	mow	mowed	mown
deal	dealt	dealt	pay	paid	paid
dig	dug	dug	put	put	put
do	did	done	quit	quit	quit
draw	drew	drawn	read [ri:d]	read [red]	read [red]
dream	dreamt, dreamed	dreamt, dreamed	rid	rid	rid
drink	drank	drunk	ride	rode	ridden
drive	drove	driven	ring	rang	rung
dwell	dwelt	dwelt	rise	rose	risen
eat	ate	eaten	run	ran	run
fall	fell	fallen	saw	sawed	sawn
feed	fed	fed	say	said	said
feel	felt	felt	see	saw	seen
fight	fought	fought	seek	sought	sought
find	found	found	sell	sold	sold
flee	fled	fled	send	sent	sent
fling	flung	flung	set	set	set
fly	flew	flown	sew	sewed	sewn
forbid	forbade, forbad	forbidden	shake	shook	shaken
forecast	forecast	forecast	shed	shed	shed
forget	forgot	forgotten	shine	shone	shone
forgive	forgave	forgiven	shoe	shod	shod
forsake	forsook	forsaken	shoot	shot	shot
freeze	froze	frozen	show	showed	shown

Infinitive	Past tense	Past participle	Infinitive	Past tense	Past participle
shrink	shrank, shrunk	shrunk	stink	stank, stunk	stunk
shut	shut	shut	stride	strode	stridden
sing	sang	sung	strike	struck	struck
sink	sank	sunk	string	strung	strung
sit	sat	sat	strive	strove	striven
sleep	slept	slept	swear	swore	sworn
slide	slid	slid	sweep	swept	swept
sling	slung	slung	swim	swam	swum
slink	slunk	slunk	swing	swung	swung
slit	slit	slit	take	took	taken
smell	smelt, smelled	smelt, smelled	teach	taught	taught
sow	sowed	sown	tear	tore	torn
speak	spoke	spoken	tell	told	told
speed	sped, speeded	sped, speeded	think	thought	thought
spell	spelt, spelled	spelt, spelled	throw	threw	thrown
spend	spent	spent	thrust	thrust	thrust
spill	spilt, spilled	spilt, spilled	tread	trod	trodden
spin	spun, span	spun	upset	upset	upset
spit	spat	spat	wake	woke	woken
split	split	split	wear	wore	worn
spoil	spoilt, spoiled	spoilt, spoiled	weave	wove	woven
spread	spread	spread	weep	wept	wept
spring	sprang	sprung	win	won	won
stand	stood	stood	wind	wound	wound
steal	stole	stolen	wring	wrung	wrung
stick	stuck	stuck	write	wrote	written
sting	stung	stung			

7.9   Appendix XI: Verbs in -ify, -ize and -ate

All the verbs in this appendix are words which you are likely to hear or to read in the media (advertising, television and the press). The ones which we consider most useful are in bold type.

-ify

amplify	mollify
beautify	mystify
certify	notify
clarify	nullify
classify	pacify
codify	personify
diversify	purify
dignify	**qualify**
edify	quantify
electrify	ratify
exemplify	**rectify**
falsify	**satisfy**
fortify	**signify**
gratify	**simplify**
horrify	solidify
identify	**specify**
indemnify	stratify
intensify	stultify
justify	**terrify**
liquify	testify
(or liquefy)	typify
magnify	unify
modify	

-ize (or -ise, ← Section 7.4.2)

apologize	idolize
anglicize	immunize
authorize	immortalize
centralize	individualize
characterize	**industrialize**
colonize	institutionalize
compartmentalize	jeopardize
criticize	legalize
decentralize	liquidize
computerize	**materialize**
dramatize	**maximize**
economize	**minimize**
emphasize	mobilize
energize	**modernize**
externalize	**monopolize**
familiarize	moralize
fantasize	motorize
finalize	**nationalize**
fraternize	naturalize
generalize	neutralize
glamorize	normalize
harmonize	optimize
	organize
ostracize	**tranquillize**
patronize	trivialize
personalize	vandalize
polarize	**victimize**
pressurize	**visualize**
publicize	
recognize	**-ate**
regularize	**accelerate**
revitalize	**accommodate**
romanticize	**accumulate**
scandalize	activate
scrutinize	adjudicate
sensationalize	advocate
sensitize	affiliate
serialize	**aggravate***
socialize	**alienate**
specialize	alleviate
stabilize	**allocate**
standardize	**alternate**
sterilize	**anticipate**
stylize	**appropriate**
sympathize	articulate
terrorize	**assassinate**

Aggravate is widely misused to mean *irritate* or *annoy*.

associate	deliberate	**eradicate**	**impersonate**	irrigate	radiate
automate	**demonstrate**	**estimate**	**indicate**	**irritate**	recapitulate
captivate	**depreciate**	**evaluate**	indoctrinate	**isolate**	repudiate
collaborate	designate	**exaggerate**	infiltrate	**legislate**	**retaliate**
complicate	**deteriorate**	exterminate	inflate	liquidate	rotate
concentrate	detonate	fabricate	innovate	masturbate	**segregate**
confiscate	**distintegrate**	facilitate	inoculate	**moderate**	separate
compensate	domesticate	**fascinate**	instigate	operate	**simulate**
congregate	**dominate**	**generate**	insinuate	orientate	**stimulate**
contaminate	**educate**	gesticulate	**integrate**	originate	**terminate**
contemplate	elaborate	gravitate	interrogate	**penetrate**	**tolerate**
co-operate	**eliminate**	hibernate	intimate	perpetuate	validate
co-ordinate	**emigrate**	**humiliate**	**intimidate**	prefabricate	violate
deflate	**emulate**	**illuminate**	invalidate	proliferate	
delegate	**enumerate**	**imitate**	**investigate**	propagate	

7.10 Appendix XIII: Matrix of verbs on the pattern LATIN PREFIX + ROOT

Each ● indicates a verb composed of the prefix from the vertical column, and the verb root from the horizontal row. For example, the first row produces ad- + cede = *accede*, con- + cede = *concede*, etc. Where the prefix is modified, this is indicated in the matrix, as in the case of ad- with -cede, where the prefix becomes ac-. (This can be a help with spelling. For example, the word *accommodate* is often misspelled. It comes from ad- + con- + modate→ → (*adconmodate*) → *accommodate*.)

	ab-	ad-	con-	de-	dis-	ex-	in-	inter-	ob-	per-	pre-	pro-	re-	sub-	trans-
-cede		ac-	●					●			●		●		
-ceed						●						●		suc-	
-ceive			●	●						●			●		
-cept		ac-		●		●									
-cline				●			●						●		
-clude			●			●	●				●				
-cord		ac-											●		
-cur			●				●		oc-				●		
-dict		●					·				●				
-duce	ad-		●				●					●	●		
-duct	●	●	●												
-fect			●				●			●					
-fend				●					of-						
-fer			●	●			●		of-		●		●	suf-	●
-fine			●	●									●		
-firm		af-	●												
-flect				●									●		
-form			●	●			●			●			●		●
-fuse			●	●			●						●	suf-	●
-ject			●			e-	●	●	●			●	●	●	
-late						e-							●		●
-lude		al-	col-	●		e-									

	ab-	ad-	con-	de-	dis-	ex-	in-	inter-	ob-	per-	pre-	pro-	re-	sub-	trans-
-mand			com-	●									●		
-mise												●		sur-	
-miss				●											
-mit		●	com-			e-			●	●			●	●	●
-pel			com-	●	●		im-					●	●		
-plain			com-			●									
-plete			com-	●											
-port				●	●	●	im-						●	sup-	
-pose			com-	●	●	●	im-	●	op-			●	●	sup-	●
-press			com-	●		●	im-		op-				●	sup-	
-rect			cor-			e-									
-rupt			cor-		●	e-		●							
-scend		a-		●											●
-scribe		a-		●			●				●	●		●	●
-sent	●	as-	●								●		●		
-serve			●	●					●		●		●		
-sign		as-	●	●									●		
-sist		as-	●	●			●			●-			●	●	
-solve	●				●								●		
-struct			●				●		●						
-sult			●				●						●		
-sume		as-	●								●		●	●	
-tain		at-	●	●					●	●			●		
-tend		at-	●		●	●	●				●			●	
-tribute		at-	●		●										
-vene			●					●							
-vent			●				●				●				
-verse			●										●		
-vert	a-		●				●			●			●	●	
-vide												●			
-vise		●		●									●		
-voke			●			e-	●					●	●		
-volve			●			e-	●						●		

8 Contents

8 Verbs – Meaning and uses

Silverlocks and the Three Bears

The three bears had been working very hard and were looking forward to a nice hot dish of soup each and a good night's sleep. What they did not know was that, while they were out, a pretty girl called Silverlocks had got into their cottage. She had tried the soup in each dish, and had drunk up all the soup in the smallest one. Then, because she was feeling very tired after her meal, she had gone into the other room, where there were three comfortable chairs. She tried them all, but chose the smallest one to curl up in, because it had the softest cushions. She was still there, fast asleep, when the three bears returned. The bears noticed at once that somebody had been in.

'Who's been drinking my soup?' shouted the big and the middle-sized bears at the same time.

'Somebody has drunk up *all* my soup!' squeaked the small bear. Then they went into the next room, where the comfortable armchairs were.

'Who's been sitting in my chair?' said the two bigger bears simultaneously. The small bear looked down at his chair, which was in the darkest corner of the room. He said nothing, but waited patiently for the other two bears to go away.

Moral: Two's company; four's a crowd.

Preface

In this and the following chapters, we shall use these names for the different forms (**tenses**) of the verb:

	Simple	Continuous
Present	He moves	He is moving
Past	He moved	He was moving
Future	He will move	He will be moving
Present perfect	He has moved	He has been moving
Past perfect	He had moved	He had been moving
Future perfect	He will have moved	He will have been moving
Conditional II	He would move	He would be moving
Conditional III	He would have moved	He would have been moving

8.1 The two elements of meaning

Every verb form (**tense**) has two elements of meaning:

 Time   – the time when the action happens

 Attitude – our interest in the action, the way we see it

8.1.1   Time

We can refer to the **present** (*now* – the moment of speaking), the **past** (*before now*) and the **future** (*after now* or *later*). We can refer to a *point* (moment) of time, or to a *period* of time, and we can specify whether the period of time is completed (i.e., whether the action has definitely ended) or whether it is incomplete. e.g.

Point	*Period*	
	incomplete	*complete*
they went upstairs	they had been working	he waited patiently until

8.1.2   Attitude

We choose the verb form which expresses our point of view about the activity, i.e., which expresses the way we interpret the situation. e.g.

Action incomplete	*Definitely past*	*At some time before now*
she was feeling tired	they went upstairs	somebody has drunk my soup

Or we may express Ø attitudes about events that are always true:
e.g. It rains a lot in the north of England.

Attitude plays a large role in talking about the future
(→ Chapter 9).

It may rain	– estimating the probability (guessing)
It is going to rain	– interpreting the signs
It will rain	– stating the future as if it were a fact

> Summary: Meaning of any verb form   =   Time + Attitude
> 🕐 + ◀

A   The tenses

8.2   The present tenses

8.2.1   Present continuous

> 🕐 *Time*   Now, the moment of speaking, this week, this period of time we are in.
>
> ◀ *Attitude* We are talking about an action which is unfinished, incomplete, in progress, going on during the period of time we are in.

Examples

a *Going on at this moment*
What *are you doing*?
I'm making a birthday cake for my brother.
What is that music *you're playing*?

b *Going on during this period of time*

What *are you doing* nowadays?

Oh, *I'm still working* at the same place.

I'm learning to play the guitar.

Are you taking lessons?

Everyone *is talking* about the new James Bond film.

People *are eating* less meat nowadays (i.e., you are describing a *trend* which is going on.)

c *Everything is ready for something which will happen soon* (see also→ Section 9.8).

I'm on holiday at the moment, but *I'm starting* a new course next week.

Hurry up! The train *is leaving* soon. (i.e. it will leave at any moment)

What *are you doing* tomorrow night?

I'm having dinner with Nick and his girlfriend.

d *Describing something which is temporary* (i.e. something which is true at the moment of speaking, but which may not be true later.)

John is normally a sensible man, but he *is being* very stupid at the moment.

e *Describing, and emphasizing, a never-ending series of events*

In this use of the present continuous, the adverbs (→ Chapter 12) *always, forever* or *constantly* are usually added:

You never do your homework on time: you*'re forever making* excuses.

She *is always trying* to show that she knows more than everyone else.

I'm constantly having to remind you to tidy up your room.

Summary

All the actions in a–e above are *unfinished, incomplete,* as far as the speaker is concerned (i.e. the *attitude* element). Compare the following views of the same situation.

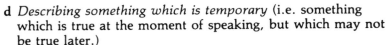

he is sensible   he is being stupid

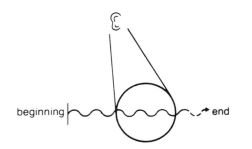

I heard him *playing*
the Moonlight Sonata
(i.e., a part of it, not
necessarily all)

I heard him *play*
the Moonlight Sonata
(i.e., the whole sonata)

8.2.2. Present simple

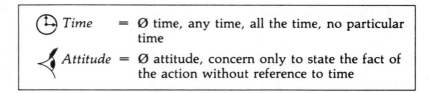

Time	=	Ø time, any time, all the time, no particular time
Attitude	=	Ø attitude, concern only to state the fact of the action without reference to time

Examples of the present simple are

a *General, universal, true statements* (including scientific statements)
    The Earth *goes* round the Sun.
    French people *drink* more wine than English people.
    Most of us probably *eat* too much meat.

b *Describing the regular or permanent features of one's life*
    I *live* in a small town on the south coast. I *work* at home, but I often *go* abroad on business. I *have* two children, one *is* still at school and the other *goes* to college. I *speak* French and Spanish, and I *know* a bit of German. I *don't like* sport but I *enjoy* the open air. I *don't smoke*, but I *drink* a lot of wine when I *go* to France.

Note: because the present simple is used in this way, it is often used with frequency adverbs (→ Section 12.11.2–3) like *often*, *sometimes, always, regularly, never, frequently*.

c *Describing an event which depends on a fixed timetable or schedule*
    There is a train to London from here every half hour. The next train *leaves* at 15.40.
    I've been accepted by Birmingham University. My course *starts* on Monday week.

Note: in such cases, you could say *I will leave* and *will start* as they refer to events in the future (see → Section 9.2.5).

d *Describing a demonstration, events in a play etc.*, where time is of no interest.
    First *I fill* the beaker with 100 cc of distilled water. Then *I add* the crystals and the acid. *I heat* the beaker and in a few seconds the mixture *turns* deep yellow.
    At this moment, Hamlet *enters*. He goes over to Laertes and *speaks* to him. Meanwhile, Polonius *decides* to . . .

Note
Sometimes, people will describe something that happened to them using the present simple (instead of the past tense), because it sounds more dramatic,
e.g. 'So, this old man *comes up* to me and *asks* me the way to the Town Hall. I *look* him straight in the eye and *tell* him there isn't a town hall in Hadley. Immediately *he starts* shouting . . .
We do not advise you to imitate this style.

8.2.3 Present continuous or present simple?

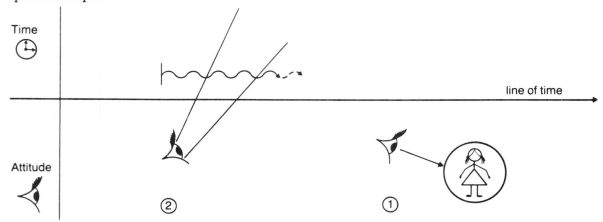

Note the difference between:

1 Mary (usually) *lives* alone.

The eye looks at Mary but not at the line of time.

but

2 At the moment, she *is living* with her parents.

The eye looks at the line of time and is interested in what is happening (*living with her parents*) at the time of speaking. Note that the activity (*living*) is incomplete, unfinished.

Similarly, John works in a bank.

A fact about John like saying 'John is a bank clerk. That's what he does'.

but John is working in a bank.

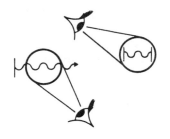

A fact about what is happening in John's life nowadays. It could be the reply to a question like 'What is John doing now? Where is he working?' and suggests that he *was* doing something else before, and/or that his job in the bank is not a permanent one.

Some actions by their nature are more likely to be seen in progress while others are more likely to be seen as single completed acts (see diagram on left).

Compare the descriptions of the actions in a football match and a horserace:

Jones *traps* the ball and *heads* it across to Smith. Smith *passes* it to Brown, who *kicks* it downfield. Baker *intercepts* and *passes* to . . .

i.e. a series of single completed acts

trap　head　pass　kick　intercept

Goodboy *is leading* at the moment, but Brownwindsor *is coming* up very fast on the inside. Blacksheep *is falling behind* now, but the other horses *are keeping up* well with the leaders. Goodboy *is slowly pulling away* . . .

i.e., a series of activities in progress (changing and unfinished)

leading   falling behind   pulling away

coming up   keeping up

Process   **State**

eating   he is full!

Verbs which describe *processes* (where things change) will be used in both the **simple** and the **continuous** forms (depending on our interest in the time and the process). Verbs which describe *states* (i.e. the results of processes) are more likely to be used in the **simple** form.

e.g. The *process* leads to the *state (result)*.

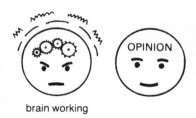

brain working

The difference between the process and the *state (result)* can be seen in the two uses of *think*:

   I'm thinking about what you said. *I think* you're right.
(brain working)   (opinion)
   'I think you are right' means *'I am of the opinion* that you are right'.

For this reason it is usual to say, for example:
   I *don't think* it *is* going to rain (rather than 'I *think* it *isn't* . . .')
   i.e. *I am not of the opinion* that it *is* going to rain.

More examples of *process* and *state (result)*

Process	*Result*
a *I'm falling* in love with her.	I'm in love with her.
	=*I love* her.
b *I'm studying* the problem.	At last *I understand* it.

Notes

1 A similar contrast occurs with verbs to do with **perception**.
   i.e. the use of our senses:

Like *study*	Like *understand*
look at	see
listen to	hear
touch, feel	feel
taste	taste
smell (=sniff)	smell

Compare:

He *is tasting* the wine (i.e. to find out if it is good) *and*
The wine *tastes* sour (i.e. it has a sour taste).
The verbs like *understand* often occur with *can*
      e.g. *I can see* a strange light in the sky.

2 Verbs which, like *see, hear,* etc. are more likely to be used in the simple form because they refer to *states* rather than to *processes* include:

Opinions	*Mental states*	*Emotions*	
assume	expect	care	mind
believe	forget	detest	prefer
consider	imagine	envy	regret
feel (=think)	know	fear	want
find (=consider)	mean	hate	wish
suggest	notice	hope	
suppose	remember	like	
think	understand	love	

3 The following verbs occur in the simple form because they express states rather than processes:

Have (=possess)

Possession	*Measure*	*Others*	
belong to	contain	appear	look (=resemble)
have	cost	apply to	matter
hold	hold	depend on	represent
own	measure	deserve	resemble
possess	weigh	differ	seem
		exist	stand for (=represent)
		interest	

WARNING!
Verbs like those in the notes above which normally occur in the simple form can also occur in the continuous form in these cases:
a When you want to emphasize the *process*:
      I have had too much wine: *I'm seeing* double!
b When the verb is used with a different meaning:
      Are you seeing Anna tonight? (seeing=meeting)

A note on **have**
Take special care with the verb **have**. In the sense of *possess*, it is used in the simple form,
e.g. I *have* a present for you.

In these cases, it is often replaced by *have got* in speaking:
e.g. *I've got* a present for you.
Strictly speaking, the negative form is
  I have not a present for you.
and the interrogative
  Have you a present for me?
However, it is becoming common to treat **have** (=possess) as an ordinary verb, i.e., to use **do/does/did** to form negatives and interrogatives.
e.g. *I don't have* a present for you.
  Do you have a present for me?

The verb **have** is used in a number of expressions where it does not mean *possess*. In these cases, it is used equally in the simple and the continuous form, and it forms negatives and interrogatives in the simple tenses with **do**:
  What time *are we having dinner* tonight?
  We went to the party but *we didn't have a very good time.*
  Did you have a look at the article I told you about?
  You cannot see John at the moment: *he's having a bath.*

8.2.4 Adverbials used with the present tenses

Because the present simple refers to regular or repeated events, it often occurs with frequency adverbs (→ Section 12.11.2) like *often, sometimes, always, seldom* and *never*. Because the present continuous refers to events happening at the moment of speaking, it often occurs with adverbials like *now, at the moment, today* and *this week*.

On the other hand, these adverbials are not *the reason* for choosing the simple or continuous form. It is just that in many cases they are associated with the particular circumstances which *are* the reason for choosing the verb form.
In other words, *now* often goes with the continuous form, but it can also go with the simple form:
e.g. He used to live in a flat but *now* he lives in a house.
Similarly, *always* often goes with the simple form, but it can also go with the continuous:
e.g. He is *always* giving me presents. Do you think he loves me?

The decision about which form to choose depends on the situation, not the use of particular adverbials.

8.2.5 The special use of the present simple and the present continuous in newspaper headlines

In order to say as much as possible in a few words, newspaper headlines have developed what is almost a special language. For example, they use short words instead of long ones even when those short words are never or rarely used anywhere else (e.g. *probe* for *investigation, rap* for *criticize, bid* for *attempt, hit* for *badly affected*, etc.). They also use nouns as adjectives in strings (e.g. GOVERNMENT RAILCRASH ENQUIRY ROW, which (probably) means *'There is an argument (row) about the enquiry which the government have set up to find out the cause of the railcrash.'*)

Verbs rarely appear in headlines, but when they do, the convention is:

the **present simple** is used to describe a past event,

the **present continuous** is used to describe a future event.*

e.g. PM ANNOUNCES NEW PLAN = The Prime Minister has recently (just) announced . . .

BL MOVING TO NEW PREMISES = British Leyland are going to move soon to . . .

The **to-infinitive** is used to describe a planned future event as well:

CHAIRMAN TO RESIGN = The Chairman will resign . . . (he has announced this)

*No verb = present tense. e.g. NEW STRIKE THREAT = There *is* the threat of a strike again.

8.3   The past tenses

8.3.1   Past simple

> *Time*   a time before now, earlier than now.
>
> *Attitude*   describes something which began *and ended* before the present, i.e. it describes a completed act.

e.g. The small bear *looked* down at his bed.

We *left* Orleans at eleven o'clock and *drove* straight to Amboise. We *had* lunch there, and then *decided* to go to Tours. We *found* a small hotel near the station . . .

The duration of the act (i.e., how long it lasted) is not important:

I was born in a little village in the Midlands, and *went* to school there until I was eighteen. We *didn't have* much money so we never *had* any holidays.

The tense can describe something which happened a long time ago, or which happened a moment ago:

The French Revolution *broke out* in 1789.

What was that noise? I *didn't hear* anything.

What *did you do* at school today? We *watched* a film about Africa.

Note: For the difference between 'What *did you do* today?' (Past simple) and 'What *have you done* today?' (Present perfect), see → Section 8.4.6).

8.3.2   Past continuous

At the time of speaking often means at that point in the story (the narrative), as in the examples.

> *Time*   a time before now, earlier than now.
>
> *Attitude*   describes something which began in the past but which had not finished at the time of speaking*, i.e. it describes an unfinished, incomplete action.

e.g. They were looking forward to a nice hot dish of soup.
Because she was feeling very tired after her meal...
She was still lying there, fast asleep, when the three bears returned.

The past continuous is

a often used to give a descriptive background to a narrative (a story) in the past tense, e.g.

It *was raining* when we left Orleans. Because the roads were wet I drove quite slowly even though everyone else *was driving* at their usual speed. Just outside Amboise we had to stop because of an accident. A crowd of people *were standing* at the roadside and the police *were taking* statements from them...

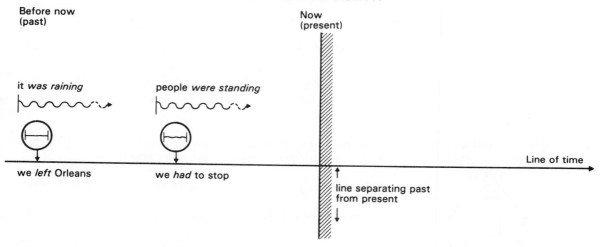

b Note the difference between these two sentences
  A The children *were standing* when the teacher came into the room. (when = at the same time)
  B The children *stood up* when the teacher came into the room. (when = immediately after)

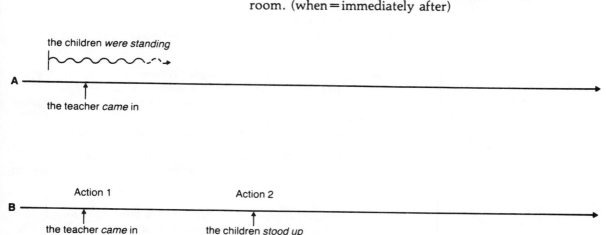

The **past continuous** is used in speaking in these cases.

a When you want to show deference to another person's wishes or ideas, i.e. when you want to suggest that they are more important than yours are:

'What are you doing this evening?'
'Well, *I was thinking* of going to the pictures . . .'
This suggests ' . . . but I am sure you have a much better idea.'

b It can also be a way of showing your interest in the other person:

'What are you doing this evening?'
'I *was thinking* of going to the pictures.'
This could suggest (the intonation would also be important)
'Would you like to come with me?'

c *I was wondering if . . .* is a way of asking a favour very politely:

I was wondering if you could lend me a fiver till payday.

d It is used to show a change of mind:

I *was going* to stay in this evening *but* I've decided to go out instead.

8.3.3   *Used to and would*

ODEON CINEMA

If you want to emphasize or draw attention to an activity in the past which no longer happens, use the pattern USED TO+MAIN VERB

When I was young, I *used to go* to the football match every Saturday.
'Does Nick smoke?' 'He *used to*, but I think he has given it up.'
'What a funny-looking cinema!' 'Well, it *used to be* a church!'

Notes

1 You cannot use **used to** with an expression of a *definite* period of time.

I used to go to school in Wellington *when I was a boy.* (indefinite time)
but I went to school in Wellington *for eight years.* (definite time)

2 **Used to** is a fixed expression with no present tense, i.e. there is no form *use to*. The equivalent is the present simple.

Nick *used to smoke* heavily.   He *used to be* a heavy smoker.
Nick *smokes* heavily.   He *is* a heavy smoker.

3 The negative form of **used to** is generally **never used to**.

e.g. Julia has become very aggressive lately. She *never used to be*.

You will also meet a past tense form with **would**. It is mainly a written form used in stories. It means the same as **used to** and is really a way of providing variety in a narrative.

Every Saturday evening, Father *would take out* his old violin and *start* to play old music hall songs. We had to listen politely and pretend to enjoy his playing. Mother used to look at us severely if we laughed or made a noise. Sometimes Father *would go on* for hours . . .

We advise you to use **used to** rather than **would**.

8.3.4 Adverbials used with past tenses

Adverbials of time which are used with the past tenses include those:

a *referring to frequency*
e.g. We *often* stayed up late.
She was *constantly* trying to make ends meet.

b *referring to a point of time*
e.g. It arrived *last week/yesterday*.
Why didn't you tell me *earlier/before*?
The adverbial *ago* is very useful: it fixes the moment in the past. It is used in the pattern X+AGO, where X is an expression of time.
Definite: three weeks ago, two hours ago, a century ago
Indefinite: some time ago, ages ago, a long time ago

c *referring to a period of time*
e.g. We lived there *for a number of years*. (of course, we no longer live there)
My father had a small business *then/at that time/during the war*.

8.4 The perfect tenses

8.4.1 Present perfect (simple)

⏱ *Time*	A moment or period of time *between* 'before now' and 'now'.	
🔱 *Attitude*	We are talking about an action which took place at an *unspecified* time before now. We are usually more interested in the *result* of the action rather than in the action itself.	

I can see the result:

e.g. Somebody *has drunk up* all my soup! empty dish, no soup

Why are you crying? *What has happened?* tears streaming down your face

The government *has increased* the price of cigarettes. **dearer cigarettes**

Who *has eaten* the apples? **no apples**

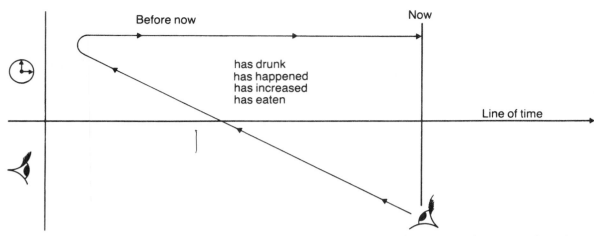

Note that we do not know, specify or care about exactly *when* the actions (*has drunk, has happened, has increased, has eaten*) took place, so we use the **present perfect**. If we are interested in the actions themselves (e.g., we want details about when, where, who and how), we use the **past simple**.

Focus on the result	*Focus on the action*
Someone *has broken my pen*	*When* did it happen?
	Who did it?
	Did you lend it to someone?

Similarly,

BILL '*Have you ever been* to Italy?'   (ever = at any time between 'before now and now')

JOE 'Yes, *I have been* there several times.'   (note that the times are not specified/definite)

BILL '*Were you* there in 1979?'   (our interest now focuses on a particular time)

JOE 'Yes *I was.*'   (past simple, because time is now specified)

BILL 'Which cities *did you visit?*'   (i.e. in 1979. 'Which cities have you visited?' would be another general question)

8.4.2 Present perfect
continuous

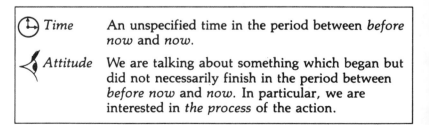

Time	An unspecified time in the period between *before now* and *now*.
Attitude	We are talking about something which began but did not necessarily finish in the period between *before now* and *now*. In particular, we are interested in *the process* of the action.

Have you been waiting long?

What on earth have you been doing?

e.g. He's *been sitting there for hours* just staring at the wall.
The rate of inflation *has been falling* slowly since the beginning of the year.
Have you been waiting long?
I've been working on this problem since nine o'clock this morning and I still haven't solved it.

In each case, the activity (*sitting, falling, working on*) is still going on. In the following examples, the activity itself has ended, but the *results* are clear and of great interest to us:

Who *has been drinking* my soup? (i.e. the dish is only half full now)
It's been raining. (the streets are still wet)
Have you been working in the garden? (you look tired and your boots are dirty)
What on earth *have you been doing*? (said by a mother to her child who has come in covered in mud)

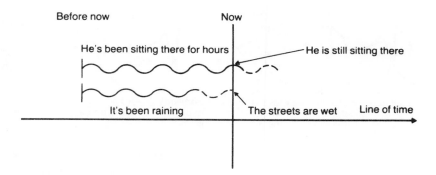

8.4.3 Past perfect simple

🕐 *Time*	*Earlier than* a time before now.
Attitude	We use this tense when we want to make it clear that action A took place in a time before and separate from the time when action B took place.

e.g. *I gave* my wife the present which *I had bought* her the day before.
(Action B)   (Action A)

When *I arrived* at the station, the train *had already left*.
(Action B)   (Action A)

While they *were out*, a pretty girl *had got into* their cottage.
(Action B)   (Action A)

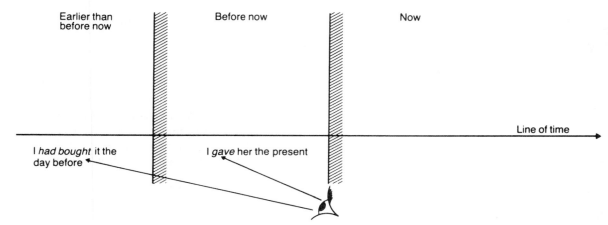

Or think of each past action as a man taking a step forward. When he wants to refer to an action which happened earlier, he looks back over his shoulder.

The actions in the story are *got up* → *looked out* → *phoned* → *told*. The actions in brackets ( ) took place *before* the actions of the story, so we refer back to them by 'looking over our shoulder' to an earlier time:
(← had stolen)   (← had already found)

Note the difference between
     The film *started* when I arrived.
     Action A *I arrived*; Action B *the film started*
and
     The film *had started* when I arrived.
     Action A *the film started*; Action B *I arrived*

8.4.4 Past perfect continuous

The commonest use* of this verb form is to provide the **past** form of the **present perfect continuous**:

HAS
          BEEN . . . ING ⟶   HAD BEEN . . . ING
HAVE

---

*For the use of **past perfect simple** and **continuous** in reported speech
(e.g. I *have worked* hard today   He said that he *had worked* . . .
      I *have been working* hard today   He said that he *had been working* . . .
      see ➔ Chapter 14B)

The three bears *had been* working hard (i.e. at a time before this story started) and *were* looking forward . . .

It *had been* raining heavily and the streets *were* still wet.

8.4.5 Adverbials used with perfect tenses

All the adverbials of time which are used with the perfect tenses are adverbials of *unspecified, indefinite time.* As soon as you specify a time (last year, in 1979, a few minutes ago, then,) your attention shifts to the past.

The following adverbials are commonly used:

Frequency adverbs (→ Section 12.11.2)
I have *often* wondered what would happen if women ran the world.
Their father had *occasionally* taken them to Blackpool when they were young.

The pair **ever*** and **never**, meaning *at an* or *at any unspecified time before now* and *at no time before now* respectively, are very common.
    Have you *ever* seen anything like it?
    This is the first time I have *ever* been in an aeroplane.
    I have *never* seen anything like it.
    I have *never* been in an aeroplane before.
    It was the first time anyone had *ever* kissed her.

***Ever** is now used (1) in questions; (2) in the pattern . . . THE FIRST TIME (THAT) . . . EVER; (3) in negative patterns, e.g. NOTHING/NOBODY HAS EVER . . . where NEGATIVE + EVER = NEVER

Recently, lately, in the last few
    He had *recently* bought a car, and was feeling very proud of himself.
    Have you seen any good films *lately*?
    There have been quite a few accidents in *the last few* weeks.
With the past perfect, *last* changes to *previous* (see also → 14.5.4 note 2).

Just
This is a very common word to express the idea that something happened in the period of time immediately before the time being referred to.
    'Where is Paul?' He has *just* left.' (= He left a moment ago.)
    They had just *finished* dinner when their friends arrived.
It is often used in the sense *simply, nothing more important etc. than that*:
e.g. I can't do any more for him. I've *just given up*.
    She *just picked up* her coat and walked out of the room.

Already *and* **yet**
(For the difference between **still** and **yet**, see → Section 12.12.1).

Already is used to indicate that something has happened at an unspecified time before now:

> Don't bother. I've *already done* it.
> He *has already fallen off* his bicycle three times this month. (i.e., and he is likely to do it again!)
> By the time their friends arrived, they *had already finished* dinner.

It can also be used in questions:

> *Have you already had* dinner?
> *Has she finished already?* (or *Has she already finished?*)

Yet is used in questions and negative statements to mean (not) in period of time between before now and now, (not) up to and/or including the present:

> *Have you ironed* my shirt *yet?*
> *Haven't you finished yet?*
> I *haven't had* a chance to see the boss *yet.*

With the past perfect, it is better to use the expressions *up to that point/moment* or *until then*:

> I *had not had* a chance to see him *up to that moment.*

Since *a point or* **for** *a period of time*

We can specify the length of the period of time between *before now* and *now* using

$$\text{PRESENT PERFECT} \ + \ \begin{cases} \text{SINCE} & \text{a point of time} \\ \text{FOR} & \text{a period of time} \end{cases}$$

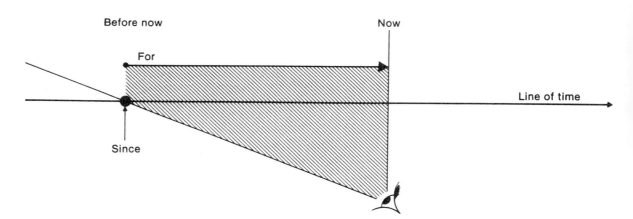

e.g. I have known her *for years*.
      I have lived here *since 1975*.

Note the question and answer with *How long?*

> 'How long have you been here?'   'I've **been here for three months**.'

The question *How long are you here for?* can easily be misunderstood. It means

> *What is the total length of your stay here?* That is
> *How long are you here for?* = *How long have you been here?* + *How much longer will you stay here.*

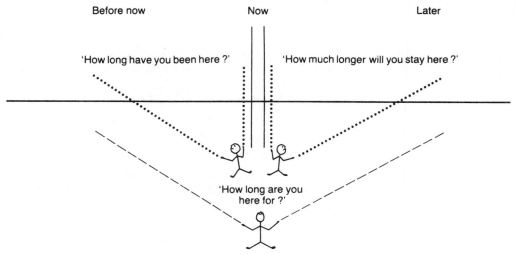

Before now   Now   Later

'How long have you been here ?'   'How much longer will you stay here ?'

'How long are you here for ?'

Other expressions with **since** *and* **for**

since last July/last year/I was a boy/1980/the 14th century/the time we . . ./the last time we . . .

for X years/several months/a long time/ages

These expressions with **since** and **for** can also be used with the past perfect:

> They *had been working* hard *since* first light, and **were feeling** tired . . .
>
> Judging by the mess, the squatters *had been* there *for* several days

Note: **since** is used only with the perfect tenses; **for** can be used with any tense.

8.4.6 Present perfect or past simple?

That

SCHOOL

There are cases, especially involving recent times like *today* or *this morning*, when either verb form is possible, but with a very slight difference of meaning.

A What did you do at school today?

A mother might ask her child this question after the child has come home from school. The past tense (*did you do*) shows mother's attitude that 'school' is finished, and is separate from 'home' and 'dinner' and the other things which belong to the rest of the day.

(Tell me) what you *did* at school today

(Show me) what you *have done* at school today.

B What have you done at school today?

Mother's attitude is that 'school' is not quite over, **even though** the child is now at home. She wants to hear the child's **answer** and to look at his/her work.

Compare this with the 'sphere of interest' using **this** and **that** (← 2.5.2).

Similarly, imagine that the child had lost something and went out to look for it. When he comes home, someone might ask him
A *'Did you find* your notebook?'
B *'Have you found* your notebook?'

A seems to show more interest in the action (finding) and might lead to such questions as 'Where was it?'   'Where did you look for it?'

B seems to show more interest in the result of the looking, and is perhaps another way of asking 'Where is your notebook?' or of saying 'I hope you have got your notebook back, and I'm glad if you have.'

Listen for these uses of the two verb forms, but remember that the difference in meaning *in these cases* is very small.

8.4.7   Present perfect simple or continuous?

There are also cases where you can use either the **simple** or the **continuous** form with a very slight change of meaning:

A The rate of inflation *has been falling* rapidly since the beginning of the year.
B The rate of inflation *has fallen* rapidly since the beginning of the year.

Sentence A seems to be interested in the *process* and suggests that the activity (falling) is still going on and will continue to do so.

Sentence B seems to be interested in *the result* of the process at a given moment (i.e. it is concerned with judging the situation at that moment), but it does not suggest that the rate of inflation will continue to fall so rapidly in the rest of the year.

Perhaps a member of the ruling party would say sentence A (to be optimistic), and a member of another party would **agree** to sentence B (less confident that the government's anti-inflation policies are working!).

Future and **future perfect** are dealt with in Chapter 9.
Conditionals are dealt with in Chapter 10 together with modals.

B The imperative

8.5 The basic imperative

The **basic imperative** consists of the base form of the verb:
Go! and the negative *Don't go!*
It is used in a variety of situations.

Public notices
Public notices telling you what to do or what not to do may take
the form NO+ . . ., as in NO SMOKING or NO ADMITTANCE. More
often they are in the form of an imperative:

CROSS NOW   DO NOT TALK TO THE DRIVER   DO NOT TOUCH
KEEP TO THE LEFT   KEEP OFF THE GRASS   DO NOT FEED THE
ANIMALS

Politer notices may use the **passive** (→C) as in PASSENGERS ARE
REQUESTED TO (or NOT TO) . . .

Graffiti are full of 'notices' which in most cases we cannot obey:
Save trees – eat more beavers   Preserve wildlife – pickle a
squirrel

Spoken imperatives
The basic imperative can be rude or friendly depending entirely
on the situation and the tone of voice used. It can express:

a *Orders*   Get out!   Don't do that!   Answer the phone!
Many expressions of rudeness use the imperative. Amongst the
less vulgar are
Get lost!   Shut up!   Don't be stupid!

b *Requests*   Pass the salt.   Don't make a noise.   Help me with
this suitcase.
It is common – and advisable if you are not English – to use the
word *please* with imperative requests:
Please help me.   Please don't make a noise.

c *Invitations*   Come in!   Help yourself!   Sit down!   Make
yourself at home!   Drop in any time!   Don't go yet!

d *Advice*   Don't work too hard!   Mind you don't fall!   Watch
out!   Be careful!   Don't hurt yourself!
You can also offer encouragement, make suggestions etc.:
Keep going!   Pass the ball!   Don't give up now!   Give her a
kiss!

Instructions
Instructions for operating a machine, carrying out a scientific
experiment, making a cake (i.e. following a recipe), etc., are
written in the imperative form.

Examples:

Recipe for Date and Nut Loaf
Put dates and soda in a basin and *pour* hot water over them. *Leave* to cool. *Mix* dry ingredients together and *add* them to the mixture. *Bake* in a greased tin until firm. *Keep* at least a day before eating.

Scientific experiment
Place a drop of bromine in a gas-jar with a greased rim, and *place* a similar jar on top. *Hold* a piece of paper behind the jars and *observe* the results.

8.6   'Coloured' imperatives

Imperatives can be modified or softened in a number of ways, e.g. by adding *Please*, or by changing from the basic form to expressions like *Would you mind . . .?   Could you . . .?   I wish you would/n't . . .*

There is an imperative form with **do**, e.g. *Do come in! Do lend me that book when you've finished with it!* The word *do* is always stressed, (see also ← 7.5.1, Note 4). This form expresses a number of feelings.

Do come in! suggests that I am really pleased to see you. It might be that you are a little nervous or shy, and I want to make you relax and feel welcome.

Do lend me that book when you have finished it! tells you that I was really serious when I told you earlier that I wanted to borrow it.

Do be more careful in future! is trying to persuade you politely but forcefully to change your ways.

There is an imperative with **you**, which emphasizes that *you* in contrast to someone else must do something. The word *you* is stressed.
BILL   'Make the tea, Joe!'
JOE   "*You* make the tea! I'm busy.'

'*You* spend all day looking after three screaming children, and see how *you* like it!'

WARNING!
Imperatives with *do* and with *you* are used between people who know each other: you would not say to your boss, for example: '*You* do it!' or '*Do* sign these letters!' (unless you had a special relationship with him/her). When talking to people you do not know very well, or people you need to be polite to, soften the imperative with a form such as 'Would you . . .?' or 'Could you . . .?' or 'Would you mind . . . ing?'

8.7 Imperatives with *let*

We use **let** in the pattern LET + ME/US/HIM/HER/IT/THEM + VERB to express a kind of imperative referring to ourselves or other people.

Let's go! means *I suggest that we go*, and the idea of suggestion can be strengthened by adding ...*shall we?*: *Let's go, shall we?*

When used with pronouns other than *us* (usually shortened to '*s*), **let** is more truly an imperative:

Let me have a look!
Don't let me leave without my briefcase!
Let them go as soon as they have finished.
Don't let her see what you are doing.

C The passive

8.8 Form

(See also ← Section 7.3).
The general relationship* between the ordinary (**active**) form and the **passive** form is:

$$X \underset{\text{is done}}{\overset{\text{does}}{\times}} \begin{matrix} Y \\ \text{by } X \end{matrix}$$

The active and passive forms are:

moves	is moved
moved	was moved
has moved	has been moved
had moved	had been moved
will move	will be moved
will have moved	will have been moved
(etc.)	(etc.)
is moving	is being moved
was moving	was being moved
to move	to be moved
to have moved	to have been moved
moving	being moved

Note also the way the indirect object (← Section 5.4.2) in an active sentence becomes the subject in the passive sentence:

X   gave   Y a present.
Y   was given   a present. (by X)

*This does not mean that every active form has a passive form or vice versa: only transitive verbs can have a passive form (→ Chapter 13A).

8.9 Meaning of the passive

The **subject** of any sentence (→ Chapter 13A) is the subject because it is what we are mainly interested in. It is what we are talking about. In these sentences we are talking about a house, a lot of books, a meeting and some shoppers.

This house was built in 1850.
A lot of books have been written about this subject.

The meeting will be held in the Town Hall.
Several shoppers were injured in the explosion.

It is true that someone built the house, someone (a lot of different people) wrote the books, someone (or some group) will hold the meeting, something injured the shoppers. Our main interest is not in who or what performed the actions (build, write, hold, injure). If we were talking about these people or things, we would use the active:

My great-grandfather built this house in 1850.
Several important people have written books about this subject.
The Council will hold their meeting in the Town Hall.
The bomb injured several shoppers.

8.10   Uses of the passive

8.10.1   Putting the important things first

To describe the use of the passive, we could begin this paragraph by saying:

We use the passive to . . .
The passive is used to . . .

Because *the passive* in this case is more important than *we*, it would be logical to make the passive the subject of our sentence.* In other words, the most important item becomes the subject of our sentence.
The passive is used to make the object of the verb into the subject of the sentence.

A number of attempts have been made to raise the Titanic.
The meeting has been postponed until further notice.

The passive is especially useful when the originator (the doer) of the action is not just less important, but is actually very difficult or impossible to identify (specify):

Materials from the Earth's interior *are continually being brought* to the surface.
The ocean floors *are recycled* into the Earth's interior, and *are replaced* in less than 200 million years.

It is difficult to say *what* brings the materials to the surface or *what* recycles and replaces them.

There is an important difference of emphasis between the active and the passive when talking about the same situation. For example, we have a dog, called Brandy. He is, in theory, Sarah's dog, and she usually feeds him. I ask two questions regularly:

A 'Has Sarah fed Brandy?'
B 'Has Brandy been fed (yet)?'

In question A, I want to know if my daughter has done what she ought to do. In question B, I simply want to know if the dog is all right (no matter who might have fed him).

*It is really a matter of style. In this grammar, for example, we often use the direct, friendly 'author-to-reader' style by using the active voice (*We advise you to . . .*) rather than the more formal, impersonal passive (*You are advised to . . .*). Check for yourself!

8.10.2 Formal, especially scientific, writing

The passive is used in serious and formal writing (and speaking), e.g. in descriptions in encyclopaedias, reports of meetings, and in reporting experiments. For example, the experiment with bromine (see the instructions on page 168) would be written up afterwards like this:

> A drop of bromine *was placed* in a gas-jar with a greased rim, and a similar jar *was placed* on top of it. A piece of paper *was held* behind the jars, and the results *were observed*.

The only other way to record the experiment is to use the doer as the subject: *We placed*... or *I placed*... or *The students placed*....

If you have a choice, we advise you to use the direct style (i.e. use the active form) rather than to try to make what you say or write sound important by using the passive.

8.10.3 Notices

These are common examples of notices which use the passive:
ENGLISH SPOKEN – KEYS CUT WHILE YOU WAIT – NO CHANGE GIVEN – CHILDREN UNDER 14 NOT ADMITTED – SECOND-HAND BOOKS BOUGHT AND SOLD – CHEQUES NOT ACCEPTED WITHOUT A BANKER'S CARD.

Notice that the parts of **to be** are left out (*is* spoken, *will be* given, etc.) Newspaper headlines are similar.
e.g. West Country *cut off* by snowdrifts! (for *has been cut off*)

General notes

1 Expressions of the type THEY/PEOPLE+SAY/BELIEVE, etc., are frequently used in the passive in formal speaking and writing: *It is said that*... *It is believed that*...
A much more useful pattern is:

THE PERSON OR THING	IS	said believed etc.	TO (BE)... TO HAVE (BEEN)...

I	am considered	to be an expert on cricket.
'The Slits'	are reported	to be making a tour of the USA.
The report	is expected	to be published in May.
Pablo Casals	is acknowledged	to have been the world's finest cellist.
A camel	is said to be able	to go without water for 28 days.
John Lennon	is known	to have been interested in oriental religions.
Da Vinci	is said	to have designed the first submarine.

Other verbs which are used in this pattern are: assume, feel, find, presume, repute, understand. Note also:
> He is expected/required to (do something)...

The passive *supposed to be* is ambiguous (has two meanings): *You are supposed to be in class* could mean *Everyone supposes (thinks, assumes) that you are in class*, but it probably expresses an obligation – *You ought to be in class*.

2 The passive infinitives can cause problems. Note how they are used in these sentences:

A   It was the first/last/second/ best/etc. one | to be made.
    | to have been made.

There is no important difference between the two infinitives.

B i) I would like to be invited.   =Please invite me!
   ii) I would like to have been invited.   =I was not invited, and I am sorry about that.

Sentence B(ii) can also be expressed *I would have liked to be invited*. Some people would even say *I would have liked to have been invited* but we do not advise you to imitate such a complicated form.

C   IS/ARE TO:
   i) These cakes *are not to be eaten* until they are ready.
   ii) I *was to have been* invited, but they lost my address!
   iii) NOT TO BE OPENED BEFORE CHRISTMAS DAY
   iv) TO BE TAKEN THREE TIMES A DAY BEFORE MEALS (on a medicine bottle)
   v) The books *to be catalogued* are on your desk. (=which must be catalogued)

Notice the difference of construction between:

{ There are a lot of letters *to be written*.
{ I have a lot of letters *to write*.

{ There is a lot *to be done*.
{ We have a lot *to do*.

The construction THERE IS/ARE . . . TO BE DONE can also be used with the active infinitive,
e.g. *There are* a lot of letters *to write*.
    There is a lot *to do*.
with no important change of meaning.

In some cases, the difference is more marked:

{ There is nothing *to do*. =I have nothing to do, I'm bored.
{ There is nothing *to be done* (about it). =I can do nothing about it, I do not have any power or authority to act.

{ Here are some books *to read*. =for you to read (for your pleasure)
{ Here are some books *to be read*. =which you must read (as a task)

3 The useful constructions GET/HAVE SOMETHING DONE and X
NEEDS...ING are passive in meaning:

> **I must get/have my teeth examined.** } =My teeth must be
> My teeth need examining.   }   examined.

(See also → Section 13.6.2, Cat. d.)

8.11   *By* and *with*

The pattern is   X /WAS DONE $\begin{matrix} \text{/BY} \\ \text{/WITH} \end{matrix}$ /Y

8.11.1   By

Consider these sentences.

A

X	did	Y.		
Fleming	discovered	penicillin	in 1928.	a fact about Fleming

B

Y	was done			
Penicillin	was discovered	–	in 1928.	a fact about penicillin

If we wish to include Fleming's name in our talk on penicillin, we
use **by**:

C

Y	was done	by X.	
Penicillin	was discovered	by Fleming	in 1928.

In grammatical terms, *Fleming* is the subject of sentence A and
the agent in sentence B.

Other examples
Many towns in Central Italy were destroyed *by the earthquake.*
The building was occupied *by security forces* after a short gun
battle.
The helicopter, which arrived ten minutes late, was piloted *by
the Prince of Wales himself.*

8.11.2   With

The word **with** means using (a/the), i.e. it goes with the tool,
instrument or means you use to do something:

> Use a sharp knife to cut the meat (with). = The meat should be
> cut *with* (=using) a sharp knife.

Note the difference between these two sentences:
He was killed by a (falling) brick. = A (falling) brick killed him.
(it was an accident)
He was killed with a brick.   = The man who killed him
used a brick. (it was no
accident!)

Note

It is sometimes difficult to decide whether certain past participles are part of a passive, or whether they are being used as adjectives:

I was amazed by his suggestion.	=His suggestion amazed me. (**passive**)
I was amazed at his suggestion.	=When he suggested X, I was amazed (or happy or sad or any other suitable adjective).

Other words like *amazed* are:

    amused disappointed embarrassed excited fascinated frightened pleased satisfied shocked surprised worried

If you are not sure which preposition to use (satisfied with? worried about? shocked at?), use **by**, which will always fit. The difference in meaning is slight.

9 Contents

9 The future

The Cat, the Tortoise and the Law of Gravity

A cat and a tortoise were having an argument.

'I'm very fast and you're very slow,' said the cat.

'All right,' said the tortoise, 'we'll have a competition.'

'I'll win,' said the cat at once.

'We shall see,' replied the tortoise, quietly smiling to himself. 'I bet you that I can travel 100 metres in the same time as you.'

The cat agreed, sure that he could travel much faster than any tortoise. They shook hands, and the tortoise led the cat to the top of a tower which was exactly 100 metres high. You see, the tortoise had learned about the law of gravity at school. One day, his teacher had said '*Force = mass × acceleration*.'

'What does that mean?' the tortoise had asked. (He was not usually very curious about things, but gravity sounded like something a tortoise could make use of.)

'It means', said the teacher, 'that two bodies of different mass will fall at the same speed, and will reach the ground at the same moment.'

The cat looked down anxiously at the ground far below them.

'What are we going to do?' he asked in a small voice.

'We're going to jump when I count three,' replied the tortoise. '1-2-3, go!'

They jumped and, thanks to the law of gravity, fell together and hit the ground at the same moment exactly. The cat landed beautifully on his feet, but the tortoise landed on his back, breaking his shell and most of his bones. He was in hospital for a long time afterwards.

Moral: Gravity is strictly for cats.

9.1 Introduction

We can be certain about the past (e.g. *X happened, X was happening*), about the results of past actions (e.g. *X happened*), about the present (*X is happening*) and about general truths (e.g. *X happens*). We cannot be certain about the future (the time after or later than now), because we are talking about things that have not yet happened. For this reason, we express the future in different ways: *Attitude* (← Section 8.1) is much more important than *time*. The form we choose depends on such things as:
- how sure we are that something will happen
- whether we want something to happen
- whether we are talking about ourselves (I, we) or others (he, she, they).

All the following sentences are about future events, but our *attitude* is different in each case:

The film starts in five minutes' time.
I'm starting a new job on Monday.
What are we going to do?
You're going to fall!
We'll have a competition.
We shall see.
Will it make any difference?
The plane will be landing shortly at Heathrow Airport.
Will you be coming to the party tonight?
He is to leave at once.
The concert is about to begin.
It will have finished by the time you get there.

We can also use some **modal verbs** (→ Chapter 10) to talk about the probability of future events (e.g. *may, might, should, could*).

A Future with *will/shall* (-'ll)

9.2 Simple future

The 'classical' or 'simple' form of the future is usually given as:

I
we } shall (move)   you will (move)   he, she, it
they } will (move)

The meaning of this form is:

🕐 *Time:*   a moment or period later than now
Attitude: we are making a simple statement of fact about something which will definitely happen or not happen. Our attitude is Ø: it is the time of the event which matters.

---

e.g. Two bodies of different mass . . . *will reach* the ground at the same moment.
We shall see who is faster.
There will be time for questions after the lecture.
If it rains, *we shall go* by car.*

*The pattern IF/WHEN ETC + PRESENT (*rains*) . . . FUTURE (*shall go*) is dealt with in Section 9.15.

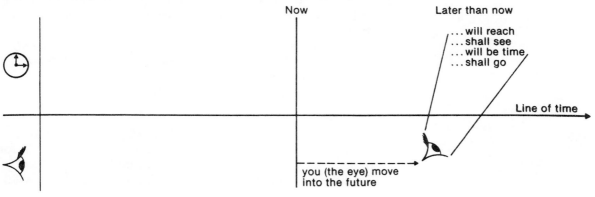

This simple pattern is complicated by several things:

a *Will* and *shall* have other meanings.
b We express *attitude* as well in certain cases e.g., with different persons, or when asking questions.
c *Will* is also used with *I* and *we*.

For this reason, it is better to consider *will/shall* with each person separately.

9.3 First person: *I/we*

9.3.1 Form

Here are all the possible forms. For meaning, see Sections 9.3–9.7.

a with shall

	+	−	+?	−?
Full Form	I / we *shall* (move)	I / we *shall not* (move)	*Shall* I / we (move)?	Shall I / we not (move?)
Short Form	*I'll* / *we'll*	*I'll* / *we'll* I / we not *shan't*		*Shan't* I / we ...?

b with will

	+	−	+?	−?
Full Form	I / we *will* (move)	I / we *will not* (move)	*Will* I / we (move)?	Will I / we not (move?)
Short Form	*I'll* / *we'll*	*I'll* / *we'll* I / we not *won't*		*Won't* I / we ...?

Notes
1 You are most likely to meet and to use the forms in italics.
2 The full forms are used in formal writing. The short forms are used in speaking and in informal writing such as personal letters.
3 Distinguish the pronunciation of *won't*, [wount], from *want*, [wɒnt], so that your listener can clearly hear the difference between *I won't go* and *I want to go*.
4 *Shan't* is pronounced [ʃɑːnt], i.e. with a *long a*.

9.3.2 Meaning

The differences in meaning between I/we **shall** and I/we **will** are no longer clear, partly because we now use the short form -**'ll** for both, and partly because usage is different in different parts of the English-speaking world (e.g. many Americans only use **will**.)

The most useful distinctions are:

a *I'll do it* = willingness

I will/we will (in the spoken form *I'll/we'll*) is used very much in English to mean *I am ready to I am happy to I am willing to*:

e.g. 'Who will do the washing-up?' *'I will.'*

'I need some bread.' 'All right, *I'll go* and get some for you.'

'Mr Smith is very busy at the moment.' 'That's all right. *I'll wait.'*

'All right,' said the tortoise, *'we'll have* a competition.'

(i.e. I am willing if you are willing. Compare 'Let's have . . . ' in Section 8.7.)

b *I won't do it* = unwillingness, refusal

I won't/we won't is a common spoken form to say that you refuse to do something:

e.g. Who will do the washing-up?' 'Well, *I won't!*'

'I won't leave until I have seen Mr Smith!'

You could use *shan't* in these cases, and your listener would know from your intonation or your tone of voice whether you were simply stating a fact or expressing a feeling.

Note: There is a clear difference between **will/won't** and **want to/don't want to**:

A 'I want to go and get the bread.' B 'I'll go and get the bread.'

A simply informs your listener about what you would like to do; B offers to do it. The reply to A is likely to be 'All right, go then.' or 'No, you can't'; the reply to B is likely to be 'Thank you' or 'That's all right, I already have some.'

A 'I don't want to leave.' B 'I won't leave.'

Similarly, A states a fact; B expresses a strong feeling (refusal).

c *Shall I . . .* = offering

Shall I?/shall we? is a very common way of asking someone if you can do something for them, i.e., help them; or if they want you to do something:

e.g. That parcel looks very heavy. *Shall I carry* it for you? (=Let me . . .)

Shall I lock up, or will you do it? (=Would you like me to . . . ?)

Shall we do all the exercises on page 23? (=Do you want us to . . . ?)

Shall I/shall we? can also be used of course in simple questions about the future,

e.g. What time *shall we* meet tonight?

Will I/will we?, if they are used at all in British English, are used in asking simple questions about the future (perhaps to take away the suggestion of offering contained in *shall I?*). The forms **will I/will we?** are often used with *be able to, have to* and *need to*:

e.g. *Will I be able to* take my dog with me?
Will we have to take an examination at the end of the course?
Will I need to change trains?*

*Negative statements and questions are also more common with **won't** than **shan't**:
e.g. We won't be able to come tomorrow.
   I won't need to change any more money.
   Won't we have to apply for a visa first?

d *Shan't I/shan't we?* and *won't I?/won't we?*

These forms are not often heard, and the difference in meaning between them is slight. They are most useful as echo questions.

e.g. 'You won't be able to get in.' 'Won't we?' (or 'Shan't we?'); and with *be able to, need to* and *have to* to ask 'coloured' questions (← Section 7.6.2):

e.g. Won't (or shan't) I be able to take my dog with me?

9.4   Second person: *you*

9.4.1   Form

	+	−	+?	−?
Full form	*you will* (move)	*you will not* (move)	*Will you* (move)?	*Will you not* (move)?
Short form	*you'll*	*you'll not* or *you won't*	-	*Won't you?*

9.4.2   Meaning

You will can be used for a simple statement of fact about the future with Ø attitude expressed:

You will find everything you need in the cupboard (You'll find . . .)

You will not find another one like it anywhere. (You won't find . . .)

When I am talking about myself, I express such things as my intentions, my wishes and my willingness. When I am talking about **you**, I am more likely to express the following things:

a *telling or ordering you to do or not to do something*
You will go immediately to headquarters. You will go alone, and you will tell no-one about this.
(Compare the imperative: *Go immediately . . . go alone . . . tell no-one . . .* See Chapter 8B)

b *making predictions about your future*
(i.e. telling you what I think will or will not happen to you)
Don't worry! You won't feel a thing!
You'll make yourself ill if you eat all those cakes!

c *making predictions about your present situation*
(this is a kind of intelligent guesswork)
> You will be tired after your long journey, I expect.
> Have you already eaten? In that case, you won't need anything else to eat, will you?

d *testing your willingness to do something*
> Will you just hold this for me a second?
> Will you look after the children while I go to the shops?
These are *polite requests* which can be made even politer by using **would you . . .?** instead of **will you . . .?** Note the way I test your willingness, i.e., I ask for your help and co-operation, in the sentence:
> *I'll* do the washing up *if you'll* put the children to bed.

The construction I'LL /DO X/ IF YOU'LL /DO Y/, is different in structure and meaning from the simple conditional construction I'LL /DO X/ IF YOU /DO Y/, as in the sentence *I'll scream if you touch me.* (See →Section 10.9).

e *giving an invitation*
  i) Will you stay for dinner?
  ii) Won't you stay for dinner? – this is a more pressing invitation than the first. It really says **Please** *stay . . .* or **Do** *stay . . .* (→Section 8.6)
  iii) Will you come to the cinema this evening?
  In the sense of *Would you like to . . .?*, this is an invitation, but the sentence is in fact rather *ambiguous* (i.e., it has two meanings). It could be an *invitation* (We want you to come with us . . .) or it could be a *request for information* (What are your plans for this evening?).
  For this reason, it is very common to use the continuous form **will be . . . ing** when we are simply asking someone for information. For example:
  Will you come to the dance? is ambiguous, but is most likely to be an *invitation* – *Would you like to . . .?*
  Will you be coming to the dance? is simply a question to get the *information* – *What do you intend to do . . .?*

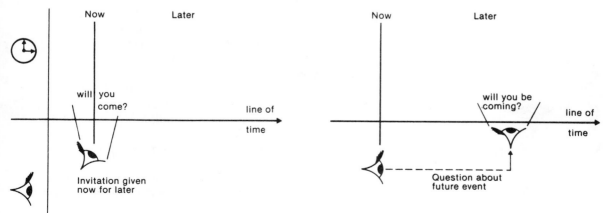

9.5 Third person: *he, she, it* and *they*

9.5.1 Form

(For convenience we use **s/he** to stand for he and she)

Full form	s/he it *will* (move) they	s/he it *will not* (move) they	*Will* s/he it (move)? they	Will s/he it not (move)? they
Short form	*s/he'll* *it will* *they'll*	s/he'll not s/he it *won't* they'll not they		*Won't* s/he it ? they

9.5.2 Meaning

The third person can be used in a simple statement of fact with Ø attitude expressed:

e.g. There will be time for questions after the meeting.
They will not be able to come tomorrow. (They won't . . .)
How long will she stay in Athens?

When we are talking about other people or things, we may want to express other ideas:

a *Making predictions about their future* (i.e., saying what we think will or will not happen to them)
e.g. He's very intelligent. He will do well in life. (He'll do . . .)
They will be ill if they eat any more. (They'll be . . .)
She will not walk very far in those high-heeled shoes! (She won't . . .)

b *Making predictions about the present*
(this is a kind of intelligent guesswork)
e.g. 'Where is Joe?' 'Oh, he'll be in his office, I should think.'
'He won't be back from lunch yet.' (=I don't think he will be back yet)
(See also→Section 9.6.d)

c *Saying that someone is unwilling (refuses) to do something*
e.g. He won't eat his breakfast (=He refuses to . . .)
They won't tell me anything about their experience.
Things can also be very unco-operative:
e.g. My car won't start!

My car won't start

A similar use occurs in the positive form, but it is not so common as the **won't** =*refuses to* expression:
She's a very annoying person: *she will keep* interrupting when I'm trying to work.
More common and more useful is the similar expression with **would**:
e.g. John has told everyone about our meeting. *He would*!
(=That is typical of him, it's the sort of thing he always does.)

d *Taking a particular interest in other people's activities*
Won't they come with us? could be a simple request for
information, or it could express the idea *I should like them to
come with us.*
Notice the difference between the simple and the continuous
form in such sentences as:
A   Will John bring his girl friend?
B   Will John be bringing his girl friend?
A shows a particular interest, and could suggest I hope he will (or
he won't!) bring her. B is simply a request for information.

Note on **shall** *with second and third persons*
Although constructions with **shall** and **shall not (shan't)** to
express promises, permission and prohibition do occur, we advise
you to use the much commoner ways of expressing the same
things given in the right hand column of this table:

Using *you shall/shan't, he shall/shan't* etc.	Modern equivalents
You shall have a dog for your birthday.	I promise you you will have . . . I'll buy you a dog . . .
You shan't go to the party.	You can't go the party I forbid you to go . . . I won't let you go . . .
He shall have everything he needs.	I will give him . . . Let him have Give him . . . I want him to have . . . I promise that he will have . . .
They shall not (shan't) come here again.	They mustn't . . . I forbid them to . . . I don't want them to . . .

Shall is still used in legal documents to describe what must and
must not happen in accordance with the law:
e.g. The purchaser shall return or pay for the goods within
thirty days. After this time, the purchaser shall be liable to a
surcharge if he has failed to return or pay for the goods.
The vendor shall have the right to . . .

9.6   Future continuous: *will
be (mov)ing*

a As we have seen (← Section 9.5.2 d), this form is used in
questions to show that we are simply asking for information
and not making an invitation, as in the pair:
Will you bring Jill with you? (could mean *Please bring
Jill . . .*)
Will you be bringing Jill with you? (means *I simply want to
know if . . .*)

b The action may be going on now, and we think of it
continuing into the future:
e.g. I wonder if *it will still be raining* this afternoon.

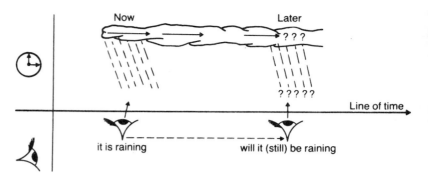

c It is also used when we project ourselves into a future time and
see something happening:
e.g. In a few minutes *we shall be landing* at Barcelona airport.
I'll be seeing Julia this evening. I'll give her your love.

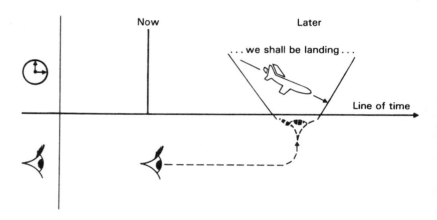

d Like the simple form (← Section 9.5.2 b), it is used in
predicting (guessing) what someone is doing now or will be
doing at a later time:
e.g. Where is Joe?

Simple	(fact)	He is in his office.
	(guess)	He'll be in his office, I suppose.
Continuous	(fact)	He is having his lunch.
	(guess)	He'll be having his lunch, I expect.
	(fact)	You're feeling hungry.
	(guess)	You'll be feeling hungry after all that exercise, I expect.

Referring to a coming event:
     The funeral is next Friday. Will Mr Wasp be there?
Using the present continuous to express an **arrangement**
(← 8.2.1c):
(fact) Oh yes, he is coming to the funeral, of course.
(guess) Oh, he'll be coming to the funeral, surely.

9.7 Future perfect: *will have (moved)/been moving*

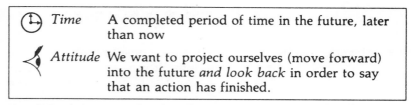

Time A completed period of time in the future, later than now

Attitude We want to project ourselves (move forward) into the future *and look back* in order to say that an action has finished.

This form is often associated with the expression *by a point of time in the future*:

e.g. By the time you receive this letter, *I will have left* England.*

I'll call for you at seven. *Will you have finished* dinner by then?

*Notice that the tense in the *by the time*...clause is the present simple (...*receive*...) and not the future perfect (...*will have received*...). The use of the present tense in such clauses is dealt with in Section 9.15.

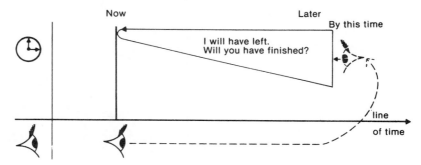

Note

It is possible to have a continuous form (**will have been doing**) to talk about something which is happening at the moment of speaking. If it will still be happening at a particular moment in the future, you can say, for example *how long it will have been going on* by then.

e.g. It is 6 o'clock. I am reading the novel *War and Peace*. At (or by) 8 o'clock, I will have been reading for more than two hours.

On the other hand, it is not often that you need to say such things: note only that the English tense system allows you to say them when the need arises.

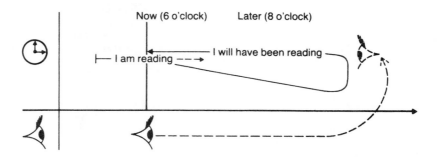

B   Future with *going to**

9.8   Meaning and use

The form **going to (do)** is common in speaking and in informal writing. It is a way of referring to a future event which expresses a strong *attitude*; the *time* of the event is less important.

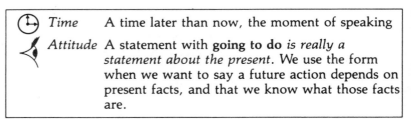

🕐	*Time*	A time later than now, the moment of speaking
👁	*Attitude*	A statement with **going to do** *is really a statement about the present*. We use the form when we want to say a future action depends on present facts, and that we know what those facts are.

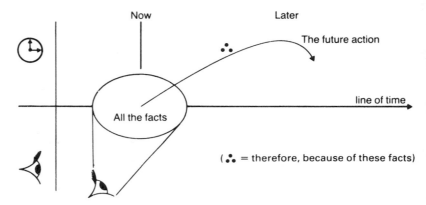

Examples
> *I'm going to sell* my car and get a new one.
> What *are you going to do* when you leave school?
> John has changed his mind. *He isn't going to marry* Stephanie after all.

In the nature of the essential meaning of **going to**, we are often concerned with our own and other people's *plans, decisions, intentions*:

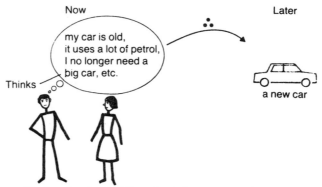

says - 'Darling, I've decided. I'm going to buy a new car.'

*Note also the useful past form **was/were going to**:

It's going to rain soon.
You're going to fall off if you're not careful!
She's going to make an excellent nurse.

In these examples, we are using present facts to make predictions (to say now what we feel sure is going to happen): black clouds = rain; a boy riding a bicycle without holding the handlebars = accident; good progress during training = an excellent nurse.

As with all predictions the result (rain, accident, excellent nurse) is probable but not absolutely certain: *we can only be certain about the present facts* (cloud, bicycle, progress).

As we have seen (← Section 8.2.1 b), we can also use the present tenses for future statements;
e.g. Tomorrow *is* Thursday.
The new term *starts* next week. (present simple)
I'm leaving for America soon.
I'm starting a new job on Monday. (present continuous)

Like the *going to* construction, these statements are based on *present facts*.

9.9 *Going to* or present simple?

When the present facts are something published or fixed like a calendar or a timetable, use the present simple. *Tomorrow is going to be Thursday.* makes no sense. The sentence *The train leaves in 5 minutes' time* is a simple statement of fact; *The train is going to leave in five minutes' time* is likely to be said if you want to say *'Hurry up! You're going to miss your train!'*

9.10 *Going to* or present continuous?

When you are talking about plans, decisions or intentions on the basis of the present facts, the difference in meaning between the two forms is often very slight.
A I'm going to start a new job on Monday.
B I'm starting a new job on Monday.

A perhaps emphasizes more my decision (I'm telling my listener something about *myself*); B perhaps emphasizes more the change which will now take place according to plan (I want my listener to know about *my new job*). We advise you to use **going to** in these cases if you are not sure.

But, when you are using the present facts to make predictions or to give warnings/advice, you must use **going to**. (*It's going to rain soon* or *You're going to fall off*) could not be said with the present continuous (*it is raining, you are falling off*).

Note:
We try to avoid **going to** with the verbs *go* and *come* simply because *going to go* and *going to come* do not sound very elegant:
e.g. I'm going to Manchester next week.
Are you coming to the concert this evening?

9.11   *Going to* or future with *will/shall*?

There are many cases where you can use either **going to** or **will/shall**, *depending on your attitude*:

A It will rain soon – statement of fact, (Ø attitude), time is important

B It's going to rain soon – prediction (definite attitude), time is not important.

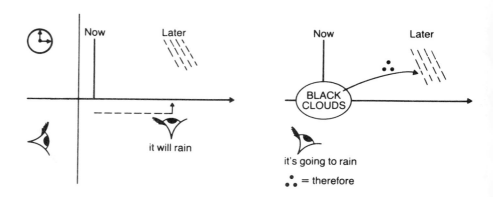

it will rain

it's going to rain

∴ = therefore

A What will you do when you leave school? = tell me the facts about your future.

B What are you going to do when you leave school? = tell me what you have decided about your present intentions.

There are many cases where only one form would be suitable in the situation you are referring to:

A I'm going to buy a new car. – this is what the man would say *to his wife*.

B I'll buy a new car.   – this is what he would say *to himself*.

A ⎰ SALESMAN: '*I'm going to* visit Stevenage tomorrow.'
   ⎱ COLLEAGUE: 'Why? Surely there's more business in Luton.'
B ⎰ SALESMAN: 'OK. *I'll visit* Luton instead.'

The salesman announces his decision (*I'm going to Stevenage*). When he replies to his colleague, he expresses an agreement (*I'll go* = this will happen, and I am willing to do what you suggest.) He could not reply *I'm going to Luton instead* because he is no longer talking about his intention but about what will happen as a result of his colleague's suggestion.

A I'm going to have a baby. This is the usual expression.
B I'll have a baby. This suggests the woman has made a conscious decision to have a baby; she is not just making a simple statement of fact.

C Other ways of expressing the future: *is to*, *is about to*

9.12 Is to

🕐	*Time*	A time later than now
◣	*Attitude*	We are talking about an *obligation* (→ Section 10.4) to do something. It is similar in meaning to *must* or *have to* (→ Section 10.4), but it emphasizes the fact that certain plans or arrangements have been made for us.

Examples
These are your instructions. You *are to go* at once to London to meet our agent. You *are to tell* no-one about these plans.
Nobody *is to leave* the room until the examination is over.

It is not a common spoken form and we advise you to use **must/have to** (*You must go to London...*, *You mustn't tell anyone...*) or simple imperatives (*Don't leave the room...*).

9.13 Is about to

🕐	*Time*	A time shortly or immediately after now, the moment of speaking
◣	*Attitude*	We want to emphasize that something will happen very soon

Examples
The boat *is about to* leave. Would all visitors please leave the boat right away. Thank you. (public announcement on cross-Channel ferry.)
Ladies and gentlemen, you *are about to* see the most amazing spectacle that the world has ever witnessed! (the showman wants to increase the audience's curiosity.)

9.14 Expressing probability

One of the things we most often do when we are talking about the future is to say how probable (likely) it is that something will or will not happen. To express probability, we need a wide range of patterns to cover every possibility. Think of a horse race:
　　The favourite *will almost certainly win*.
　　The others *may/might/could win*.
　　The outsider *won't win* (unless a miracle happens!).
Ways of expressing probability are dealt with in → Chapter 10.

9.15   The tense used in time clauses

(See also→Section 14.3, note, for a full description.)

In a sentence like *I shall meet you when I next visit London*, both events (*meet* and *visit*) are future events, but the verb in the *when*-clause is in the present tense, e.g. *when I next visit London*. The verb in the main clause (→13A p. 255, footnote), e.g. *I shall meet you...*, may be in the future tense, or it may be an imperative: e.g. *Put them away* before you leave.
The verb in the time clause

e.g.   ... *when I next visit London*,
is always in the present or the perfect tense:
e.g.   Put them away *before you leave*. (not ... *you will leave*)
         You can go *as soon as you have finished*. (not ... *you will have finished*)

The conjunctions (→Chapter 14A) which introduce time clauses include:
    as soon as, as long as, after, before, when, until, while
The same *sequence of tenses* applies to conditional clauses (→10.9) beginning with *if, unless* and *in case*.

10 Contents

10 Modals (including conditional sentences)

can/could (able to) may/might will/would shall/should ought to must (have to) need.

The Hippopotamus and the Mathematical Problem
(*Part 1*)

There was once a hippopotamus who was a mathematical genius. He could do any calculation in his head, and he always got the right answer. One day, he was lying in his mudhole, humming to himself and working out π to 300 decimal places using the Fibonacci series, when he felt a terrible pain behind the eyes.

'It must be all this calculating that is giving me such a headache,' he thought, 'I really ought to go and have my eyes tested.'

To tell you the truth, the hippo was very, very short-sighted, but he refused to admit it, even to himself. The optician gave him a strong pair of glasses, and said (because he did not want to hurt the hippo's feelings): 'You don't need to wear them all the time, but I think you should wear your glasses whenever you feel like doing any sums in your head.'

The hippo caught sight of himself in the mirror, and thought how intelligent he looked in glasses, so he kept them on, stopping to admire his reflection in every pool as he walked back to his mudhole. On the way, he caught sight of a notice nailed to a tree. Thanks to his wonderful new glasses, he could also make out what was written on it. It said, quite simply: $2+2=5$.

10.1 Introduction

We have seen (Chapter 9) how *will* and *shall* are used to express our *attitude* to future events. The other modals are used to express many other attitudes to events. The main areas are:

Probability: when we want to say how certain we are that something will happen (e.g. *may, might, should*)

Obligation: when we want to say that something will definitely happen because the situation demands it (e.g. *must, have to*); or to say that it is desirable or 'correct' for something to happen (e.g. *should, ought to*)

Necessity: when we say that something is or is not necessary or useful (e.g. *need(n't), need to*)

Ability/success: to say that something is possible (e.g. *can, able to*), or that an action was successful (*was able* to)

Permission: to ask whether (or to say that) something is allowed (e.g. *may, might, can, could*)

Condition: when we want to say that one action depends on another (i.e. **if** sentences)

WARNING!:

In this chapter we describe the *main, common* uses of modals. Modals are subject to changes of *fashion* (e.g., *That's got to be Simon* for *That must be Simon*) and *social* or *regional* preferences (e.g., *Have we to?* or *Have we got to?* or *Do we have to?*). Imitate the forms given in this Grammar, but be prepared to hear or read variations!

10.2 Form

For the combination of modals with other verb forms, see the table on page 128. **Can** and **must** use *able to* and *have to* respectively (a) as alternative forms in the present and past, with some change of meaning; (b) to supply parts for other tenses.

Can	*Present*	*Past*	*Conditional*
I, we you, they he, she, it	**can**	**could**	**could**
I	**am able to**	**was able to**	**would be able to**
he, she, it	**is able to**		
we, you, they	**are able to**	**were able to**	

Other forms with **able to**:

to be able to	has		must be able to
being able to	had	} been able to	should be able to
will be able to	would have		etc.

For differences in meaning between **can/could** and **is/was/would be able to**, see → Section 10.7.

Must	*Present*	*Past*
I, we you, they he, she, it	**must**	**(must)***
I, we you, they	**have to**	**had to**
he, she, it	**has to**	

Other forms with **have to**:

to have to
having to
will have to
would have to
has
had } had to
would have
may have to
might have to
etc.

For differences in meaning between **must** and **have to**, see → Section 10.4.

Note
To talk about a future event which depends on present facts, we usually use **can** (instead of *will be able to*) and **must** (instead of *will have to*):

e.g. The boss says that we *can* have next Tuesday off. (rather than *will be able to*)

I *must* stay in tonight and finish my essay. (rather than *will have to*)

10.3   Probability

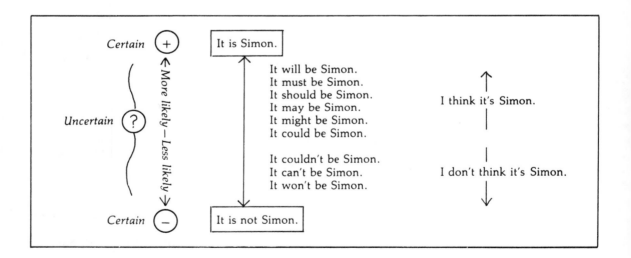

Notes

1 The table puts the expressions of probability (*Perhaps it's Simon*) in order of 'strength', i.e. *it will be* expresses greater certainty than *it might be*. The order is not fixed, but will vary according to such factors as dialect, personal preference, tone of voice, situation.

2 *It will be Simon/it won't be Simon* are almost the same as *It is/it is not Simon*, i.e. nearly certain. It suggests that you have information which allows you to feel sure about the situation (e.g. Simon said he would call at this time, or you know that Simon usually goes to Karate class on Wednesdays).

3 *It must be Simon/It can't be Simon* are very similar in meaning to *will/won't* as described in Note 2. It suggests that the *logic* of the situation leads to the conclusion that it is/is not Simon (e.g., nobody else would call at this hour of the night, or Simon is away on holiday at the moment).

Other examples
It must be all this calculating that is giving me such a headache.
You must be tired after your journey. Come and sit down.
'I've decided to give up my job.' '*You can't be* serious! It's such a good job.'

To talk about past events, there are the forms *must have been* and *can't/couldn't have been*:
e.g. 'Look at Richard's black eye. *He must have been* in a fight!'
'She brought up six children on her own.' '*It can't have been* easy for her.'

4 *It should be Simon* is less certain. It suggests a conditional: *If everything has gone according to plan* . . . but, for example, Simon might have forgotten his promise to come tonight. The meaning is illustrated well in the past form *should have been*:

Situation: Simon has promised to come round at eight o'clock.
Time 7.55: You say 'Simon should be here soon.'
Time 9.00: You say 'I wonder what has happened to Simon. He should have been here ages ago.'

5 May/might/could. May expresses a stronger probability than **might**, but the strength of **could** varies with the situation and the speaker. All three express a 'middle point' between *certain+* and *certain−*, i.e. they are *open*:

    I might come round this evening. = equally I might not, I
                                          haven't decided yet.
    I may come round this evening. = I am thinking of coming
                                          round; you can expect to
                                          see me.
    I could come round this evening. (in the sense of expressing probability) = it is possible, but not very likely; I have a number of things to do.

Notice that *it couldn't be Simon* expresses a strong doubt, similar to *it can't be Simon*. Compare this with:

| It's probably Simon | But it | may not | be him because he |
| I expect it is Simon | | might not | usually phones first. |

That is, we use **may not/might not** to contradict an expectation: the sentence *But it may/might not be . . . because . . .* is like an afterthought.

6 To express probability about something which is past, we use the modals with **have** (moved). The most usual expressions are:

> must
> may
> might $\left.\right\}$ have (moved)
> could   (been moving)
> couldn't
> can't

Examples: Imagine that the person who knocked on the door has gone away now. We continue to wonder who it *might have been*:

'It must have been Simon – nobody else would call at this time of night.'
'No, it can't have been Simon – he is away on holiday at the moment.'
'It might have been Ivor.'
'No, it couldn't have been Ivor. He is in America at the moment, I believe.'
'It could have been Joe, couldn't it?'
'Yes, it may well have been Joe. I wonder what he wanted?'
'I must have been thinking of something else at the time: that's why I forgot to phone her.'
'Joe might have been drinking lemonade, but it looked like beer to me.'

7 The forms **will/won't have** (moved) and **would/wouldn't have** (moved) can also be used to express probability about a past event, but they are less common than the ones in note 6.
e.g. 'It won't have been Simon, because he said he would never come here again.' (instead of *'can't/couldn't have been . . .'*)

10.4 Obligation: *must/have to*

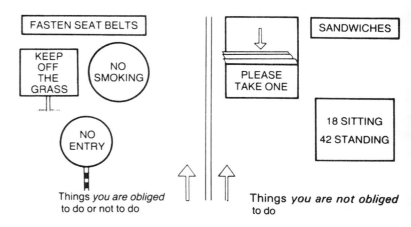

FASTEN SEAT BELTS

KEEP OFF THE GRASS

NO SMOKING

NO ENTRY

Things *you are obliged* to do or not to do

SANDWICHES

PLEASE TAKE ONE

18 SITTING
42 STANDING

Things *you are not obliged* to do

You have
no choice

You have
a choice

The two kinds of notices illustrate the difference between
obligation and *no obligation.*

Obligation	*No obligation*
You must fasten your seat belt.	You do not have to take a
You must keep off the grass.	leaflet.
You must not smoke.	You do not have to buy
You must not enter.	sandwiches.
	You do not have to sit.*

*It is true that you must *either* sit *or* stand; but you don't have to sit if you prefer to stand

The forms which we recommend you to use are given in bold
type:

		Obliged to/not to	*Not obliged to*
Present		**must** **must not**	
		have to	**do not have to**
		have got to	haven't got to
		are to are not to	————
Past		**had to**	**did not have to**

Notes

1 In the left hand column (*obliged to/obliged not to*), notice that
the only forms which express the idea that you are obliged *not
to do* something are
must not and **are not to**
The forms *have not to* and *had not to* to express the idea of
mustn't are no longer used, except in dialect.

2 The forms with **got to**, *have got to* and *haven't got to* are very
common spoken forms:
e.g. Sorry, I can't stop. I*'ve got to* go out again.
At least we *haven't got to* go to work tomorrow, thank
goodness.
'I don't want to do this.' 'But the teacher says *we've got
to.*'

3 **Have to** – *question form.* There are two question forms:

I you we they	have to	Have	I you we they	to . . . ?	Do	I you we they	have to . . . ?
he she it	has to	Has	he she it	to . . . ?	Does	he she it	have to . . . ?

There is no difference in meaning between these forms. The
form with **do/does/did** is commoner and we advise you to use
it.

4 Must *or* **have to***?*

In the present tense you have a choice between **must** and **have to**. The difference in meaning is not big but it can be useful:

> Choose **must** if you want to suggest that the obligation comes from you.
>
> Choose **have to** to suggest that the obligation comes from somewhere else.

It is her own idea.

That is an order from me: I want you to leave

I don't mind if you stay, but I have just been given a telephone message for you.

i.e. The doctor has told her to lose weight.

What is it that causes them to be so noisy?

I wish they would be quieter.

Note: The difference between **must** and **have to** is much clearer with the first person (I, we) and the second person (you) than it is with the third person (he, she, they).

The same difference of meaning occurs between **must not** and **have not to/are not to**:

e.g.   You must not speak to him again.=I don't want you to.
You are not to speak to him again.=That is an order from a higher authority.

5 The forms **will have to** and **will not (won't) have to**.
A You must take an umbrella if it rains.
B You will have to take an umbrella if it rains.
In sentence A **must** is used by the speaker to show that he is

personally involved – he is giving advice to his friend, perhaps.

In sentence B, the speaker is stating a fact. *Rain = need for umbrella*.

C At least he won't have to take any more examinations.

In sentence C, **won't have to** is a simple future form of **don't have to**.

10.5 Obligation: *should* and *ought to*

We use **must/have to** to describe an obligation where you have *no choice*: **must/have to** let you know what is allowed ,and what is forbidden, prohibited, against the law, against the rules.

We use **should** and **ought to** to describe a sort of obligation where you have a *choice*:

ADVERTISEMENT
The best cigarette in the world!
Government Health Warning
Cigarette smoking is dangerous.

ROAD SAFETY COUNCIL
If you drink, don't drive.
If you drive, don't drink.

HEALTH COUNCIL
Take up a sport today — you'll feel better for it!

COUNCIL OF CHURCHES
HELP OLD PEOPLE!

In these illustrations, we are free to do or not to do such things as smoke cigarettes, drink, drive, take up a sport, help old people – we do not have to do any of those things. But the government is giving us good advice when it advises us not to smoke: in everyday language it is saying 'You *should not* smoke cigarettes'. In the same way we are told:

'You *should not* drink if you intend to drive.'
'You *should* take up a sport.'
'You *should* help old people.'

In other words, **should** (and **ought to**, see below) expresses *moral obligation*: it says what would be good for us or for others.

Other examples

'I think you *should* wear your glasses whenever you feel like doing any sums.'
You *should* always wash your hands before you eat.
'I'm tired out!' 'It's your fault. You *should* get to bed earlier.'
'I haven't heard from Evelyn for ages. Do you think I *should* give her a ring?'

The past is formed with SHOULD + HAVE (moved):

'I feel ill.' 'It serves you right – you *shouldn't have* eaten so much.'
This library book is overdue – I *should have* returned it last week.

She wants to lose weight –
it is her own idea

She knows that it is bad to be
overweight – doctors say so

Use of **ought to**

In theory, you could use **ought to** (negative **ought not to**) in all the examples in Section 10.5 with little or no change of meaning. Only the question form, *Ought I to* might sound a little unusual. In practice, **ought to** can suggest something more than *should*. It comes originally from the verb *owe*, and still carries the idea *that we owe something to other people*, i.e. that there is *a moral obligation*:

a when you have *not* done your duty:
I really ought to go and have my eyes tested. (I owe it to myself)
John really *ought to* visit his parents more often. (He rarely sees them)
I *ought to* get more exercise. (I am very unfit – my doctor told me)

b when the obligation comes from outside (compare *have to*) rather than inside (compare *must*):
They ought to ban smoking in public places. (i.e. 'they' – the people in power – should ban smoking.)

Note: the difference between **should** and **ought to** is very subtle (=difficult to see and to choose). If you are not sure, we advise you to use **should**.

10.6   Necessity

10.6.1   Need

The verb **need** (which is not technically speaking a modal), is regular in all tenses, and takes the construction TO NEED TO+VERB. In the present tense only, there is an alternative form which behaves like *must* or *can*, i.e., it does not change, and it forms the negative **need not** and the question form **need I**?* This special form takes the construction NEED+VERB, i.e. without *to*:

I, you, we, they	need to (go)	Do not need to (go)	do	I you we they	need to (go)?
he, she, it	needs to (go)	does not need to (go)	does	he she it	

I, you, we, they he, she, it	(not used in +)	need not (go)	need	I you we they (go)? he she it	

*The verb **dare** is like **need** in that it is a regular verb having the pattern DARE TO (DO SOMETHING). However, in the present tense there is an alternative form which is used in the negative, e.g. *I daren't do it* instead of the regular *I don't dare to do it*. Note also the fixed expression *I daresay* . . . when you are saying that you believe that something could be true:
e.g. I daresay you are feeling tired after your long journey.

Use **need to** for all other tenses:
  I did not need to
  You will need to
  Would they have needed to . . . ? etc.
For the meaning and use of the past form **need not have (gone)**,
see → Section 10.6.3).

Meaning
Need to says that something is necessary or useful. It is similar to
must or **have to**.

Do not need to
or   } says that something is not necessary. It is
need not   }   similar to **do not have to.***

*The forms **needn't/don't need to/don't have to** are, of course quite different in
meaning from **mustn't** (See ← Section 10.4).

Examples
1 You need to work much harder.
2 She needs to improve her handwriting.
3 Do I need to get a visa?
4 You don't need to wear them all the time but . . .
5 He can go now: he does not need to wait.

10.6.2 *Need to go or need go?*

In theory you could use the irregular **need (go)** form in sentences
1–5. In practice, **need (go)** is not used in positive sentences (i.e.,
1 and 2) except in a few expressions such as *All you need do
is* . . . (Even there you could also say *All you need to do is* . . .).
It can be used in questions
e.g. 3 Need I get a visa?
and in negative sentences
e.g. 4 You need not wear them all the time but . . .
      5 He can go now: he need not wait.

The difference between *you don't need to* and *you needn't* is
very slight* and we advise you to use the regular form (*don't
need to, Do I need to* . . . ?). You will most often hear the
irregular form in the following situations:
a as a response to the question *Must I* . . . ? or *Do I have to* . . . ?
  'Must I do it right away?'
  'No, *you needn't do* it now; leave it until tomorrow if you
  like.'
b to say that it is useless to try to do something:
  You needn't imagine that I don't know what you have been
  doing.
c to say that something is not expected or not possible:
  You needn't give me a lift on your scooter – I'm much too
  heavy anyway.

***Needn't** expresses a freedom from obligation/necessity which originates from the
speaker (It is not necessary because *I* say it is not necessary). **Don't need to** expresses
a freedom which originates from somewhere else (I am reporting to you the fact that
it is not necessary). Compare **mustn't** and **don't have to**.

10.6.3 The past forms *did not need to (go)* and *need not have (gone)*

Need not have (gone) has a particular meaning: it says that you did something which was not necessary (i.e. you wasted your time!). **Did not need to (go)** says that it was not necessary to do something, but it does not say whether you in fact did it or not.
e.g. I *needn't have bought* a French-English dictionary.
I *didn't need to buy* a French-English dictionary.

	Was it necessary?	Did she buy one?
Needn't have bought	No	Yes
Didn't need to buy	No	?

10.7   Ability/success: *can/could* and *able to*

We use **can** to say what someone knows how to do (Sentence 1 *He can speak several languages*), or what is possible (Sentences 2 and 3 *Can you lift it?*, *I cannot eat any more.*). In these sentences you could also use **able to** without any important change of meaning, but we advise you to use the commoner form **can/cannot**.

Could is the past form of **can** to express the same idea:
e.g. He *could* do any calculation in his head.
Thanks to his new glasses, he *could* make out what was written on the notice.

He can speak several languages!

There is a useful difference of meaning between **could** and **was/were able to**: the latter form says not only that you could do something (it was possible for you), but also that you did it.

Can you lift it?

		Was it possible to go in?	Did he go in?
A	The door was open and he could go into the room.	Yes	?
B	The door was open and he was able to go into the room.	Yes	Yes

In Sentence A (could), we only know *for sure* that it was possible; Sentence B (was able to) tells us *also* that he *managed to* get in, he *succeeded in* getting in. (Compare the difference between *didn't need to* and *needn't have*, ← Section 10.6.3).
For the use of **could** in the conditional (=*would be able to*), see → Section 10.9. For all other forms you will need **able to**.

I *can't*   eat any more.
cannot

Examples
I *will not be able to* see you tonight, I have to go to night school.
Wouldn't you like *to be able to* speak as many languages as he can?
They *have not been able to* find out yet what caused the epidemic.

Note: there is a slightly more formal expression with the same meaning as *not able to*, that is, **unable to**.

e.g. I shall be unable to see you tonight ...

They have been unable to find out ...

10.8 Permission:
may/might **and** *can/could*

When we are talking about *permission* (asking for it, or saying whether we or other people have it), grammarians used to say that we should use **may**; in practice most people nowadays use **can** or **could**:

*or I'm not allowed to have a bicycle
(See Note 1.➔)

Notes

1 ***May not** is rarely used in this sense. Either use **cannot** or expressions like *I am **not allowed to***... or *They **will not let** me* ..

The forms **may not** and **might not** are of course used to express the probability that something will not happen (◄ Section 10.3);

e.g. I have bought a ticket for the Segovia concert, but *I may not go* if I am feeling too tired.

'Correct' form	Form most often used
Asking permission for yourself/ves DIRECT May $_{\text{we}}^{\text{I}}$ (go)? –	Can $_{\text{we}}^{\text{I}}$ (go)? Could $_{\text{we}}^{\text{I}}$ (go)? (more polite)
INDIRECT (formal) I wonder if I might (go)?	I wonder if I could (go)?
Asking whether someone has permission May you (go)?	Can you (go)?
Asking permission for others May $_{\text{they}}^{\text{he she}}$ (go)?	Can $_{\text{they}}^{\text{he she}}$ (go)?
Permission given $_{\text{he she they}}^{\text{I we you}}$ may (go).	$_{\text{he she they}}^{\text{I you we}}$ can (go).
Permission not given $_{\text{he she they}}^{\text{I we you}}$ may not (go).	$_{\text{he she they}}^{\text{I we you}}$ cannot (go).

2 **Can you . . . ?** and, more politely, **could you . . . ?** are common ways of making a request (asking someone to do something for you):

e.g. *Can you tell* me the exact time, please?
Excuse me, *could you tell* me where the Don Giovanni restaurant is?
Could Sarah come with us? (compare illustration 2 *Can Sarah come . . . ?*)

10.9   Condition: *if* sentences

We use conditional sentences to show how one action or event depends on another. We express our *attitude* by using the modals: in this way we can show whether we are *certain* (*it will happen*), or whether we are only *expressing the probability* (*it may happen, it could happen* etc.).
There are three basic types of conditional sentence:

I   If I **do** X, Y **will be** the result.

II   If I **did** X, Y **would be** the result.

III If I **had done** X, Y **would have been** the result.

10.9.1   Type I

Type I: IF I DO X, Y WILL BE THE RESULT

Examples
If it rains, we shall stay at home. (*or* '...we will...' ◄ Section 9.3)
If I have enough time, I may go and see Jennie this evening.
If you study really hard, you should pass your examinations.
If they don't come soon, they might miss the first act.
If you don't make an effort, you cannot expect to be successful.

Form

Certain	If I do X,	Y	would	be the result.
↑ more | *probable* | less ↓	If I do X,	Y	must can may should ought to could might	be the result.

You can make either side negative to say *If I (do not) do X, Y will (not) be the result.*

If X is ⟶ Y will be
If X is not ⟶ Y will not be

All the modals except **must** can also be made negative.

Meaning
The Type I conditional sentence makes statements about the real world, i.e. statements of fact as in the illustration *If you drop it, it will break.*

Notes

1 There is a type of if-sentence which has the pattern IF X IS, Y IS. It is the sort of sentence which states a general truth, such as a scientific fact.
Compare A If you *drop* eggs, they *break.*
                        = a general truth about eggs

                 B If you *drop* that egg, it *will break.*
                        = what will happen to this particular egg

In such cases, if really means whenever or every time that...

2 Another common variation has the pattern IF X IS, DO Y, where the second part of the sentence is an imperative (Chapter 8B). In other words, the speaker is telling you what to do if a certain thing happens:

e.g. If Penny *calls, tell* her I've gone to the hairdresser's.

If *I'm not* here by seven, *don't bother* to wait for me.

3 The pattern IF YOU WILL DO A, I WILL DO B is explained in ← Section 9.4.2.

10.9.2   Type II

Type II: IF I DID X, Y WOULD BE THE RESULT

Examples

If I were you, I would take up a sport to keep fit.
If you saved your money, you could afford a holiday abroad.
If we could (i.e., *were able to*: past) get to London before midday, we might be able to do some shopping in Oxford Street.

Form

Certain	If I did X, Y	would	be the result.
more ↑ *probable* ↓ less	If I did X, Y	should ought to could might	be the result.

You can make either side negative to say *If I did (not do) X, Y would (not) be the result*. Similarly with **should (not)**, **ought (not) to**, **could (not)** and **might (not)**.

There is an alternative verb form in the **if** part of the sentence, **were to do**:

IF I WERE TO DO X, Y WOULD (ETC) BE THE RESULT.* The difference in meaning between *If I bought a new car* and *If I were to buy a new car* is slight: **were to** is used with action verbs (buy, go, leave) rather than with state verbs (be, have).

We advise you to use the simple past form *If I bought* etc.

Meaning

The Type II conditional sentence makes statements about things which are not real, or are not known to be true.

A statement about what might be real, but is not at the present:

e.g. *If I lived in America*, I would earn a lot of money. (One day I might go)

If *I lived* in America, I would earn a lot of money...

---

*The special forms *If I were* and *If he/she/it were* are still common, although *If I was* and *If he/she/it was* are now considered to be correct. We recommend you to use the form *I/he/she/it were* in these conditional sentences, and also in the expression *I wish I were*. You must use it in the expression *as it were*.

A statement about what is not real, and never could be real:

e.g. *If I were you, I* would take up a sport and keep fit. (I could never be you)

A statement about what might be real, but we are not sure:

e.g. *If you added sulphuric acid* to the mixture, it ought to turn blue.

(i.e. you said that you added it, but so far there is no sign of blueness. Are you sure you added it?)

10.9.3 Type III

Type III: IF I HAD DONE X, Y WOULD HAVE BEEN THE RESULT

Examples
If I hadn't come to Liverpool, we would never have met, darling.
If you hadn't reacted so quickly, we might well have had an accident.
If she had not been so hardworking, she might not have been manager today.
If they had only asked us, they could have used the caravan with pleasure.

Form

Certain	If I had done X, Y	would have	been the result.
Probable	If I had done X, Y	could have might have	been the result.

This type of conditional sentence is based on the facts: *I did not do X, so Y did not happen.* Similarly, from the facts *I did X, so Y happened* you can get the conditional sentence in the negative *If I had not done X, Y would not have happened.*
There is another possible Y result:

I $\begin{array}{c}\text{did}\\\text{did not do}\end{array}$ X, so Y $\begin{array}{c}\text{is}\\\text{is not}\end{array}$ (now) the result.

e.g. If she had married, she would not be manager today.
　　If you had listened to me, you would be a rich man by now.

Meaning
Type III conditionals are about what *might have been* or what *might be* now if only something had or had not happened the way it did. They are about such things as:
regret: If only I had studied harder when I was young...
missed opportunities: If you had arrived earlier you would have seen the procession.
criticism of others: If you hadn't spent so much money, we would be well off now.

It is perhaps most useful when we try to explain why things are

If *you had arrived* earlier, *you would have seen* the procession.

as they are (in the way that scientists form *hypotheses* to explain what they do not yet fully understand):

e.g. Perhaps if I had added a little less flour, the cake would not have been so hard.

If you hadn't taken plenty of Vitamin C, you might have caught my cold.

10.9.4   General notes on conditionals

1 The conditional clause can also come second. The change is one of emphasis. The information which interests you most comes first. For example:

He wouldn't be rich if he had not worked hard.

suggests that your first thought about him is '*He* is a rich man';

If he had not worked hard, he wouldn't be rich.

suggests that your first thought about him is that he worked hard.

Notice that the comma (,) is left out when the conditional clause comes second.

2 The following expressions are also used to introduce conditional clauses, especially of the first type:

unless (=*if . . . not*, but see ➧ 14.3), in case, provided *or* providing, on condition that.

Supposing is mostly used with second and third conditionals:

e.g. *Supposing* everyone behaved like that, (what would happen then)?

Supposing you had married a foreigner and had gone to live in her country, do you think you would have been happy?

Here's a five-pound note. Don't spend it *unless* you have to.

I'll give you some money *in case* you need to buy some food.

You can go out tonight, *provided* you have finished your homework.

He said that we could have the evening off *on condition that* we were back by midnight.

3 You may read a form of conditional clause which is formed by inverting subject and verb.

e.g. *Had I* known you were coming . . . *for* If I had known you were coming . . .

Were I to be invited, I would . . . *for* If I were invited . . .

Should you see him, tell him his results have arrived. *for* If you see him . . .

It is only used with **had, were** and **should** and it is a rather old-fashioned written form. We advise you not to use it.

11 Contents

11 Phrasal verbs

The Hippopotamus and the Maths Problem
(*Part 2*)

The hippo looked up at the notice board once again. $2+2=5$?
He scratched his head (not an easy thing for a hippopotamus to
do) and began to mutter to himself:

'That can't be right. There must be some mistake.'

He sat down (which can also be a problem for a hippo) and
tried to work out for himself how $2+2$ could be made to equal
5. He thought too about the person who had written the
expression up on the board. *Somebody* had written it, and they
must have had a good reason for doing so. There must be
something in it. Finally, he got very angry, tore the notice down,
and took it back home with him. He put it on the ground and
continued to stare at it for days on end, no longer bothering to
eat or drink, or even to roll in his beautiful mudhole. $2+2=5$.
He took off his new glasses to wipe off some mud. Immediately
the board and the crazy expression became a blur – he could no
longer see the figures 2 or 5; nor could he make out the plus or
the equal signs. Suddenly, he began to feel much better, as if a
big weight had been lifted off his shoulders. He smiled (which is
a VERY difficult thing for a hippo to do), rolled over in the mud,
and began to sing. He no longer had a problem, and the world
looked beautiful again. After that, he gave up maths and took up
singing instead.

Moral: If you want to see things really clearly, take your glasses
off.

Note: in this chapter, we use the expression **phrasal verb** to
describe both the pattern VERB+ADVERB and the pattern
VERB+PREPOSITION (sometimes called *prepositional verbs*). We
refer to the adverb and/or preposition which follows the verb as
the **particle(s)**.

11.1 Introduction

11.1.1 What are phrasal verbs?

Phrasal verbs consist of a simple verb +1 or 2 particles, where
the meaning of the *compound* is often different from the meaning
of the individual parts (compare a chemical compound where,
for example, sodium chloride, $NaCl$, – common salt – is quite
different from the basic elements, sodium (Na) and chlorine (Cl)).

The three basic compounds are:

VERB + PREPOSITION   look after

VERB + ADVERB   give up

VERB + ADVERB + PREPOSITION   get down to

Most of the verbs used in phrasal verbs are common ones which, apart from **to be**, generally refer to *physical activities.*

be, break, bring, call, carry, catch, *come,* cut, *do,* draw, drop, *fall, get, give, go,* hold, *keep,* lay, let, look, *make,* pass, pull, *put,* run, see, *send,* set, *stand, take, turn,* work

The commonest verbs are in italics.

11.1.2 Understanding phrasal verbs

If the parts of a phrasal verb have their *literal* meaning or only a *slightly transferred* meaning, you can easily understand what the compound means:

ADVERB   He sat down.   (literal meaning)
ADVERB   He tore the notice down.   (slightly transferred)
ADVERB   *Take* these plates *away.*   (literal meaning)
ADVERB   *Take* three *away* from ten. (i.e.,
            $10 - 3 =$) (slightly transferred)
PREPOSITION *Look into* the microscope.   (literal meaning)
PREPOSITION *Look into* the matter. (=investigate)   (slightly transferred)

On the other hand, many phrasal verbs have a meaning which you cannot easily deduce from the meaning of the parts:

e.g. After that, he *gave up* maths.   (=stop, abandon – difficult to connect with *give* and *up*)
Please *look after* this for me.   (=take care of, protect – not easy to connect with *look* and *after*)
You should *get down to* work right away.   (=begin, apply yourself to – not easy to connect with *get, down* and *to*)
. . . nor could he make out the plus or equal signs.
    (=separate, identify, see clearly – not easy to connect with *make* and *out*)

Sometimes a phrasal verb can have several meanings:

e.g. If you want to see things clearly, *take* your glasses
    off.   (=remove)
When does the plane *take off*?   (=leave the ground)
He's a wonderful mimic: he can *take off* most
people.   (=impersonate)
Do you think this book will *take off*?   (=be a success)

The fourth sentence is a transferred or *metaphorical* use of *take off* (as applied to aeroplanes), and is typical of the way in which the meaning and use of phrasal verbs grow and change.

11.1.3   Are phrasal verbs important?

There are several reasons why you should pay attention to phrasal verbs.

a They are very common and widely used by English-speaking people, both in everyday speech and in writing (they are particularly common in the media – newspapers, magazines, etc.).

b There is often a single verb, usually of classical (Latin or Greek) origin, corresponding to a phrasal verb (e.g., give up=abandon, break in=interrupt, cut out=delete, leave out=omit, do without=economize on, but the single word can often sound odd or much too formal in everyday speech:

c Phrasal verbs are *dynamic*, that is, we are constantly inventing (making up) new ones and giving new meanings to old ones – slang and the conversation of young people are full of such things:
e.g. He's *into* meditation.=deeply interested in
It *turns me on*.=excites me;
He keeps *plugging away at* the same old arguments.=repeating and insisting.

d Phrasal verbs provide many common and useful nouns and adjectives in everyday use,
e.g. breakthrough, input, make-up, outburst, takeover, go-ahead, standby. See ← Section 1.10, Appendix II.
We advise you to learn to recognize phrasal verbs and words derived from them, and to try to use the commonest ones (See → Section 11.5, Appendix XIII).

11.2   Word order in phrasal verbs

11.2.1   VERB+PREPOSITION

If the particle is a preposition, the phrasal verb *will always have an object*, which follows the preposition in the usual way:

[VERB]+[PREPOSITION+OBJECT]

{ *Noun object*	look	after	the dog
{ *Pronoun object*	look	after	it
{ *Noun object*	see	to	the other people
{ *Pronoun object*	see	to	them

11.2.2 VERB + ADVERB + PREPOSITION

If the phrasal verb has two particles (adverb + preposition) the pattern is the same as in → Section 1.11.2.

[VERB + ADVERB] + [PREPOSITION + OBJECT]

{ *Noun object*	look	down	on	your enemies
{ *Pronoun object*	look	down	on	them
{ *Noun object*	catch	up		with	the girl on the other side
{ *Pronoun object*	catch	up		with	her

The commonest two-particle combinations are:
up to, up for, up with, down on, down to, in for, in on, in with, out for.

e.g. get up to, stand up for, put up with, look down on, talk down to, be in for, be in on, fall in with, look out for.

A list of common three-part phrasal verbs is given in → Section 11.6, Appendix XIV.

11.2.3 VERB + ADVERB

If the particle is an adverb, the word order depends on (a) whether there is an object; and (b), if there is an object, whether the object is a **personal pronoun** or a **noun**.

a *Without an object*:

VERB + ADVERB

go	away
set	off
stand	up
get	down

This pattern is very common with *verbs of movement.*

b *With a personal pronoun as object* (me, you, him, her, it, us, them)

VERB	+	PRONOUN OBJECT	+	ADVERB
put		them		away
bring		it		up
take		us		out
send		them all*		off

The pronoun must always come between the verb and the adverb. Contrast this with the pattern in Section 11.2.1, where the object always comes after the preposition.

*also each of them, every one of us etc.

c *With a noun as object.*

When the object is a **noun** or an **indefinite pronoun** (everything, everybody, etc. ← Section 5.10), there are two possible patterns. The first is exactly the same as for Section 11.2.3b, i.e., when the object is a personal pronoun:

VERB	+	NOUN OBJECT	+	ADVERB
put		your toys		away
bring		the matter		up
take		the children		out
send		all the letters		off
tore		the notice		down

There is a second pattern, in which the object follows the adverb particle:

put away	bring up	take out	send off
your toys	the matter	the children	all the letters.

Unfortunately there are no simple rules to say which pattern is 'correct' in any particular situation – the choice may depend on a slight change of meaning*, on the rhythm of the sentence, or sometimes on the personal preference of the speaker.

*In general, the phrasal verb is more likely to have the literal meaning of its parts when the verb and adverb are kept together: and a transferred or changed meaning when they are separated.

We advise you to use the first pattern VERB+OBJECT+ADVERB:

  i) *with short, simple nouns*   pay *the money* back
        put *your toys* away
 ii) *with indefinite pronouns*   hand *everything* over
        leave *nothing* out
iii) *with the names of people*   pick *John* up
 iv) *with idiomatic expressions* (that is, where the meaning is in the whole expression rather than in the individual words)
        Don't *give the game away.*
        His speech *brought the house down.*

You usually have to use the second pattern VERB+ADVERB+OBJECT in the following cases:

  i) when the object is a long one:
      e.g. He tried to *work out how 2+2 could be made to equal 5.*
      Pay back *the money you borrowed.*
      (He could not) make out *the plus or the equal signs.*

 ii) when the object is followed by a contrast or a second object:
      e.g. Pick up *John, but not Philip.*
      Bring round *your girlfriend, and anyone else who wants to come.*

11.3 Is the particle an adverb or a preposition?

11.3.1 Prepositions only

These common particles are only **prepositions**:
   after against at for from into like to with without
They always occur in the pattern VERB + PREPOSITION + OBJECT
e.g. look after someone, go against the rules, get at the meaning, (not) stand for your nonsense, come from Italy, go into the question, look like it, get down to work, put up with your complaints, go without food.

11.3.2 Adverbs only

These common particles are only **adverbs**:
   away back forward out
They usually (◄— 11.2.3) occur in the pattern
VERB ± OBJECT + ADVERB
e.g. run away, take it away, answer back, answer him back, bring forward, bring the date forward, go out, put the light out.

11.3.3 Either preposition or adverb

Most other particles may function either as **prepositions** or as **adverbs**. The commonest are:
   about across along around before behind by down
   in off on over round through under up

Compare these two sentences:

A Look the word up. ——→ Look it up.   *Up* is an **adverb**
B Look up the street. ——→ Look up it.   *Up* is a **preposition**

In A *to look up* (a word) means to find the meaning of the word in a dictionary.
In B *to look* is the verb; *up the street* tells us where to look.

From this we see the particle behaves differently:
As an **adverb** it is part of the verb, and gives it its special meaning:
LOOK UP + THE WORD.
A relates to a question like *What must I look up?*
As a **preposition** it relates* the verb to the following object:
LOOK + UP THE STREET**
B relates to a question like *Where must I look?*

There is also a difference in the *stress pattern*, which will help you to separate the two kinds of phrasal verb:

VERB + PREPOSITION : stress on the verb
VERB + ADVERB   : stress on the particle (or equally on **verb** and particle)

---

*Prepositions express relations of time, space and other things. See ◄— Sections 6.3 – 6.5).
**UP THE STREET* is an adverbial phrase having the pattern PREPOSITION + NOUN (see Chapter 12).

Examples
PREPOSITION: This is exactly what I am *look*ing for.
ADVERB: I smoke, but I am trying to give *up*.
PREPOSITION: *Jump* over it.
ADVERB   Think it *over*.

11.4   Meaning of phrasal verbs

11.4.1   Literal meaning

Phrasal verbs made up of VERB OF MOVEMENT + ADVERB usually have the *literal* meaning of the two parts, and are therefore easy to understand:

stand up

lie down

Similarly,
go out,
come round

You can guess the meaning of many other verbs where the movement is not so literally expressed:

> get up, get off, go up or down (in price), send away, take away, bring back

11.4.2   Transferred meanings

The same verbs as in 11.4.1 may have other, *transferred* or *metaphorical* (i.e. not literal) meanings, and these can only be learned by experience and with the help of a good dictionary:
e.g. *Stand up* for what you believe
in.   = defend
Don't let the fire *go out*.   = die
She fainted, but she is *coming
round* again.   = regaining consciousness

As a guide only, we describe below the transferred meanings of some of the commonest particles*:

> away   back   down   forward   off   on   out   over
> round   through   up

*Particles not included here tend to keep their literal meaning.

11.4.3   Common particles

————————➤

– – – – – –➤

Away
a *Literal meaning*: from here to another place
e.g. be away, go away, keep away, stay away

b *Slightly transferred*
e.g. give away, put away, throw away; send or write away for something
Note the expressions *give the game away* = reveal a secret
explain something away = to make it seem as if it never happened

c *Slowly getting less, weakening, disappearing*
e.g. die away (e.g. of sound), fade away, fall away, be eaten away
Note the expression *do away with*=destroy, get rid of, murder

d *Continuously and without hesitation*
e.g. work away (at a task, at a problem), fire away (=fire a gun freely; the invitation *Fire away!*=ask questions if you want to)

Back

a *Literal meaning*
   i) returning to an earlier place or time
   e.g. be back, come back, go back, get back (=arrive), turn back
   Note the idiom *fall back on something*=use something which you had kept in reserve
   ii) not at the front
   e.g. stand back, keep back, stay back, get back (=go to the back of the crowd, etc.)

b *Slightly transferred*
e.g. give back, hand back, keep back(=not say, not reveal), look back (e.g. look back on your childhood), put back, take back (e.g. I take back what I said=I did not mean it, I am sorry I said it.)

c *In return, one thing for another*
e.g. pay back (e.g. money which you have borrowed.) Note also the expression *pay someone back*=take revenge on them, answer back (especially rudely)

Down

a *Literal meaning*: moving from a higher to a lower position or being in the lower position
   e.g. get down (off a horse, etc), go down, fall down, lie down, keep down, stay down

b *Slightly transferred*
   e.g. put down, turn down (e.g. the corner of a page), bring down

c *Destroying, no longer in working order*
   e.g. burn down, cut down, knock down, pull down, shut down, tear down; break down (e.g. of a machine or a system)

d *Refusing, denying, rejecting*
   (Compare the *thumbs down* sign to show refusal or rejection)
   e.g. look down on (=despise), put someone down (=humiliate), shout someone down, turn down (e.g. a proposal, an application or a request)

e *Recording something* (in writing, etc.)
e.g. write down, note down, copy down, take down (notes), set down

Forward

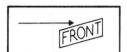

a *Literal meaning*: movement to the front
e.g. come forward, go forward, run forward, step forward

b *Slightly transferred*
=into a more obvious or important position
e.g. come forward, bring forward (e.g. choose an earlier date than the one originally suggested). Look forward (to)=get pleasure now from thinking about something which will happen later.

Off

a *Literal meaning:* moving from a surface or in a position which is no longer on the surface
e.g. fall off, get off (e.g. a bus), jump off, step off (e.g. an aeroplane)

b *Slightly transferred*
e.g. take off (=leave the ground), set off (=leave a place in order to start a journey), drive off (e.g., leave the scene of an accident)

c *Disconnecting or disappearing*
e.g. die off (e.g. Flies die off during the winter, i.e., they are *killed off* by the cold.), switch off (e.g. a light), turn off (e.g. a radio. Note that the slang expression *It turns me off*=It does not give me pleasure. Compare *turn on*), wear off (e.g. the effects of a drug)

It is not easy to derive the idiom *take someone off* (=impersonate) from the basic meanings of *off*.

On

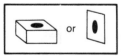

a *Literal meaning*: in contact with a surface (opposite of **off**)   or
e.g. get on (e.g. a bus), sit on, stand on

b *Slightly transferred*
e.g. put on (e.g. clothes), go on (=perform in a theatre)

c *Fixing or connecting*
e.g. fit on, fix on, nail on, screw on, sew on, stick on, switch on (e.g. a light), turn on (e.g. a radio or a tap)

d *Making progress, continuing*
e.g. carry on, drive on (i.e. without stopping), get on (=make progress or succeed), go on (=continue), hold on (e.g. when the telephone line is engaged, the operator might ask you to 'Hold on, please'), keep on.
Note the expression *Come on!* which you say to someone

to encourage them to start or to continue; and *He does go on about it!* which means that he will not stop talking about something which he finds interesting, or which makes him angry.

Out

a *Literal meaning*: movement from inside or in a position no longer inside
e.g. go out (=leave a building), get out

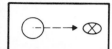

b *Slightly transferred*
e.g. hang out, hold out (e.g., your hand), pull out, put out (=expose, show), reach out, stand out (=be obvious), stick out (=project), take out, throw out.
Note the expression *walk out on someone*=leave them for good

c *Fading or disappearing completely*
e.g. die out (=become extinct. Compare *die off*), fade out, go out (e.g., the fire has gone out=it is dead), knock out, put out (=extinguish), rub out, wear out, wipe out (=destroy)

d *Appearing or happening suddenly*
e.g. burst out (e.g. burst out laughing or crying), break out (e.g. a fire or a war breaks out)

e *Becoming or being clearer, louder*
e.g. call out, copy out, cry out, find out (=discover) read out (i.e., read aloud), set out (e.g., set out written work neatly), shout out, speak out (this suggests to speak frankly or honestly: *to speak up* suggests to speak more loudly), spell out, work out (=solve), write out.

f *Distributing, giving to each one*
e.g. hand out, give out, pay out, share out

It is not easy to derive the phrasal verb *to make out* (=to identify, as in the phrase *nor could he make out the plus or the equal signs*) from the basic meanings of *out*.

Over

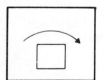

a *Literal meaning*: from one side or place to the other
e.g. fly over, get over, go over, climb over

b *Slightly transferred*
e.g. bring over, carry over, hold over (=postpone), make over (=transfer), take over.

c *Considering, reviewing, inspecting*
e.g. go over (=review and discuss), look over (=inspect), talk over, think over (=review and consider).
Note that *go over* is a VERB+PREPOSITION compound; so is *look over* in the sense of *My house looks over the river*. The others are VERB+ADVERB compounds, i.e., we

say *go over it*, but *look it over, talk it over, think it over* (See ◄ Section 11.2.3).

d *The idea of excess or surplus (more than you need)*
be left over

Round

a *Literal meaning*
   i) movement in a circle or curve, to face the opposite way
      e.g. come round, turn round
   ii) make a circle
   e.g. gather round, stand round

b *Slightly transferred*
   e.g. go round (as in *Have we enough food to go round?*), hand round, look round, pass round

c *To a place where someone will be, visiting*
   e.g. call round, come round, go round, pop round. The usual invitation is 'Come round and see us some time.'

Through

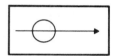

a *Literal meaning*:
   e.g. go through, pass through, step through

b *Slightly transferred*:
   = through to the very end, all the way to the finish
   e.g. be through (=have finished); get through (e.g. on a telephone) look through, read through, see through. Note that you can say either *look through it* and *read through it* or *look it through* and *read it through*. *See through it* means *not to be deceived by it*; *see it through* means *stay with it* (a plan or project) until it is finished.

c *From one side to the other*:
   e.g. come through (=survive), get through to someone (=make him understand), pull through (=survive an illness), see through (=not be deceived by).

d *Telephone communication*:
   e.g. I'll put you through to Mr Smith (=connect) I can't get through (=the line is engaged or out of order)

Up

a *Literal meaning*: moving from a lower to a higher position or being in a higher position
   e.g. get up, go up, pick up, rise up, stand up, step up

b *Slightly transferred*
   e.g. bring up (=rear children), come up (=arise, as in *A problem has just come up*), grow up (=become adult), wake up (i.e., come out of a deep sleep).

To *take up* a hobby, as in the sentence *he took up singing instead*, comes from the idea of taking up in the sense of *picking up*.

c *Coming nearer, approaching closely*
  We usually mention the object approached, and use the pattern
  VERB OF MOVEMENT + UP TO + OBJECT
  e.g. come up (to), dash up (to), drive up (to), run up (to), rush up (to), walk up (to).

d *Appearing unexpectedly*
  e.g. crop up (compare *come up*), turn up (=arrive unexpectedly), pop up.

e *Increasing*
  e.g. hurry up (=move more quickly), play up, speak up (=more loudly), step up (=increase), speed up, turn up (e.g. turn up the volume on the TV set).

f *Doing a thing fully and completely*
  e.g. clear up, do up (=fasten), drink up (i.e., finish the whole drink, or stop drinking after you have finished that one), eat up, fill up (e.g. you ask the attendant at the petrol station to 'fill her up', that is, you want to have a full petrol tank), pack up, save up, store up, tear up (i.e., tear something to pieces, until it is completely destroyed), tidy up, use up, wash up, wrap up.
  Note the expressions *make up*=apply cosmetics to the face
  make up=settle a quarrel and become friends again
  make up=invent, create
  make up your mind=make a definite decision
  make up for=compensate
  make up=invent, create

It is not easy to derive idioms like *put someone up* (=accommodate) and *put up with* (=tolerate, suffer) from the basic meanings of *up*.

11.5   Appendix XIII: A list of common phrasal verbs

The matrix shows the possible combinations of thirty-two verbs with thirty common particles. To interpret the matrix, find, in the vertical column, the verb that interests you, e.g. *keep*. Then, reading across the page, look at the top of any column which contains a P/p or an A/a to find the particle:
e.g. keep at, keep from, keep to, keep away, keep back, keep out, etc.
Where both A/a and P/p occur in the same square, it means that

the phrasal verb exists in the adverbial and a prepositional form, with, of course, a change of meaning:

e.g. *get across*:

Get across the river⟶Get across it i.e. go from one side to the other

Get your meaning across⟶Get it across i.e. make the other person understand.

*Other useful phrasal verbs not included in the matrix**

add up	fill in	miss out	split up
ask out	fill out	mix up	stick out
back up	fill up	own up	sum up
beat up	finish off	pack up	talk over
blow out	fit in	patch up	talk round
blow up	fix up	pay up	tell off
book up	follow up	pay out	think over
brush up	grow up	pick up	think up
build up	hand down	play down	throw out
butt in	hand in ·	pop in	try out
clear off	hand out	read on	use up
clear up	hand over	reckon up	warm up
close down	hang about	rule out	wear out
cover up	hang on	show off	wear off
doze off	help out	show up	weigh up
dress up	last out	shut up	win over
end up	laugh off	slip up	wind up
even up	live down	speak up	write off
explain away	live in	speak out	write out
(be) fed up	lock up	spin out	

*The meanings of a number of these phrasal verbs are explained in ← Section 11.4.3.

11.6   Appendix XIV   List of the commonest phrasal verbs having the pattern VERB + ADVERB + PREPOSITION

be up to	What are you up to? = What (bad) things are you doing?
be up on	He's well up on maths. = He knows the subject of maths well.
add up to	What it adds up to is that . . . = to summarize the situation
back out of	He wants to *back out of the scheme.* = withdraw from the scheme
bear down on	You must *bear down heavily on* him. = use strong discipline on
bear up under	We're *bearing up under* the strain. = We are managing.
boil down to	What it *boils down to* is . . . = The essential thing is . . .
break in on	Sorry to *break in on your conversation.* = interrupt
build up to	It is *building up to* a climax. = rising to
burst in on	Sorry *to burst in on* you like this. = interrupt without warning
carry on with	*Carry on with* what you were doing. = continue

	Prepositions										Adverbs				Both															
Verb / Particle	after	against	at	for	from	into	like	to	with	without	away	back	forward	out	about	across	along	around	before	behind	by	down	in	off	on	over	round	through	under	up
	p	P	p	p	P	p	P		p	P	A	A		A	P					A			A	A	A	A		A		A
eak		p		p	P				P		A			A							A	A	A		P			P		A
ing		p						p				A	A	A	A			A	a			a	A	A	a					A
ll	p		P								a	A		A						A			A	A	A	A		A		A
rry											A	A	A	A			a								A	A	a	A		A
tch		p												A											A					A
me	p	p	p		P	p		P			A	A	A	A	a	AP	A		a		a	a	A	AP	A		AP	AP		AP
t						p					a	A		A	AP							A	a	A						A
									P	P												a	ap							a
aw						p					a	a	a	a									A							A
op											a	a		a				A	A	a		a	A							
l			P			p					a	A	a	A						A			A	A	A	a		A		
t		P				P	p				A	A	a	A	a	AP	a	aP		ap	A	A	AP	A	AP	P	aP	aP		AP
ve											A	A		A									A	a			a			A
		P	p	p	p	P			P	P	A	A	A	A	P	P	A	Ap	p	p	P	A	A	A	A		AP	P	A	AP
ld								p	p		A			A							p	A	A	A	A	A				A
ep		P		P				P			A	A		A						a	a	A	a	aP	A					A
y						p								A							a	a	a	a						a
														a							A	A	A	A	A			A		a
ok	P		P	P		P	P	p			A	A	A	A	p			p				A	A		a	AP	AP	P		AP
ake	p	p									a			A										a	a					A
ss			p								a	a	a	A			a	a			A			a	A		A	P		a
ll		p	p								a	A		A								A	A	a			a	a		A
t											A	A	A	A	a	A			a	a	A	A	A	A	A	a		a		A
n	P	p	p	p		P		p			A	a	a	A	P		a	a				AP	a	a	a	A	a	P		AP
e				P	P										a	P		p					A		p	p		AP		
d				P							A	A	a	A				a				a	a			a	a			a
		p	p						p			a		A	P			a		a	a	a	a							A
nd				P							A		A	A	A		A	A			P	a	a		P					A
ke	P			P		P					A	A		A			a				A	A	A	a	a					A
rn		P		P		P	p				A	A		A				a				AP	a	Ap	A	A	A			Ap
rk		p	p	p										A									a	P	a	ap	p			a

Key   A or a = adverb   A and P = common, useful, worth learning
          P or p = preposition   a and p = less useful, because less common, or slang

cash in on	They are *cashing in on the video craze.* =taking advantage of video to make money from it
catch up on	I'd like to *catch up on the news.* =bring myself up to date
catch up with	He ran to *catch up with her.* =arrive where she was
check up on	They have *checked up on him.* =investigated his background
come down to	the same as *boil down to*
come down with	The children have all *come down with* measles. =caught
come in for	We have *come in for* a lot of criticism. =suffered
come out against	My party has come out against VAT. =decided to oppose
come out in	*Mione has come out in spots.* =Mione is covered with spots.
come out with	He finally *came out with* the truth. =admitted, revealed
come up against	We've *come up against* a serious problem. =met
come up with	Can't you *come up with* a better idea? =suggest, propose
cry out against	Everyone should *cry out against* the arms race. =protest about
cut down on	We need *to cut down on* our consumption of meat. =reduce
do away with	I see they've *done away with* the old filing system. =got rid of
drop in on	I just *decide to drop in on* them. =visit without previous warning
face up to	*Face up to* your responsibilities. =Realize and accept
fall back on	If A doesn't succeed you can always *fall back on B.* =use B as a reserve/substitute
fall behind with	He is *falling behind* with his work. =failing to go fast enough
fall in with	They will *fall in with* our suggestions. =agree to
fit in with	I'll *fit in with your arrangements.* =adjust to suit your arrangements
get away with	He cheats and *gets away with it!* =succeeds in doing something wrong
get down to	I must *get down to my studies again.* =start work in earnest
get on with	*I get on with John very well.* =John and I have a good relationship.
get (a)round to	I'll mend the radio when *I get round to it.* =finally make the effort
get up to	He gets up to all sorts of mischief. Compare *be up to*
go along with	similar to *fall in with.*
go back on	You should never *go back on your word.* =fail to honour a promise
go down with	go down with an illness, i.e., similar to *come down with*
go in for	I *don't go in for* team sports. =play, am not interested in/keen on
go on with	similar to *carry on with*
go through with	He's engaged to be married, but he says he cannot *go through with it.* =fulfil the commitment which he has made
hit back at	She *hit back at him* by refusing to cook his dinner. =retaliate
hit out at	The Press has *hit out at* the Government. =attacked
hold out for	The men are *holding out* for better wages. =persisting in their struggle
join in with	Why don't you *join in with us?* =come and do what we are doing
keep away from	*Keep away from* the dockside area. =Do not go into . . . because it is a dangerous spot
keep in with	*Keep in with* people who can help your career. =Maintain good relations with

keep on at	=persist; similar to *carry on with*
keep out of	Try to *keep out of* trouble. =avoid, stay away from
keep up with	*I can't keep up with the course.* =The course is too much for me.
lead up to	Get to the point. *What is all this leading up to?* =What do you really want to say to me?
live up to	He is *living up to his reputation.* =doing what we expect of him
look back on	When I *look back on* my schooldays . . . =recall
look down on	She's a snob: she *looks down on* ordinary people. =despises
look forward to	I'm *looking forward* to seeing you. =anticipating with pleasure
look out for	*Look out for* bargains when you go shopping. =Try and find
look out on	Our house *looks out on* Hyde Park. =has a view over
look up to	I *look up to* people who are educated. =admire, respect
make off with	The thief *made off with all the money.* =took all the money and escaped
make up for	We must *make up for* lost time. =compensate for
put in for	He has *put in for* a promotion. =made an application for, requested
put up with	I can't *put up with* her rudeness any longer. =tolerate
run out of	*We've run out of money.* =We have no money left.
run up against	similar to *come up against*
send away for	I have *sent away for* a catalogue. =written to ask for
settle down to	similar to *get down to*
speak up for	*Speak up for* what you believe in. =Declare, defend publicly
stand in for	Chris is ill, so I'm *standing in for him.* =acting as his substitute
stand up for	*Stand up for* your principles. =Defend yourself and what you believe in (compare speak up for).
stand up to	You should *always stand up to* a bully. =never run away from or submit to
stay away from	similar to *keep away from*
stick out for	similar to *hold out for*
take up with	He's *taken up with* some strange people. =become friendly with
talk down to	Teachers should never *talk down to* their students. =treat as inferior
walk off with	She *walked off with* the prize. =easily won
walk out on	*She just walked out on her family.* =She left her family.
watch out for	similar to *look out for*
write off for	similar to *send away for*

12 Contents

12 Adverbials

The Sad Story of the Cobra and the Boa Constrictor*

Frankly, I do not expect you to believe this story of how a cobra and a boa constrictor fell deeply in love, but I will tell it to you just the same. They met by chance one afternoon during the rainy season when they were sheltering from a storm, and were immediately attracted to each other. (You see, *snakes* generally like snakes, even if *people* do not like snakes).

The cobra greatly admired the boa's muscular body, and the boa declared that he had never seen anything so beautiful as the cobra's head markings. Naturally they soon fell in love, and even began to talk seriously of marriage. But there was a big problem, which could not be so easily resolved.

'If you hold me too tightly, you might kill me,' said the cobra anxiously.

'And if you kiss me, you might bite me and poison me,' retorted the boa, equally worried.

Anyway, they promised to be very careful, and to behave sensibly. It was no good, though. The first time they met in the moonlight and embraced passionately, the boa squeezed too hard, and the cobra bit the boa's lip.

They died before either of them could even say a word: only their eyes silently expressed what they were feeling at that moment.

Moral: Love is not having time to say you are sorry.

*Scientific note: most snakes kill either by poisoning, as the cobra does, or by squeezing, as the boa constrictor does.

A General introduction

12.1 Meaning of adverbials

As their name suggests, **adverbials** are closely connected with the verb (← Chapters 7 and 8) in a sentence. The **verb** describes the state of things (e.g., *be*, *seem*, etc.) or the activity (*go*, *put*, *think*, etc.), and **adverbials** add information about such things as the *manner*, *place*, *time* and *view* of the state or action.
They answer such questions as *how? where? when? how often?*
e.g. *They began to talk seriously* of marriage.
  How did they talk?
  They met *in the moonlight*.
  Where did they meet?
  They met *one afternoon during the rainy season*.

When did they meet?
He had *never* seen anything so beautiful.
How often had he seen . . . ?

There are also a number of adverbs (= adverbials which consist of one word) which in general answer the question *how much*?, and which modify adjectives or other adverbs:
They promised to be *very* careful.
If you hold me *too* tightly, you . . .
Adverbials which add information about our *view* of the event are like a comment on the whole sentence:
e.g. *Frankly*, I do not expect you to believe this story.
Anyway, they promised to be careful.
Naturally they soon fell in love.

12.2 Form of adverbials

Adverbials may have the following forms:
a *A single word* (called an **adverb**)
e.g. often, soon, out, slowly, probably, very
b *A prepositional phrase* (i.e. having the pattern PREPOSITION + NOUN)
e.g. by chance, during the rainy season, across the road, by car
c *A phrase without a preposition* (especially *time expressions*)
e.g. one afternoon, all day, every morning, tomorrow, a week on Friday
d *A clause* (i.e., a longer group of words, see → Section 13A.)
e.g. when they were sheltering from the storm

12.3 Position of adverbials in a sentence

A basic sentence has the pattern SUBJECT + VERB + (∅ or OBJECT or COMPLEMENT); see Chapter 13A. An adverbial might go at the beginning, in the middle or at the end of the sentence:

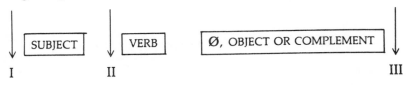

In this chapter, we use the symbols I II and III to describe the following positions:
I   *Soon* they decided to leave.
II   They *soon* decided to leave.
III   They decided to leave *soon*.

Some adverbials regularly go in the same place in the sentence (e.g. *frequency adverbs* like *always* go in position II); others go in different places depending on meaning or emphasis (e.g. adverbs of manner like *carefully* may go in positions I, II or III.)

Symbol	Position	
I	*At the beginning*	before the subject of the sentence
II	*In the middle*	i) after *main* verb *to be* – am, is, are, was, were; ii) before the main verb (i.e., the part denotes the activity or event which: speak, speaks, speaking, spoke, spoken) iii) where there are two or more auxiliary/modal verbs, after the first one
III	*At the end*	after VERB+Ø, OBJECT OR COMPLEMENT

Notes

1 Notice that we do not normally place an adverbial between a verb and its object or complement. For example, we say 'She speaks English *very well*', '*Surprisingly* she speaks English *very well*' and '*Surprisingly* she *sometimes* speaks English *very well*', but VERB+OBJECT – *speaks English* – stay together.
It is only safe to put an adverbial between a verb and its object/complement when the object/complement is a very long one.

2 In position II, variations occur in special cases.
The adverb can come immediately after the subject in short answers;
e.g. 'Who does the washing-up in your house?' 'I usually do.'
 (as well as 'Usually I do' and 'I do usually');
Have to, used to and *ought to* may be considered as part of the main verb, so that we say *He usually had to go* (rather than *He had usually to go*), *I definitely used to have one* (rather than *I used definitely to have one*) and *You really ought to leave now* (rather than *You ought really to leave now*).

Examples of main verb **be** *with adverbials in position II*

Subject	Main verb **be**	II	Complement
I	am	never	nervous.
he	is	often	in trouble.
we	are	just	good friends.
she	was	definitely	the best student.
they	were	still	in bed.

Note on negative inversion
For special effect or emphasis, certain adverbials with a negative meaning can be put at the beginning of the sentence (position I) instead of in their usual II or III position. In these cases it is necessary to *invert* subject and verb (as you would do for a question).

Examples of adverbials in Positions I, II and III

I	Subject	First auxiliary/ modal	II	Main verb (or other aux/modal +main verb)	Ø, Object or complement	III
Carefully,	John			opened	the box.	
Every Friday	she			visits	her parents.	
Frankly,	I	do not		like	his wife.	
	John		carefully	opened	the box.	
	People		often	say	things like that.	
	They		never	bothered	to reply.	
	He	did not	even	say	goodbye.	
	You	will	sometimes	be	amazed.	
	I	have	just	seen	him.	
	We	cannot	really	blame	her.	
	I	am	still	having	private lessons.	
	The new theatre	is	actually	being built	on the site of the old one.	
	The children		always	used to enjoy	themselves.	
	We		hardly ever	had to do	any homework.	
	You		really	ought to be	more careful.	
	John			opened	the box	carefully.
	The audience			applauded		politely.
	She			plays	the piano	very well.
	There			is	a funny smell	in here.
	I			hope	to see you	tomorrow.
	He	did not		do	it	on purpose.

For example:

                  adverbial

Normal position He not only *composes* music, but he also plays brilliantly.

                  adverbial

With inversion: Not only **does he** compose music, but he also plays ...

Other adverbials which can be used in Position I, causing inversion, are:

> hardly, never, rarely, seldom, scarcely *and the expressions* not only . . . but also, no sooner . . . than, not until . . . *and* under no circumstances.

When the word *only* is used at the beginning of the sentence and it restricts *the whole sentence*, the verb and subject are inverted:

Not restricted: Only the older children were allowed to go. (i.e. *only* refers to the children)

Restricted: Only then did I realize how much I loved him. (i.e. *only* then refers to and restricts the whole sentence)

Negative inversion is a written rather than a spoken form, and we advise you to recognize it but not to imitate it.

B   Adverbials of place (movement and location)

12.4   Movement and location

There are about 25 common adverbs which describe *movement towards* or *location in/at* a place. In most cases they can also function as prepositions. (Refer to ← Section 11.4. for an explanation of the meaning of these prepositional/adverbial particles).

When they are used with *a verb of movement* (e.g. *go, come, walk, climb*), they describe movement.

When they are used with verbs like *be, stay, remain*, they describe location (position):

Movement: go away, come back, walk around, climb up

Location: be away, stay back, stand around, wait up

(See table on p. 233. When the use is not common, the adverb is shown in brackets.)

Note

Many of these adverbs (especially *away, back, out, down, in, off, on* and *up*) combine with simple verbs to form **phrasal verbs**, see ← Section 11.4, for a description of the *transferred* (i.e. other than *literal*) meaning of these adverbs of place.

12.5   Other useful adverbs of place

a *Adverbs ending in* -**ward(s)**:

These adverbs describe movement *towards* or *away from* a place.

backward(s)	northward(s)
forward(s)	southward(s)
inward(s)	eastward(s)
outward(s)	westward(s)
upward(s)	onward(s)
downward(s)	homeward(s)

Note: towards is a preposition; *afterwards* is an **adverb of time** corresponding to the preposition *after*.

Movement	Location	Examples, comments
⟶ come/go ⟵	⊙ BE	
across	across	walk across; be across
along	(along)	He'll be along shortly. = He will arrive shortly.
away	away	go away; stay away, be away (from home/work)
back	back	come back; be back (from work), keep back
behind	behind	walk behind; stay behind, be behind (with your work)
(below)	(below)	on a ship only: to go/be below (cf. *downstairs* in a house)
(beyond)	(beyond)	rare as an adverb. Use *farther* (away)
by	(by)	go by; for location use *nearby*
down	down	jump down, get down; stay down
in	in	come in; be in, stay in
in front	in front	wa'k in front; be in front
inside	inside	run inside; be inside, stay inside
near	near	come near; be near, stay near (also use *nearby* or *close*)
off	(off)	get off, jump off; be off = not available, not fresh as well as *leave* (Well, I must be off)
on	on	get on; be on, stand on
–	opposite	For movement, use *across/over* (to the other side)
out	out	go out, walk out; be out, stay out
outside	outside	go outside; be outside, remain outside
over	(over)	walk over; it is over = it is finished
past	(past)	drive past; it is past = it is finished
(a)round	(a)round	walk around; She is around. = She is here somewhere.
through	(through)	step through; I'm through = I have finished
under	(under)	go under; for location, use *underneath*
underneath	underneath	walk underneath; be underneath
up	up	climb up, stand up; be up, stay up

b *Various*:

indoors, outdoors (*or* out of doors); upstairs, downstairs; uphill, downhill; sideways; inland, overseas, ahead, abroad, ashore.*

All can denote both movement and location (go indoors, and stay indoors, etc.), except for *uphill* and *downhill*, which describe movement (run uphill, roll downhill).

Note also the closely related phrases like:

next door; upside down, inside out; back to back, back to front, face to face, side by side; up and down; in and out

---

*A number of adverbs of place are connected with ships and the sea: *ahead, ashore, abroad*, aloft, astern, alongside; below; *overseas*, overboard; *underway*. The ones in italics are in common everyday use.

12.6   Prepositional phrases of place

Adverbials referring to place (movement or location) on the pattern PREPOSITION+NOUN are very common:

at home, in school, on the bus, in the country, on holiday, across the street, along the road, over the hill, etc. See the list of prepositional phrases in ← Section 6.8, Appendix IX.

12.7   The adverbs *here* and *there*

(For the meaning and use of the expressions *there is* and *here is*, see Sections 5.3.2 and 13.1.2).

Used in Position III, **here** and **there** describe either movement or location. Their meaning is like the meaning of *this* and *that* (← Section 2.5), so that **here**=*this* place, and **there**=*that* place:

Movement
come here   go there
bring it here   take it there
(to me)   (away from me)

Location
Here it is.   There it is!

Here and **there** combine with prepositions to make many useful adverbial phrases to describe movement to/from a place or location in/at a place:

across away from back down in near out of over round through under up	here there

Examples

It's through here.
(i.e. Come with me).

It's through there.
(i.e. Go by yourself).

put it
down here

put it
up here

put it
up there

put it
down there

The circle represents the speaker's 'sphere of interest' (see ← Section 2.5.2).

12.8 Position of adverbials of place

12.8.1 Adverbs of place (position)

The adverbs of place listed in Sections 12.4, 12.5 and 12.7 normally go in position III (go away, fall forwards, stay indoors, etc.). The adverbs in Section 12.4 can go in Position I, usually with the verbs *come* and *go*, to provide a slightly dramatic effect (*and* **away** *they go!* describing the start of a race), or a gentle command (**out** *you go!*).

We advise you not to imitate this form, except in the common and useful expressions with **here** and **there**:
Here you are is used when showing or offering something which someone has asked for.
Here it is, here they are more literally describe location.
There you are is similar to *here you are*, but seems to suggest reassurance, i.e. *Don't worry, everything is all right, your problem is solved.*
There it is, there they are describe location.

12.8.2 Prepositional phrases (position)

Prepositional phrases also normally go in position III (*walk across the street, stay in bed, live in the country*, etc.). They may go in position I in the following cases:
a *to avoid ambiguity*
e.g. Most workers live in flats *in big cities.*
This is not a clear statement. I could mean
A Most workers (say 90 per cent of all workers) live in big cities, and they live in flats; *or*
B Those workers who live in big cities (say 40 per cent of all workers) live in flats.
To make the meaning clear, we put the adverbial in position I:
In big cities, most workers live in flats. (i.e., meaning B)

b *to draw attention or give importance to the adverbial*
e.g. Every employee is important *in this company.* – statement about the company's workers
In this company, every employee is important. – draws our attention to the company and its policy.

c *for style* (especially when there are several adverbials)
(See → 12.18.)

12.8.3 Order of adverbials of place

If there is more than one adverbial of place in a sentence, adverbials of movement usually come before adverbials of location:

He spent the whole night pacing *up and down in his bedroom.*

 movement   *location*

In a sentence like *The car rolled downhill towards the village.*

– i.e. with two adverbials of location – put first whichever is *logically* first.

When two adverbials of location occur, it is often better to put one in position I (usually the one which describes the bigger or more general location), as in the sentence
  In big cities, most workers live *in flats.*
(See also ← Section 12.8.2)

C   Adverbials of time

Adverbial expressions of time answer the questions:
  When?   e.g. now, tomorrow, next week
  (For) how long? e.g. long, all day, for/since a time
  How often?   e.g. daily, several times, often, never

12.9   Common *when?* adverbials

12.9.1   Position

Usually in Position III: again, late, now, nowadays, then, today, tomorrow, tonight, yesterday
Usually in Position II: just
In I, II or III: afterwards, earlier, eventually, finally, first, immediately, lately, next, once, presently, soon

Examples
Don't do it *again*!
I'm afraid I got up *late*.
I hope to see you all *tomorrow*.
He has *just* gone out.
You should have mentioned it *earlier*. (III)
I *first* heard about it in 1980.   (II)

Note
The position may change to give slight changes of emphasis or meaning, or to avoid ambiguity. e.g.

  I   II   III

∧ They   ∧   decided to leave   ∧

  Soon they decided to leave. = It was not long before they decided . . .
  They *soon* decided to leave. = It did not take them long to decide that it would be best to leave.
  They decided to leave *soon*. = They decided that they did not want to stay much longer.

12.9.2   Prepositional phrases

at + time   e.g. at nine o'clock
at + holiday periods   e.g. at Easter, at Christmas
on + day   e.g. on Friday, on St. Patrick's Day
on + date   e.g. on the seventeenth of July
in + month   e.g. in July

in + year   e.g. in 1988
in + season   in (the) spring/summer/autumn/winter
during the day/night/week etc.
in the morning/afternoon/evening (but *at night*)
in a few minutes' time, in X hours'/days'/weeks'/etc./time

Note also:
yesterday morning/afternoon/evening (but *last night*)
this   morning/afternoon/evening (but *tonight*)
tomorrow morning/afternoon/evening/night
the day before yesterday, the day after tomorrow X
days/weeks/months/etc./ago
These time expressions usually go in Position III.

12.9.3 Order of *when?* adverbials

As a rule, when more than one *when?* adverbial comes in Position III, the more specific (detailed) one comes before the more general:

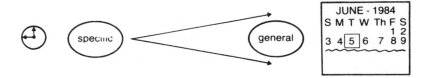

at nine o'clock on Tuesday the fifth of June, 1984

If you put the specific (e.g. *at nine o'clock*) at the *end* of the sentence, you emphasize it or draw attention to it:
    I'll see you at half past nine *on Friday*. (=See you Friday!)
but I'll see you on Friday *at half past nine*. (=Don't be late!)

**12.10 Common *how long?*
adverbials**

a always briefly long permanently temporarily

b *Time expressions*

all	morning
	afternoon
	evening
	day
the whole	night
	week

To emphasize the length of time you can say all (*time*) long as in *all night long*. The usual expression with *year* is *all year round* or *the whole year*.

since + a point of time
for   + a period of time
until + a point of time

All these time expressions usually go in Position III.

e.g. Have you been here long?
She has been very ill recently.
I've been working quite hard lately.
Mike called round about a week ago, but I haven't seen him since.
I haven't seen him all week.
I lived in Spain for several years.
Wait until dark.

12.11 Common *how often?* adverbials

12.11.1 Adverbials – number of times

Some adverbial expressions tell us the exact number of times that something happens:

hourly, daily, weekly, fortnightly, monthly, yearly*
once, twice, three times, four times, etc.
once a day, twice a week, three times a year, etc.
once every two/three etc. weeks/months/years/etc.

every	
every other	day/week/etc.
each	

These expressions usually go in Position III.

*These words are also adjectives, as in 'a daily paper', 'a fortnightly report.'

12.11.2 Frequency adverbs

Other expressions tell us whether something happens more or less often in the range of possibilities between *all the time* (always) and *none of the time* (never). These are often called **frequency adverbs**.

$\ominus$ $\oplus$

$\longleftarrow \longrightarrow$

Never	*Sometimes*	*Often*	*Always*
hardly ever	generally	frequently	constantly
← not ... ever	normally	regularly	continually
occasionally	usually		continuously
rarely			ever
seldom			forever

Frequency adverbs usually go in Position II (but see → Section 12.11.3).
There are also a few phrases which express frequency:
Like *often*: again and again, time and again
Like *sometimes*: a few times, from time to time, now and again, now and then

These expressions usually go in Position III.

e.g. I have only met him *once*.
Sarah goes to piano lessons *three times a week*.
Anne goes to folk-dancing *every other Monday*.
The boa declared that he had *never* seen anything so beautiful . . .
Snakes *generally* like snakes even if people do not like snakes.
I *seldom* go to the theatre nowadays.
You *hardly ever* write to me.
You can *usually* get a table at Don Giovannni's without booking.
He is *forever* complaining about the food. (← Section 8.2.1)
Have you *ever* been skiing?
I've told you *time and again* not to do that.

12.11.3 Further notes on the position of frequency adverbs

a These adverbs may also go in Positions I or III:

often frequently regularly generally normally usually
sometimes occasionally

If you put them in I or III, you change the meaning or the emphasis of the sentence.
In their usual place, II, they (and the other frequency adverbs) are really like a part of the verb: imagine, for example, that ther are several verbs in English to describe ways of *telling*:
to tell, to often tell, to occasionally tell, to usually tell*

*According to strict grammar, we should not split infinitives, that is, put a word between the infinitive *to* and the verb.

We use the verb *to often tell* in the sentence *Salesmen often tell lies*. This could be a response to *Tell me anything bad you know about salesmen*.

For a special effect, we can say:
III Salesmen tell lies often.
This answers a question like *How frequently do salesmen tell lies?*, that is, it draws attention to the frequency of the action.
I Often, salesmen tell lies.
This answers a question like *I know that there is something that salesmen often do. What is it?*

We advise you to put frequency adverbs in Position II, except when you really want to emphasize the frequency, as in a sentence like
They *don't* go out *very often*.
where you want to stress the fact that going out is *a rare event* for them.

b Frequency adverbs go in a different place in Position II, namely *immediately after the subject*, when you want to reply firmly to someone's suggestion (You ought not to, you should not) or instruction (Do that! Don't do that! You must not . . .).

Example (i)
Suggestion   You should always clean your teeth after meals
Replies   I always 'do!
               I always 'have done.
               I always 'have cleaned my teeth after meals.

Example (ii)
Instruction   Don't lend money to strangers!
Replies   I never 'do!
                I never 'have done.
                I never 'have lent money to strangers.
                I never 'would lend money to strangers.

Note that the stress falls on the verbs '*do*, '*have* done, '*have* cleaned, '*have* lent, '*would* lend. In normal position, i.e., Position II, the stress falls on the frequency adverb or equally on adverb and verb, as in
    I have '*always* wanted to go to America.
or I have '*always* '*wanted* to go to America.

12.12   Other time adverbs

12.12.1   *Yet* and *still*

In everyday modern English, **yet** is used in negative sentences and in questions. It usually goes in Position III:
    Has he arrived yet?   (a simple question for information)
    Hasn't he arrived yet?   (a question which expresses *slight* surprise).
    He has not arrived yet. (a simple statement of fact)

Still is mostly used in positive sentences and in questions in Position II:
1   The children are still at school.
2   Are you still working?
3   Do you still go out with Janet?
4   John hasn't come home: he must still be at work.
5   He can't still be at work: it's seven o'clock.
Sentences 1, 4 and 5 are simple statements of fact; 2 and 3 are simple requests for information.

Still can also be used in negative sentences in a different place in Position II, namely *immediately after the subject*, to express surprise, anger or worry that something is overdue (=late, i.e., it should have happened by now, but it has not happened.)

Example

John usually gets home from work at about six o'clock.

A At five past six, you say: *He isn't back yet.* – a normal statement.

B At half past six, you say: *He still isn't back.* – expressing worry, etc.

In A, the stress is on the main verb (be back): He isn't *back* yet.
In B, the stress is on the word still: He *still* isn't back.

12.12.2 No longer, not . . . any longer, not . . . any more

These expressions all mean that an activity has stopped some time before now:

Mr Jones does not work here any more. (a normal, unemphatic statement)

Mr Jones no longer works here. (a more formal, more emphatic statement)

I cannot wait any longer. = I have waited long enough.

The sentences *I can wait no longer* and *I can no longer wait* sound very formal and old-fashioned. We advise you to use the form *not . . . any longer/any more*.

12.13 Order of time adverbials

If more than one time adverbial occurs in Position III in a sentence, the usual order is

how <u>l</u>ong   how <u>o</u>ften   <u>w</u>hen   (Remember L O W)

The usual combinations are:

How long + How often: I see her *for a few hours every Friday*
                                                    L   O

How long + When   I saw her *briefly last Friday*.
                                              L   W

How often + When: He was absent *several times last term*.
                                                        O   W

The expressions at the end – *every Friday, last Friday, last term* – can also go in Position I (see → Section 12.18):

e.g. *Every Friday* I see her for a few hours.

D Adverbials of manner

Adverbials of manner answer the question *how?*, i.e., *in what way., in what manner, by what means?* They are mostly in the form of adverbs (e.g. quickly, well) and prepositional phrases (e.g. with a screwdriver, on purpose).

12.14 Adverbs of manner in -ly

A great number of adverbs of manner (and of viewpoint, see → Section 12.19 ff) are formed by adding the suffix **-ly** to **adjectives**:

12.14.1 Form

soft → softly   polite → politely   careful → carefully
easy → easily

Adjectives in **-able/-ible** change to **-ably/-ibly**:
irritable→irritably   illegible→illegibly
(For a list of adjectives in **-able/-ible**, see ← Section 4.2.1)
Adjectives in **-ic(al)** change to **-ically**
sarcastic→sarcastically   ironic(al)→ironically
(Exception: public – publicly)
(For a list of adjectives in **-ic(al)**, see ← Section 4.2.1)

12.14.2   Position of adverbs in *-ly*

These adverbs are very mobile, that is, they can appear in any of the three positions.
In *Position II*, they are really like a part of the verb (see also ← Section 12.11). Imagine that there are several verbs in English to describe, for example, ways of *opening*:
to open, to suddenly open, to carefully open etc.*

*See Section 12.11.3. If you want to avoid splitting the infinitive, put the adverb before *to* e.g.
He began *carefully to open* the door, or in Position III, *He began to open the door carefully*.

The sentence *John **carefully opened** the door* is a simple statement of fact; it answers the question *What did John do*?

In *Position III*, the adverb is what interests us, that is, we are interested in *how* the action was done.
The sentence *John opened the door **carefully*** is a statement about the way in which he opened the door; it answers the question *How did John open the door*?

Position I, as in the sentence **Carefully**, *John opened the door*, is not common in speaking, but is a favourite with writers of novels, because it seems to increase the tension (i.e., our interest in what comes next). It answers a question like *We know that something happened carefully. What was it*? or *We know that John decided that he had to be careful, but why*?
(*Note:* adverbs in **-ly** *which express viewpoint* very often go in position I, see → Section 12.19).

We advise you to use *Position II* in the pattern ADVERB+VERB+OBJECT (. . . carefully opened the door). If you really want to draw attention to the manner of the action, use Position III, ΄i.e., the pattern VERB+OBJECT+ADVERB (. . . opened the door carefully). In the pattern VERB+Ø, the adverb usually comes after the verb (They promised to behave sensibly, They embraced passionately). In the pattern VERB+COMPLEMENT, put the adverb in Position II or immediately after the verb for normal statements (They were *patiently waiting* outside the cinema. *or* They were *waiting patiently* outside the cinema.). Only put the adverb of manner in Position III, i.e., after the complement, if you really want to draw attention to it (They were *waiting* outside the cinema *patiently*.).

12.15 Other adverbs of manner

The adjective **good** becomes the adverb **well**:
e.g. He is a *good* driver. ———→ He drives *well*.
The following do not change:
He is a *hard* worker. ———→ He works *hard*.
She is a *fast* driver. ———→ She drives *fast*.

Comparatives (←4.5) of adverbs of manner have the pattern MORE+ADVERB, as in *more carefully*, except for

well   better   He drives *better* than I do.
badly   worse   He speaks French *worse* than the rest of us.
hard   harder   He works *harder* than he needs to.
fast   faster   Please go a little *faster*.

All the adverbs in this section usually go in Position III.

Note: you might also hear the adjectives *quick/quicker slow/slower* and *loud/louder* used as adverbs, as in *Come quick! Speak slower! He talks loud. Can you speak a bit louder?* We advise you to use the regular forms *quickly/more quickly slowly/more slowly loudly/more loudly*.

12.16 Prepositional phrases

12.16.1 In a . . . ly way/manner

Adjectives which already end in **-ly** should be used adverbially only in the pattern IN A (ADJECTIVE) WAY/MANNER. The commonest **-ly** adjectives are: cowardly, friendly, gingerly, leisurely, silly, surly, ungainly

Adjective: He is a friendly person.
Adverb: He always speaks to you *in a friendly manner*.

12.16.2 By/with

These adverbial phrases describe the method or the means:
Means of travel: go by car/boat/plane/ship/air
How to do something: **by**+verb*ing*
e.g. Start the engine *by turning the key*.
What you use to do something: WITH+(TOOL, INSTRUMENT, etc.)
e.g. Open the door *with the master key*.

12.16.3 Other prepositional phrases

There are a lot of prepositional phrases to describe how something happens,
e.g. by accident, at ease, without hesitation, with interest, from memory, under pressure, on purpose, in vain.
The commonest expressions are given in Appendix IV.
These phrases usually go in Position III.

E Order of different adverbials (manner + place + time)

12.17 Manner + place + time (MPT) order

When adverbials of manner, place and time occur in the same sentence in Position III, the order is usually MANNER PLACE TIME,* which gives the following combinations.

| manner | place | She was sitting *quietly* *in her armchair*. |
| | | M   P |

They were waiting *patiently outside the cinema*.

M   P

| manner | time | They met *by chance one afternoon*. |
| | | M   T |

He has worked *well this term*.

M   T

| place | time | I have to go *to the doctor's this evening*. |
| | | P   T |

He stayed *outside for several hours*.

P   T

*To remember the order *Manner Place Time*, notice that the letters M, P and T are in their alphabetical order: M n o P q r s T.

12.18 Variations in the MPT order

The M P T order can be changed in the following cases:

a Fixed expressions are not usually separated, e.g., go home, be at work, go by car, spend (time); and phrasal verbs (← Chapter 11) such as *go out, give up*.

b when we want to emphasize or draw attention to a particular adverbial, we put it *at the end of the sentence*:
She went *out of the room very quietly*. (i.e., the emphasis is

P   M

on *how* she did it. Compare ← Section 12.9.3.)

c Put the *longest* element at the end of the sentence:
I lived *for many years in one of the coldest places on earth*.

T   P

d For reasons of style, we try to avoid putting too many adverbials in Position III. We usually do this by transferring time or place expressions to Position I:

(T) [M] [P]: *Last year* I hitch-hiked *with a friend all round Europe*.

(P) [M] [T]: *In northern countries* it is dangerous to drive *quickly in winter*.

F   Other adverbials and their uses

12.19 Viewpoint, commenting and other adverbials

There are a number of adverbials which seem to express a viewpoint about the whole sentence, or to comment on the action. Others express the idea of the *extent* (or *degree*: How much?) to which the action is performed.

Those in Position I are mostly viewpoint adverbs.
Those in Position II are mostly commenting adverbs.
Those in Position III are mostly concerned with degree or extent.

I   *Frankly*, I do not expect you to believe this story. (=It is my
    frank (honest) opinion that you will not believe me.)
    Personally I don't trust him.* (=If you want to know my
    personal opinion about him, I don't think he is a person you
    could trust.)

II They died *before either of them could even say a word*.
    (=They died so quickly there was no time to speak.)
    He *definitely* needs a holiday. (=It is definite (certain) that he
    needs a holiday.)

III I like you *very much*. (=How much do I like you? Very
    much)
    I don't mind *in the least*. (=How much do I mind? Not in the
    least *or* Not to the least extent.)

*This use of *personally* is quite different from the adverb of manner in *I do not
know him personally* which means something like *I know his name, or I have heard
of him, but I have not met him.*

Here are examples of the most common adverbials which express
viewpoint, comment or degree.

12.19.1   Position I*

a *Officially*, you should not be here, so hurry up.
  Geographically, Britain was in an excellent position to develop
  as a great naval power.

  Other examples: economically, historically, ideally, morally,
  politically, psychologically, technically, theoretically.
  Some people add *speaking*: *Morally speaking, he* . . . It adds
  nothing to the meaning and we do not advise you to imitate it.
  A fashionable but not very attractive way of forming adverbs
  of this type is to add the suffix **-wise** to almost any noun:
  e.g. Charmwise, he is terrific, but brainwise, he is
       hopeless=He is a very charming person, but not very
       intelligent.
  We advise you not to imitate this form, but you should expect
  to hear it from time to time.

  Frankly
b Honestly | I do not care what other people think of me.
  Seriously

  As a matter of fact
  Confidentially
  Between you and me | I think he is a liar.
  Personally
  To tell you the truth

  Funnily enough
c Surprisingly | I have never done this sort of thing before.
  (Un)fortunately

*Note: Viewpoint adverbials in
Position I are often separated from
the rest of the sentence by a comma
(➤ Chapter 15)
e.g. Frankly, I doubt if he knows
     anything about it.

d
| Clearly |
| Obviously |
| Undoubtedly |

you do not believe me.

Surely you do not mean that?

The viewpoint adverb *surely?* is a common way of suggesting that the other person is wrong or being illogical or has forgotten some important facts. Funnily enough, the people who ask Surely . . . ? questions are themselves often the ones who are wrong, illogical or short of information.

e
| Apparently |
| Maybe |
| Perhaps |
| Possibly |
| Presumably |

he has gone away.

f *Basically* I agree with you.

'How does this machine work?' 'Well, *basically* it is like an electronic switch.'

Basically should be used to describe the basis (the essential) of for example the agreement (I agree with you in essentials, but there are one or two details I should like to discuss . . .) or the mechanism (It is like an electronic switch but there are some differences . . .). The word *Basically* is, however, commonly used to introduce any sentence where the speaker wishes to give the impression that what he is about to tell you is very important.

12.19.2   Position II

g
I
| just |
| simply |
| only |
| mainly |
| chiefly |
| especially |

wondered what on earth you were trying to do.

h I am
| also |
| equally |
| just as |

interested in books about butterflies.

Note the position of the following:

I am interested in other books
| as well. |
| too. |

i I am *not* interested in sport *at all*.

I am *not* interested in sport *either*.

j John looks quite ill. He
| certainly |
| definitely |
| obviously |

needs a holiday.

k She never said a word. She | just / literally* / simply | packed her bags and left.

l They | barely / hardly (even) / scarcely | took any notice of what I was saying.

m She | almost / nearly / practically | burst into tears when she saw the mess.

*People say *literally* for emphasis, but it often makes no sense (*She literally bit my head off.*), so we advise you to use it with great care.

12.19.3 Position III

n I admire her | enormously. / greatly. / a lot. | (=very much).

Note the use of *badly* in the sense of *very much*:

e.g. My hair badly needs cutting (=My hair is in a very bad state)

The adverb *badly* could also go in Position III, but the sentence *My hair needs cutting badly* is ambiguous, because *badly* could be an adverb of manner!

o It did not worry me | at all. / in the least. / in the slightest.

12.20 Adverbials which join or link ideas and sentences

The following adverbials are used, usually in Position I, to join the last idea or sentence to the next one:

a First, ... Second, ... Third, ... (etc.)
Next, ... Then, ... Lastly, ... Finally, ...
Firstly, ... Secondly, ... Thirdly, ... (etc.)

b Furthermore, ... Moreover, ... In addition, ... Equally, ... Similarly, ...

c Incidentally, ... By the way, ...

d Therefore, ... Consequently, ... So, ... Somehow, ...

e Namely, ... For example ... For instance, ... In other words, ... That is (to say).

Note: The abbreviation for *namely* is *viz,*; for *for example* – *e.g.*; for *that is* – *i.e.*

f On the one hand, ... On the other (hand), ...; In contrast, ... By/In comparison, ...

g After all, ... All the same, ... Anyway, ... At any rate,
... However, ... In any case, ... Nevertheless, ... Still,
...

Notes

1 In more formal speech and in writing, some of these adverbials
can go in Position II, separated by commas, or in Position III
after a comma:
e.g. I hope, therefore, that you will agree with me ...
     There are some reasons, however, for believing that ...
     I am prepared to meet him, nevertheless.

2 *Still*, ... and *Anyway*, ... are common spoken and, in
writing, informal ways of saying *In spite of what has (or has
not) happened*, ... :
e.g. *Anyway*, they promised to be careful, and to behave
     sensibly.
     I'm sorry that Jennie has left you. *Still*, you can always
     find another secretary.
     Anyway, she wasn't such a good secretary when you
     come to think about it.
Anyway, and also the word *though* can be used, after a
comma, in Position III:
e.g. She wasn't a very good secretary, *anyway*.
... , *though* usually means *all the same* or *on the other hand*:
e.g. They promised to be careful. It was no good, *though*. The
     first time they met, the boa squeezed too hard ...
     Jennie was a bit untidy and she was often absent without
     reason. She was a good secretary, *though*.

12.21   Adverbs used to modify adjectives or other adverbs

12.21.1   Very/not very

The commonest adverb used in this way is **very**:
    Your work is good.   Your work is very good.
    He types quickly.   He types very quickly.
We usually form the negative of these statements either by using
a word of opposite meaning (good – bad, quickly – slowly) or
by using **not very**:
    Your work is bad. *or* (more usual) Your work isn't very good.
    He types slowly.   *or* (more usual) He doesn't type very
                                            quickly.
In order of merit (e.g. as the expressions might be used by a
teacher to say how good or how bad your work is), the
expressions are, from best to worst:
1   very good   4   not good
2   good   5   bad
3   not very good   6   very bad

The expression **not bad** comes between 2 and 3. The expression
not very bad would be a kind thing to say after 4:
e.g. Your work is not good, but it is not very bad.
Notice that **very** is not used on its own:
    I like you Ø.   I like you very much.

12.21.2 Others

Other adverbials which are used like **very** and **not very** are:

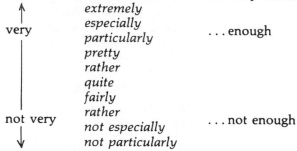

extremely
especially
particularly ...enough
pretty
rather
quite
fairly
rather
not especially ...not enough
not particularly

Examples
It was extremely cold that night.
He spoke extremely fast.
This stamp is particularly valuable.
He spoke particularly slowly.
The food here is pretty awful.
We get on pretty well together.
Your work is rather poor.
She left rather suddenly.
It's a fairly difficult exam.
The time passed fairly quickly.
I'm not particularly keen to go.
He speaks Polish, but not particularly well.

Notes

1 Although combinations of **-ly** adverbs are possible, it is better
to avoid long combinations like 'particularly carefully'. Use
very instead.
2 The meaning of **fairly**, **quite** and **rather**, and their position in
the scale between *very* and *not very*, can change according to
such things as:
a *Intonation*
'What is your new teacher like?'
'She's quite 'nice. (=I like her)
'She's 'quite nice. (=She's all right, but I am not
                     enthusiastic about her.)
b *Fashion*
The word **rather** used to suggest something negative, as in
rather careless and *rather sad*, but it is now commonly used
with positive words, when it can mean *very*:

    She's rather nice.

Stressed **rather** often suggests that you are surprised by what you find, or that you disagree with someone else's opinion about something:

> This disco's rather good, isn't it? (=it is much better than I expected it to be)
> Oh, do you really think so? I thought it was rather disappointing. (=In contrast to your opinion, I think . . .)

c *Understatement* An Englishman might say 'My brother is quite a good tennis player'. when the fact is that his brother is the European singles champion.
We advise you to use **very** and **not very**, but learn to recognize the way in which the other adverbs are used before you use them yourself.

3 The following adverbs are more like those adverbs which describe extent or degree:

I am mainly │ interested in rare books on ornithology.
    chiefly │

The adverbs **especially** and **particularly** are used in the same way.

4 These adverbs describe a sort of superlative (the highest degree):

      absolutely │
I am completely │
      totally │ exhausted.
      utterly │

Utterly tends to be used with things which you do not like (*tired out, fed up, depressed*). The others are also used with 'positive' words (*absolutely delighted, completely satisfied, totally convinced*).

5 Be careful to distinguish between **very** and **too**:
He speaks *very* quickly. This is a fact. It is not necessarily a problem.
He speaks *too* quickly. This is a fact, but it is also a problem, because he speaks so quickly that I cannot understand him.

Compare the difference between *He has **a lot of** money* (which may be a good or a bad thing) and *He has **too much** money* (which is definitely a bad thing: he has more than he should have).

13 Contents

13 Sentence patterns

The Spaniel and the Hedgehog
(*Part 1*)

One day, a spaniel was playing in the garden when he came across a strange animal with spines all over its body. He did not know what the strange creature was, but he soon found out how painful it could be to try to make friends with a hedgehog.

He sniffed at the animal but leapt back with a cry of pain as the creature's spines stuck in his nose. In the meantime, the hedgehog had curled up into a little ball, so that you could no longer tell which end was which.

Determined to get to know the animal better, the spaniel pushed it with his paw in order to turn it over, but again he got nothing but a painful jab in his flesh.

A   Note on grammatical terms

In this chapter, we use some grammatical terms.

Subject
Every full sentence has a grammatical subject, that is, a noun, noun phrase or pronoun which governs the verb:
e.g. *Brown bread* is good for you.
     He soon found out.
     Have *you* been out?
The *grammatical* subject is often, but not necessarily, the same as the main topic (interest) of the sentence:
grammatical subject and *topic of the sentence the same*:
     The spaniel was playing in the garden.
grammatical subject and *topic of the sentence different*:
     There was a hedgehog on the lawn. (*There* is the grammatical subject, but the sentence is really about *a hedgehog*.)

Verb
The verb which is governed by the subject tells us what the subject *is* (or *is like*) or what the subject *does*.
Verbs like *be, seem, appear* and *become*, and verbs which can form a complete sentence on the pattern
SUBJECT + VERB ± COMPLEMENT, are called **intransitive verbs**:
     He *left*.
     She *was sleeping* in the chair.
     Brown bread *is* good for you.

Verbs which form a complete sentence with a noun, noun phrase or pronoun as object are called **transitive verbs**:

The spaniel *pushed* it.

John *prefers* brown bread.

He *did not know* what the strange creature was.

Has anyone *seen* my scarf?

Note

Many verbs can function both transitively (i.e. they take an object) and intransitively (i.e. ±a complement). They are classified in dictionaries by the symbols **Vt** and **Vi**. These symbols are used in the rest of this chapter.

Object

The word or group of words (noun, pronoun, noun phrase or clause) which are governed by a transitive verb is the **object** of that verb:

He wanted to get to know *the animal.*

He pushed *it.*

He did not know *what it was.*

Complement

We use the word **complement** to describe the word or words (usually an adverbial or an adjectival expression) which follow an intransitive verb:

Brown bread is *good for you.*

The spaniel was playing *in the garden.*

The hedgehog had curled *up into a little ball.*

Direct and indirect object

(See ← Section 7.4 for a full description)

Examples

Give *me* *the case*   Give *it* *to me*   Give *the case* *to me*
    i.o.   d.o.   d.o. i.o.   d.o.   i.o.

Parts of the verb

(See ← Section 7.4 for a full description)

Be careful to distinguish these forms:

Present participle: The **-ing** form of the verb as in the sentence *I saw him climbing through the window.* (i.e., I SAW HIM + HE WAS CLIMBING THROUGH THE WINDOW)

Gerund

Also the **-ing** form of the verb, but used differently. It is a kind of noun* as in

Smoking is bad for you.

or I enjoy *walking. (The test* for a gerund is that you can always replace it by the pronoun *it* (Compare *It is bad for you* and *I enjoy it* with *I saw him it,* which does not make sense).

*For this reason it is correct to use the possessive form before a gerund, e.g. *I remember his doing it./Michael's doing it.* Nowadays you can use the object form: *I remember him doing it./Michael doing it.*

Past participle: see ◄— Section 7.4. *Examples*: called, left, gone, done, spoken

Infinitive: the simple base form of any verb is called the infinitive. We use the terms *to-infinitive* and *base infinitive* to separate the infinitive forms in *I want **to go*** and *Let him **go**.*

Phrase: a short group of words usually following one of the patterns
PREPOSITION+NOUN: in the dark, after school
QUESTION WORD+INFINITIVE: where to go, how to do it
PARTICIPLE+NOUN: following the request, leaving the school

Clause*: a longer group of words containing a full verb but which are different from a complete sentence in that they cannot make sense *by themselves*:
when we had finished,   how he knew,   because she told me to, whether they had had enough

> *Strictly speaking this is a definition of a **subordinate clause** as distinct from a **main clause**:
> e.g. He did not know (*main clause*) what the strange creature was (*subordinate clause*).
> For our purposes, we shall use the expression **clause** to describe subordinate clauses, i.e. clauses which cannot make complete sense by themselves.

For the meaning of the terms **noun, pronoun, possessive, adjective, adverbial, verb** and **preposition**, see the appropriate chapter.

B Summary of types of sentence patterns: key sentences

These *key sentences* illustrate the main kinds of sentence patterns. Types A–E are patterns with intransitive verbs (**Vi**); types F–J are patterns with transitive verbs (**Vt**) (see table overleaf).

13.1 Type A:
BE+COMPLEMENT

C Patterns with intransitive verbs: Types A–E

13.1.1 The complement

The complement can be a noun, a pronoun, an adjective, an adverbial or a prepositional phrase:
This is *my brother*.
Who is *it*?
He is *alive*.
He is *here*.
It is *in the garden*.

Table: sentence patterns

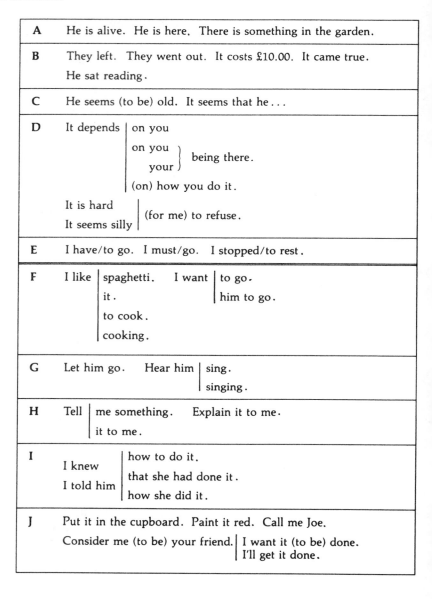

A	He is alive. He is here. There is something in the garden.
B	They left. They went out. It costs £10.00. It came true. He sat reading.
C	He seems (to be) old. It seems that he . . .
D	It depends ⎧ on you ⎫ being there. (on) how you do it. It is hard ⎫ (for me) to refuse. It seems silly ⎭
E	I have/to go. I must/go. I stopped/to rest.
F	I like ⎧ spaghetti. it. to cook. cooking. ⎭ I want ⎧ to go. him to go. ⎭
G	Let him go. Hear him ⎧ sing. singing. ⎭
H	Tell ⎧ me something. it to me. ⎭ Explain it to me.
I	I knew / I told him ⎧ how to do it. that she had done it. how she did it. ⎭
J	Put it in the cupboard. Paint it red. Call me Joe. Consider me (to be) your friend. ⎫ I want it (to be) done. I'll get it done.

13.1.2 The pattern
THERE IS + X
+PREPOSITIONAL PHRASE*

e.g. There is something in the garden.
     There is some butter in the fridge.
This pattern, THERE IS X IN Y, is much commoner than the pattern X is in Y.
Although one should use *there are* before plural complements, it is common in speaking to use the singular, usually shortened to *There's* . . . :
e.g. *There's some eggs in the fridge.* instead of the strictly correct *There are some eggs in the fridge.* We advise you to use *There are* with plural complements.

There is, of course, the *grammatical* subject; the *topic* subject of the sentence is X.

13.1.3 The pattern
IT + BE + ADJECTIVE/NOUN +
to-INFINITIVE

This pattern is very useful.

e.g. It's so nice to see you again.

It's a pity to stay inside when the sun is shining.

It would be a mistake to trust him with so much responsibility.

Note also the patterns HOW + ADJECTIVE and WHAT (A) + NOUN as in:

How nice (it is) to see you again!

What a pity (it is) to stay inside!

Similarly:

He soon realized *how painful it could be to make friends* with a hedgehog.

The pattern BE + ADJECTIVE/NOUN + that-CLAUSE is also **very** useful:

	funny		you do not know her.
	interesting		there are no Germans in the school.
	likely		they will arrive before ten.
	lucky		you got here so early.
	odd		nobody has telephoned.
	possible		he has been delayed.
It is	probable	(that)**	the Government will resign.
	strange		you both chose the same colour.
	wonderful		you were able to come to the wedding.
	a pity		they could not be here today.
	a shame		there aren't any more.
It is	time high time about time	(that)**	you started* to do things for yourself.

*Note the *past tense* after the expression 'It's (high/about) time'

**The conjunction *that* is usually left out except in formal statements.

13.1.4 Expressions with
BE + (NOT) NOUN/ADJECTIVE
+ GERUND

	(not)	
It is	no good	
	no use	
	(not) worthwhile	arguing with him.
There is	no point (in)	
What's	the use of	

13.2 Type B: Vi + Ø and Vi + complement

Vi + Ø is common with verbs of movement and actions which we do not control:

e.g. they left, she smiled, he was sleeping, it is raining, I laughed, people came and went.

It is more usual to have a complement to these and other intransitive verbs:

One day a spaniel was playing *in the garden.*
The hedgehog had curled up *into a little ball.*
He sniffed *at the animal.*
People came and went *all the time.*

13.2.1 The pattern Vi + Ø

The pattern VERB + ADVERB PARTICLE (← Chapter 11) is very common.

He *leapt back* with a cry of pain.
He pushed it in order to *turn it over.*
He *went out* at nine and *came back* at three.

13.2.2 The pattern VERB OF MEASUREMENT + UNIT OF MEASUREMENT

It lasted (for) three hours.   He weighs sixteen stone.
It takes me all day to do it.   It costs £10.00.
It measures (*or* It is) three metres long.
My watch | gains five minutes a day.
         | loses a minute a week.
The temperature suddenly | rose | several degrees.
                         | dropped |

13.2.3 The pattern VI + ADJECTIVE

a There are a number of verbal expressions which describe *a change of state.* These verbal expressions are formed by combining a verb like *get* or *turn* with an adjective. Common examples are:
become boring/difficult/hard; *come* true; *get* angry/bored/better/worse (and other comparatives); *grow* old/rich/tired; *turn* sour/green (and other colours); *fall* ill/silent; *go* bad/mad/quiet/stale/red (and other colours); *wear* thin.

b Note also the following expressions on the same pattern:
appear happy, etc.; *feel ill,* etc.; *look* tired, etc.; *seem* silly, etc.; *sound* interesting, etc.;
break loose; *keep* quiet; *die* young; *lie* still; *make* sure; *marry* young; *remain* silent; *ring* true/false; *sit* still; *stand* still.

c VERBS OF THE SENSES + ADJECTIVE: feel, look, smell, sound, taste

Sense	Verb	Adjective
touch	It feels	rough, smooth, soft, etc.
sight	It looks	delicious, good, interesting, pretty, etc.
smell	It smells	bad, funny, good, horrible, nasty, etc.
hearing	It sounds	difficult, easy, interesting, odd, etc.
taste	It tastes	delicious, funny, horrible, salty, etc.

13.2.4 The pattern VERB OF MOVEMENT/POSITION + PRESENT PARTICIPLE

e.g. He sat reading.
This pattern is particularly useful in the combination GO + ACTIVITY, where the activity is sporting or recreational (but not a team sport).
e.g. go bowling, go dancing, go fishing, go hiking, go sailing, go skiing, go surfing, go swimming, go walking.

13.3 **Type C:** SEEM (etc.) + COMPLEMENT

The verbs *appear* and *seem* can be followed by:
an adjective
e.g. He seemed depressed.
by *to be + adjective*
e.g. He appeared to be asleep.
by *to be + present participle*
e.g. They seemed to be trying to break into the house.
by *a to-infinitive*
e.g. She seems to know everything about you.
The pattern SEEM/APPEAR + THAT-CLAUSE is rather formal and we recommend that you choose a simpler form:
e.g. It appears that he has left. ⟶ Apparently he has left.
It seems that he has left. ⟶ He seems to have left.

13.4 **Type D:** Vi + PREPOSITION + OBJECT

(For a full list of verbs with following prepositions, see Appendix VI.)

13.4.1 Types of object

The object which follows the preposition can be:
a noun   e.g. Send for *some more money*.
a pronoun e.g. I do not believe in *anything* any more.
          You just cannot rely on *them*.
a gerund e.g. He finally succeeded in *passing* his driving test.
a phrase e.g. I am looking for *somewhere to stay*.
a clause e.g. It depends on *how much you want*.
          We talked about *what you had said*.

The preposition is left out before that-clauses:
e.g. I insisted on seeing her.
but I insisted that everything should be sold.

Note: for the difference between *it depends on **you doing** it* and *it depends on **your doing** it*, see p.254 (footnote).

13.4.2 BE + ADJECTIVE + FOR SOMEONE + TO-INFINITIVE

This is a very useful pattern (see table overleaf).

The phrase *for + person* can be left out.
It is difficult to understand.
The nouns *a pity* *a shame* and *a relief* can go in the place of the adjective –
e.g. It is *a shame* (for him) to be left out.
The verb *seem* can replace *be*:

| It | might be
is
was
must be

etc. | all right
difficult
difficult
easy
hard
impossible
silly
too heavy,
etc.
unusual
useful/useless
wrong | for | John
young people
anybody

me
him
her

you

them
etc. | to do. |

e.g. *It seems* silly (for us) to waste all this food.

Note the expressions with *How + adjective* and *What (a) + noun*:
    How easy it is (for all of us) to forget other people's birthdays!
    What a relief it is to know the results of the test.

13.5 Type E: VERB + to-INFINITIVE and VERB + base-INFINITIVE

The forms and uses of these modal auxiliary type verbs are described in Chapters 7–9).

13.5.1 VERB + TO-INFINITIVE

have to/has to/had to
has not to/has not to/had not to
do not have to/does not have to/did not have to
do/does/did not need to
ought to
used to
do/does/did not dare to
be able to
also be to
be (about) to
⎫
⎬ go
⎭

13.5.2 + base-INFINITIVE

will/would
shall/should
can/could
may/might
must
need not
dare not
⎫
⎬ go
⎭

The following expressions follow the same pattern:
    had better   had rather   would rather
e.g. We *had better go* now.
    I*'d rather stay* at home.
    (= I had/would rather . . .)

13.5.3 VERB + to-INFINITIVE to express intention

In this pattern, as for example, in the sentence *I stopped to rest*, the word *to* contains the idea of *in order to* or *so as to*, i.e., the pattern expresses *intention* (what we intend or want to do/not to do).

Purpose is clearly expressed in the following cases (i.e. *to* could be replaced by *in order to*) as in the sentences

push	The spaniel pushed it with his foot (*in order*) *to turn* it over.
call	I have called to *discuss* arrangements with you.
come	He has come *to inspect* the premises.
get up	She got up *to switch* the light on.
go	I went *to see* who it was.
go on	He went on *to say* how pleased he was to be there.
run	The children ran *to greet* us.
stand up	I stood up *to get* a better view of the procession.
stop	At ten o'clock they stopped *to eat* something.

Intention is also expressed in the following cases (but note that you could not replace *to* by the purpose expression *in order to* in these cases):

agree	I agree to help you on one condition . . .
aim	The company aims to improve its performance.
(not) bother	Please don't bother to see me out.
(not) care	I do not care to discuss the matter any further.
fail	He failed to get enough points for a pass.
hesitate	If you need anything, do not hesitate to ask.
long	I am longing to see the children again.
(not) see	She could not see to read.
(not) trouble	Don't trouble to come to the door with me.

D   Patterns with transitive verbs: types F–J

13.6   Type F: Vt + OBJECT

Examples: I like *spaghetti*. Do you speak *French*?
I need *a lot of new clothes*.

13.6.1 Vt + NOUN/ PRONOUN OBJECT

It frightens me. He doesn't understand *anything*.
Take *them all*. Enjoy *yourselves*.

13.6.2 Vt + GERUND OBJECT*

We can divide verbs which are followed by a gerund into four categories:
a Verbs which must be followed by a gerund
b Verbs which are followed by a gerund or by a different pattern
c Verbs which may be followed either by a gerund or by a to-infinitive
d Verbs followed by a gerund with a passive meaning

a *Verbs which are always followed by a gerund*
The commonest are

avoid	You should avoid travelling during the rush hour.
dislike	I really dislike having to get up early.
enjoy	I enjoy staying in bed on Sunday mornings.
finish	I'll be with you as soon as I've finished marking these papers.
*forbid***	The law forbids smoking in many public places.
give up	Why have you given up going to English classes?
go on	We must not go on meeting secretly like this.
cannot help	I cannot help wondering why there are so many unemployed.
keep (on)	Do I really have to keep taking these awful tablets?
mind	Would you mind holding the door open for me?
miss	I miss going for walks in the country.
practise	Practise saying 'I hit him on the head with a hammer'.
prevent	The weather prevented us (from) going out.
put off	You cannot put off going to the doctor's any longer.
recall	I don't recall (recollect) seeing you here before.
(not) resist	I couldn't resist pointing out that she was too late.
*stop***	Please stop laughing and get on with your work.
*try***	If the car won't start, try pushing it.

*See notes below. Note that the gerund itself may be followed by an object (i.e. it behaves like a transitive verb) or a complement (i.e., like an intransitive verb) e.g. Do you mind + *opening the window?*
We mustn't go on + *meeting secretly.*

The verbs *entail, involve, mean* and *necessitate* also take the gerund

I don't want to go if it { entails / involves / means / necessitates } changing trains.

Notes

1 *They forbid* **smoking** but *They forbid* **us to smoke**.
Also, in the passive: We were forbidden *to leave* the premises.

2 Compare this with the Vi *stop* as in the sentence *He stopped to* (= *in order to*) *have a rest.*

3 Note the difference between *try to push* and *try pushing*:
  A In *try to do X*, your *objective* is to do X, if you can
  B In *try doing X*, your *objective* is something else (Y), **and** your *method* is X
For example:
  A Try to do better in future.
    Try to pass your test.
    Try to stand on your head.

B You have got hiccups: try holding your breath. (*objective*: to cure hiccups)
You cannot sleep: try counting sheep. (*objective*: to get to sleep)

b *Verbs which can be followed by a different pattern*

i) Although the following verbs are usually included in lists of verbs which take the gerund, they may also be followed by some other pattern:

VERB	+GERUND	+ OTHER PATTERN
admit	he admits stealing it	... that he stole it
advise	he advises taking it	... you to take it
consider	he considered leaving	... whether to leave/ whether he should leave
contemplate	he contemplated leaving	... whether he should leave
deny	he denied seeing her	... that he had seen her
describe	he described walking	... how he used to walk
excuse	I cannot excuse cheating	... people who cheat
face	I cannot face seeing her	... the idea/prospect of seeing her
fancy	I do not fancy going alone	... the idea of going alone
imagine	I cannot imagine living there	... what it is/must be like to live there
postpone	he postponed going	... his departure
recommend	he recommended waiting	... that we should wait
regret	I regret saying it	... that I said it
suggest	I suggest leaving everything	... that you (should) leave everything

c *Verbs which take the gerund or the to-infinitive*
We can split these into four groups

i) forget	ii) hate	iii) intend	iv) begin
remember	love	propose	commence
	like		continue
	prefer		start

i) There is a difference in meaning between the two constructions in the case of *forget and remember*
A I gave it to you, but I do not remember giving it to you.
B I did not give it to you because I did not remember to give it to you.
i.e.
A I do not remember giving it to you. = I have no memory of the event.
B I did not remember to give it to you. = I was careless, my mind was on other things

Similarly,
A I forget giving it to you.   = I have no memory of the event.
B I forgot to give it to you. = I was careless, my mind was on other things.

Note the tense of the verbs *forget* and *remember* in the two constructions. The verbs *(not) recall* and *(not) reflect* could be used in the A sentences with the same meaning (← Section 13.6.2a).

ii) **The verbs** *hate, love, like* and *prefer* must be followed by the to-infinitive when you use the forms *would hate to, would like to,* etc.* Otherwise there is very little difference in meaning between the two forms. The gerund seems to be preferred in general statements (i.e., when you are not thinking about any particular time or occasion):

e.g. I hate *having* to get up on cold mornings.
   I like *cooking*.
   I love *walking* in the rain.

(The infinitive would not, of course, be wrong in these cases.)

The infinitive seems to be preferred when you are talking about a particular time or occasion:

   I hate *to have* to tell you this, but your hair is a mess.
   I like *to cook* a special meal on Sundays when all the family is at home.
   When I am in London, I prefer *to leave* before the rush hour.

(The gerund would not, of course, be wrong in these cases.)

Examples of *would like* etc. + to-infinitive are:
   I'*d like* to go out tonight.
   Are you sure you *wouldn't prefer* to stay in?
   I *should hate* to disappoint you.

*or *should* with I and we

iii) The difference in meaning between the two constructions in the case of the verbs *intend* and *propose* is slight. It is summarized in the table:

	Gerund	*To-infinitive*
intend	refers to a present event	refers to a present or a future event
propose	makes a suggestion	states an intention

Examples:
Do you intend playing (*or* to play) with that Rubik Cube all night?
Do you intend to go on doing what you are doing at the moment?
Do you intend to go out? = Is it your intention now to go out later?
I propose starting early = I suggest that we start early.
I propose to start early = I intend to start early.

iv) *Begin, commence, continue and start*
There is very little difference between the gerund and the infinitive after these verbs.

The gerund suggests the start of a long and continuous **habit** or activity:

e.g. I *began studying* French when I was young.

This suggests that I am still a student or a lover of the French language.

> I couldn't find my case, and I *began to wonder* if I had left it on the bus.

This suggests that the act of 'wondering' did not last long.

Use the infinitive when the verbs *begin*, etc., are in the continuous form. *It is starting to rain* rather than *It is starting raining.*

d *Verbs followed by a gerund with passive meaning*

The verbs in this category are: *need*, *want* and a less common verb *(not) bear*:

e.g. The house needs painting. = The house needs to be painted.

My teeth want seeing to. = My teeth need to be seen to.

It doesn't bear thinking about. = I cannot bear to think about it.

13.6.3 Vt + (OBJECT NOUN/PRONOUN) + to-INFINITIVE

a *The pattern Vt + to-infinitive*

e.g. I want to go.

In many cases, the Vt expresses a *mental act* such as deciding, intending, hoping and preferring. The infinitive expresses the *objective* of the mental act:

> decide *to go*, intend *to pay*, hope *to see you*, prefer *to live in the country*.

You can express the negative of the mental act: *I did not decide to go* or the negative of the objective *I decided not to go*. (It is possible, but less usual, to express a negative on both sides:

e.g. I *did not decide not to go*, but I did decide to think about it):

Mental act	Objective of act	Mental act	Objective of act
+	+ / −	−	+ / −
promise	*to do* something	can't	*to do* something
		promise	
	not to do something	didn't etc.	*not to do* something

I promise to bring you a present. I cannot promise to do it **again.**

I promise not to do it again. He didn't promise to **come today**

Common verbs like *promise* are:

afford, agree, arrange, attempt, bear, bother, choose, **claim,** contrive, dare, decide, decline, deserve, determine, endeavour, expect, fail, help, hesitate, hope, learn, long, manage, mean, omit, plan, prefer, pretend, refuse, resolve, seek, swear, threaten, undertake, want to, wish.

For the verbs

hate, like, love, prefer, begin, commence, continue, start, intend, propose, forget, remember, see ◄— Section 13.6.2.

b *The pattern* Vt+OBJECT NOUN/PRONOUN+to-INFINITIVE

In the pattern *I want you to go*, the main verb (Vt *want*) expresses such mental acts as wanting, persuading, **advising,** allowing, asking, obliging and telling.

Want	Persuade	Advise	Allow	Ask	Oblige	Tell
expect	bribe	help	empower	beg	cause	command
hate**	encourage	intend	enable	beseech	compel	instruct
like**	entice	mean	entitle	challenge	direct	teach
love**	incite	warn	permit	dare	drive	
	get					
prefer**	induce		forbid*	entreat	force	
	press			implore	impel	
	tempt			invite	lead	
	urge			request	require	

*See also ◄Section 13.6.2a, Note 1.
**See also ◄Section 13.6.2, Category c.

Notes

1 The verbs *hate, like, love* and *prefer* are often used in the form *would hate, would like, would love, would prefer.*

e.g. I'd like you to tell me something.

Would you like me to pour you another drink?

2 The verbs in the *want* column (except for *expect*) are different from the other verbs in that there is no passive form:

They asked him to leave.   He was asked to leave.

but They wanted him to leave.   *no passive (use* He was asked to . . .)

3 You can express the negative either of the **main verb** or of the **infinitive** (i.e., the part which expresses the objective of the action, but, of course, the meanings would be different:

Main verb   *Objective of main verb*

They allowed him { to join the union.
                                (not) to join the union.

i.e., *He was free to* join or not to join.

They did not allow him { to join the union.
                                         (not to join the union).*

i.e., *He was not free to* join (or not to join).*

*The negative in both parts, (e.g. the statement that *He was not allowed not to join*) is possible but we would probably express the idea differently: *He had to join* or *He was not allowed to remain outside the union*, etc.

4 The construction *get someone to do something* is very useful.
It suggests a range of actions from simply *asking* someone or
persuading someone to do something for you:
My car won't start: I must *get John to have a look* at
it. (=ask)
I don't like sports cars: you will never *get me to go* in
one. (=persuade)
Can you *get Mike to deliver* the photographs right
away. (=ask)
The police soon *got him to confess* to everything. (=force)
I wonder if I could *get you to check* this draft for
me? (=ask)
(also *have someone do something*, →Section 13.7.1. note 3.;
and the constructions *have something done, get something
done*→Section 13.10.4).

Examples of the pattern Vt+ OBJ + to-INFINITIVE

Subject	Main verb	Object	(not)	to-infinitive	+obj/compl of inf.
I	did not expect	you		to arrive	so early.
They	would prefer	us	not	to say	anything.
Anna	persuaded	Joe		to wear	jeans.
The committee	urged	everyone		to consider	the plan.
The boss	warned	her secretary	not	to be	late again.
Would you	allow	me		to do	it for you?
Having a car	has enabled	the family		to go	together.
The others	have asked	me	not	to say	where I got it.
I	told	the children	not	to talk	to strangers.

Passive constructions:
You *are not obliged to say* anything.
Everyone *is invited to attend* the meeting
Passengers *are requested not to leave* their bags unattended.
I *was* always *taught to obey* orders without question.

13.7 Type G: Vt+ OBJECT + base-INFINITIVE or PRESENT PARTICIPLE

The two common and very useful verbs having this pattern are
let and *make*:

13.7.1 Vt + OBJECT + base-INFINITIVE

Let/make	Object	base-infinitive	±obj/compl of infinitive
Please let	me	come	with you.
They would not let	Joe	see	his daughter.
Can you let	us	know	when she arrives?
You cannot make	people	learn	if they don't want to.
Don't make	me	laugh	!
It certainly makes	you	think	, doesn't it?

Notes

1 *Let* is also used to form a sort of imperative (← Section 8B):
e.g. Let's go (=Let us go), Let him speak, Let me see

2 *Make* (but not *let*) has a passive construction which is followed by the to-infinitive:
e.g. They *made me tell* everything. →I *was made to tell* (them) everything.

3 The verb *have* can be used in the pattern Vt+OBJ+base-INFINITIVE with the meaning cause, ask or tell someone to do something:
e.g. 'Mike hasn't delivered the photographs yet.'
'Don't worry, I'll *have him bring* them round right away!'
However this expression is not common in British English, and we advise you to use *get him to* or *ask him to* instead (← Section 13.6.3b).

13.7.2 Vt+OBJECT+base-INFINITIVE or PRESENT PARTICIPLE

This pattern is used with verbs of the senses, especially: *feel, hear, see, smell, watch* and the phrasal verbs *listen to and look at.*
There is an important difference of meaning between the **base-infinitive** and the **present participle**. The **infinitive** describes a complete action and the **participle** describes an incomplete action (cf. ← Section 8.2.1b):

complete action : I saw him *pick up* the papers and *put* them in his bag. =
I saw what he did: he *picked up* the papers and *put* them . . .

incomplete action : I saw him *walking* along the road. =
I saw him as (when) he *was walking* along the road.

Examples

		Verb	Object	Part./inf.	±obj/compl. of part/inf.
1.	*Feel*	I can feel	something	crawling	up my back.
		He felt	the bullet	penetrate	his shoulder.
2	*Hear*	I can hear	somebody	moving	in the other room.
		You could have heard	a pin	drop.	
3	*See*	Joe saw	her	sitting	in her armchair.
		Joe saw	her	sit	down and take out a book.
4	*Smell*	Can you smell	something	burning *	in the kitchen?
5	*Watch*	We watched	him	eating.	
		Watch	me	climb	up this tree!

*In the nature of the action (to smell), you are not likely to smell something from the start to the finish of the action.

13.8 Type H: Vt+DIRECT and INDIRECT OBJECTS
(See ◄─ Section 5.4)

13.8.1 Vt+INDIRECT OBJECT+DIRECT OBJECT

e.g. Tell me something.
This is the commonest pattern.
It is used with the verbs:
bring give hand leave (bequeath) lend offer owe pass pay promise read show teach tell throw.

Examples

Vt	Indirect object	Direct object
Give	John	your share.
Hand	me	a spanner.
Offer	them	a drink.
Pass	me	the salt.
Teach	the boys	football.
Tell	the children	a story.

13.8.2 Vt+DIRECT OBJECT+INDIRECT OBJECT

Sentences using the verbs listed can also be expressed with the pattern

Vt+Direct object (DO)+Indirect object (IO):

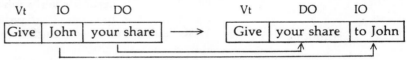

This pattern (Vt+DO+IO) is preferred when both objects are *pronouns*:

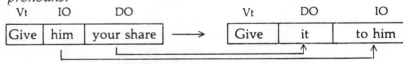

Some verbs can only be used in the pattern Vt +DO+IO:
admit announce confess declare demonstrate explain mention propose prove report say state suggest

Examples

Vt	Direct object	Indirect object
Please address	your comments	to me.
The President announced	his resignation	to the board.
Communicate	your feelings	to others.
He could not explain	the problem	to his students.
It would be better not to say	anything	to anybody.

13.8.3   Indirect object expressed with *for*

In the following, the indirect object changes to
FOR+NOUN/PRONOUN:

Buy me a drink.	Buy a drink for me.
Cook me an omelette.	Cook a meal for the whole family.
Do me a favour.	Do something for me.
Find me a place.	Find the right job for him.
Fix me a drink (slang).	Fix the drinks for our guests.
Get her a chair.	Get some stuff for everybody.
Make ⎱ him a cup of tea. Pour ⎰	Make ⎱ the tea for the family. Pour ⎰
Reserve us a table. Book us a table.	Reserve ⎱ a table for four at Book ⎰ eight o'clock.
Spare me some time.	Spare a little for the rest of us.
Save me a place.	Save a seat for me please.

Note also the expressions *ask him his name, I envy you your (looks), make me an offer, sing me a song, play me a nice tune.*

13.9   Type I REPORTING VERB (±NOUN/PRONOUN OBJECT)+ that-CLAUSE/wh-CLAUSE

Reporting verbs are verbs which describe communication between people,
e.g. tell, say, instruct, persuade, remind.
We also use the term for verbs which describe ways of thinking,
e.g. think, see, understand, hope, suppose.

13.9.1   Definitions

That-clauses are clauses which come after reporting verbs and state a piece of information:
e.g. I knew *that she had done it.*   I hope *that you will come with us.*

Wh-clauses begin with one of these words: *who, which, that, where, why, when, whether (if), how.* They may take the form WH-WORD+to-INFINITIVE:
e.g. I know *how to do* it; or the form wh-WORD+SUBJECT-VERB-COMPLEMENT:
e.g. I told him *how she did it.*

13.9.2   REPORTING VERB(±NOUN/PRONOUN OBJECT)+ that-CLAUSE

There are three types of reporting verb, depending on whether or not they require a noun/pronoun object:

a ALWAYS+OBJECT   I told *him* that she had done it.
b ALWAYS−OBJECT   I knew that she had done it.
c ±OBJECT   I promised (him) that I would do it.
I admitted (to him) that I had done it.

a Always +	b Always −		c ± Object	
advise	accept	guarantee	acknow-	propose
assure	answer	hope	ledge	prove
convince	assume	imply	admit	remark
inform	believe	know	announce	report
notify	claim	notice	complain	say
persuade	deny	observe	confess	show*
remind	discover	see	declare	signal

tell	doubt	(=understand)	demonstrate	state
	expect	specify	explain	suggest
	feel	suppose	indicate	teach*
	find	think	mention	warn*
	forget	understand	point out	
			promise*	

*If the object is included, the verbs *show, promise, teach* and *warn* are followed by the simple object:

e.g. show *me* that..., promise *me* that..., teach *the children* that..., warn *John* that...

All the others in list c must be followed (if the object is included) by TO+NOUN/PRONOUN:

e.g. He admitted *to us* that he had done wrong.

   I suggested *to her* that she should ask for a rise.

(See Chapter 14 for the relationship between the reporting verb and the form of the verb in the that-clause).

Examples

		Reporting verb	±Object	That-clause
a +	1	Simon told	everybody	that he was getting married.
	2	Can you convince	Anna	that she will do well in her test?
	3	I do not need to remind	you	that you have a job to do.
b −	4	I expect	—	that you are feeling tired by now.
	5	Don't forget	—	that have an appointment at 3.
	6	Have you noticed	—	that there aren't any people here?
c ±	7	He promised	(his teacher)	that he would rewrite his essay.
	8	The president warned	(the people)	that things might get worse.
	9	Mother suggested	(to the children)	that they should go for a walk.
	10	Did I mention	(to you)	that I have been promoted?

Note on the omission of **that**

In this pattern (REPORTING VERB+that-CLAUSE), the conjunction **that** is often left out both in speaking and in writing:

e.g. Simon told everybody he was getting married.

   I expect you are feeling tired by now.

You should keep it in in the following cases:

1 when there is a TO+NOUN/PRONOUN OBJECT, e.g., **sentences 9 and 10.**

   Mother suggested *to her children* that they...

   Did I mention *to you* that...

2 when the statement is a rather formal one, e.g., sentence 8:

   The President *warned the people* that...

3 when the reporting verb is in the passive (←Section 8.8).

   e.g. *It was announced* that all flights were running late.

   I have been told that you are an expert on computers.

   It is widely believed that the economy is slowly **improving.**

4 in certain frequently used expressions such as *the fact that,*
seeing that,
> e.g. We decided to leave *in spite of the fact that* nothing had
> been accomplished.
> *Seeing that* it was so late, they agreed to break until the
> next day.
> I'll help you *on condition that* you do not tell anyone.

5 when there is a second **that-clause** following the same reporting
verb:
> e.g. He said he was looking into the matter, *and that* he
> would announce his decision in due course.

13.9.3 REPORTING
VERB±NOUN/PRONOUN
OBJECT +wh-CLAUSE

a *Wh-clauses* of the 'how to do it' type
The reporting verbs are in the same three categories as in Section
13.9.2:

	Reporting verb	Object	wh-word + to-infinitive (±obj/com)
i)	advise inform remind show tell teach forget know see	him	how to do it where to put it
ii)	specify suggest think talk wonder about understand	–	who to talk to when to start
iii)	demonstrate explain indicate mention point out prove report	(to him)	whether to go (or not) how long to wait how many to buy

b *Wh-clauses* of the 'how she did it' type
All the verbs in Section 13.9.2a, together with the category **c**
verbs *confess, say, state* and *suggest,* can also be followed by a
wh-clause as in the sentence
He did not know what the strange creature was.

	Reporting verb	wh-clause
i)	I told him He asked me	how she did it. what was causing the problem. what the students actually needed. where Anna had gone to.
ii)	I did not know	who looked after the accounts. who he should talk to.
iii)	Nobody mentioned (to me)	when the meeting was due to start. how long the meeting would last.

c *Note on* **whether/if**

1 All the **wh-clauses** in Section 13.9.3b are really *reported
(indirect) questions* (→ Section 14.6):

Direct question: When is the meeting due to start?

Indirect question: I did not know *when the meeting was due to
start.*

If the original (direct) question is a simple *yes/no* question, such
as *Has John called?*, we use **whether** or **if** to introduce the
reported (indirect) question:

Direct question: Has John called?

Indirect question: I did not know { *whether* } *John had*
                                      {   *if*   } *called.*

2 **Whether/if clauses** usually come after a negative or
  interrogative verb:

                                                    from
I do not know *whether she will come.*   Will she come?
He could not remember *whether he had*   Did he file it?
filed it.
I do not recall *whether I told you . . .* Did I tell you?
She did not say *whether she would be*   Will she be back
back tonight.   tonight?
Do you know *whether she will come?*
Could he remember *whether he had filed it?*
Do you recall *whether I told you?*
Did she say *whether she would be back?*

3 There is no important difference between **whether** and **if**. We
  often add the words *or not* at the end of the clause, although,
  strictly speaking the expression of an alternative, *X or not*, is
  already included in the word **whether**:

e.g. I don't recall {   *if*   } I mentioned it or not, but . . .
                      { *whether* }

      Did she say { *whether* } she would be back tonight or not?
                   {   *if*   }

4 Notice the difference between the sentences:
  A I did not know *that* John had called.
  B I did not know *whether* John had called.
  A is a *fact* = John called – someone told me later.
  B is a *question* = Did John call? – the question is open.

13.10 Type J   Vt + NOUN/PRONOUN OBJECT + ADVERBIAL/ADJECTIVE/NOUN/
                    PAST PARTICIPLE

Adverbial: Put the cheese/it   in the cupboard.
Adjective: Paint the door/it   red.
Noun: Call my brother/him   Joe.
Past part: I want the work/it   done.

13.10.1   The pattern
Vt + OBJECT + ADVERBIAL

The adverbial may be:

an adverb	Put them *away.*
a prepositional phrase	Put them *in the cupboard.*
a clause	Put them *where the children cannot get them.*

The adverbial may be an adverbial of

manner	Eat it *slowly.*
place	Eat it *in the kitchen.*
time	Eat it *later.*

Examples

		Adverb	*Prep. phrase*	*Clause*
Tell me about it	M	honestly	in your own words	exactly as it happened
Put the papers	P	here	on the desk	wherever you can find space
Talk to me	T	later	after the meeting	when you get a moment

Note: variations in the order of the pattern, i.e., when the adverbial comes between the Vt and the object, are dealt with in ← Chapter 11 (Phrasal verbs) and Chapter 12 (Adverbials).

13.10.2   The pattern Vt +
OBJECT − ADJECTIVE

a The pattern is often used to describe an action (e.g., *paint*) and its result (e.g. *red*). For example, the sentence

I have decided *to grow* my hair *long.*   could be rephrased

I have decided *to grow* my hair *until it is long.*

Examples

Action	*Object*	*Result*
Paint	the door	red (and other colours).
Dye	your hair	green (and other colours).
Cut	your hair	short.
Get	your clothes	clean/dirty/wet/etc.
Get	him	interested/excited. (and other past part. adjectives)
Grow	your nails	long.
Hold	the door	open.
Keep	the shop	open/shut.
Leave	yourself	short. (i.e. of money).
Make	someone	happy/angry/sad/etc.
Make	yourself	ill/sick.

Note also the expressions *bore someone stiff*, **set someone free**, *prove someone right/wrong.*

b The pattern is also used with verbs like *consider* and verbs like *like*:

e.g. Some consider   her   = consider *that she is*
                   beautiful.   beautiful

Do you	think	it wrong?	= think *that it is* wrong
I	find	him boring.	= find (think) *that he is* boring
She	prefers	her hair long.	= prefers her hair *when it is* long
I	like	my steak rare.	= like it *to be cooked so that it is* rare
He	wants	the door open.	= wants it *to be left* open

c *The expression* **make** *something* **clear/plain** *etc. and* **find** *something* **interesting**/*etc.*

These expressions can be followed by a **that-clause** or **wh-clause**; 'find interesting' (etc.) can also be followed by a **to-infinitive**.

Notice that there is an *it* between verb and adjective:

e.g. make it clear that ..., find it interesting that ...:

i) *My objection*: the scheme is too expensive

I want to make	*my objection*	clear.
I want to make	*it*	clear.
I want to make	*it*	clear *that I think the scheme is too expensive.*

ii) *Fact*: nobody bothered to check the figures

I find	*this fact*	interesting.
I find	*it*	interesting.
I find	*it*	interesting *that nobody bothered to check the figures.*

iii) *My difficulty*: getting up early

I find	*something*	difficult.
I find	*it*	difficult.
I find	*it*	*difficult to get up early.*

Other examples
He found it hard to explain why he was there.
She made it obvious that she did not want anything more to do with him.
I find it remarkable that so many people have joined the new party.
I should like to make it clear to you why I acted as I did.

13.10.3 The pattern
Vt + OBJECT + NOUN

This pattern occurs with the verbs
appoint, call, christen, consider, declare, elect, make, name, pronounce.

Examples
a They decided to call/christen/name their son Christopher.
b He called her a liar. (Note also *to call someone names* = to insult them)

c Malcolm was appointed honorary president of the association. Similarly:

declare someone the winner; elect someone President; pronounce someone the winner; make someone the treasurer of the club

With verbs to do with appointing, e.g. elect, declare, pronounce, it is possible to add *to be*:
e.g. declare someone to be the winner

d Consider me your friend. (*or* Consider me to be your friend.) The verb *consider* can also be followed by *as* without any important change of meaning:
e.g. Consider me as your friend.
(Other verbs which have this pattern,
Vt + OBJECT + AS + COMPLEMENT, include:

accept as, class as, define as, describe as, recognize as, regard as, treat as)

13.10.4 The pattern
Vt + OBJECT + PAST
PARTICIPLE

a In the following sentences, the past participles (broken, played, stolen, scored) can be made into clauses:
e.g. I found my radio *broken*. = that my radio was broken
Have you ever heard Bach *played* on a guitar? = when it is played on a guitar
He reported his car *stolen*. = that his car had been stolen
I saw the last goal *scored* by Pele. = which was scored by Pele.
This use of the pattern is not very common.

b The pattern is most useful when it is used with the verbs *get* and *have* to express the idea that someone does something for you (Compare *get someone to do something*, 13.6.3d):

I must	*get*	someone	*to repair my car.*	
	get	–	*my car repaired*	by someone.
I'll	*have*	someone	*check it.*	
	have	–	*it checked.*	(by someone)

Examples

	Have/get		Object	Past participle	
i)	Where do you		your car	serviced	nowadays?
ii)	You should	have	your teeth	checked	every six months.
iii)	You ought to		your eyes	tested	!
iv)	I must	get	the TV	seen to:	it isn't working properly.

Notes on **have** *or* **get**?

1 In many cases, the difference between **have** and **get** is very slight. The essential difference is that **have** suggests routine, or that you do not need to make any special effort or arrangements. For this reason, you would say, for example:

The children *have* their teeth checked every six months. (i.e., it is a routine, and the children do not make the arrangements)

On the other hand, **get** suggests that you have to make an effort, that is, nothing will happen unless you do something about it.* For this reason, you would say, for example:

How on earth did you manage to *get* your car repaired so cheaply?

*The same idea can be seen in the expressions *to get it to go* and *to get it going*: e.g. My car won't start: I can't *get it to go*.
   He soon managed *to get it going* again.

2 You would not say **get** in the following sentences, because the things happened without any intention or effort on my part:

I have had my licence endorsed. (i.e., the police have recorded on my driving licence that I did something wrong)
I have had my car stolen.

It would not make sense to use **get**, because **get** suggests success (e.g. I got my car repaired cheaply), but the endorsed licence and the stolen car are misfortunes that I have suffered.

3 **Get** is also required in expressions where you yourself are going to do the work:

I must *get this ironing done* before my wife comes home!
I'm sorry about the delay with the report, sir. I'll *get it done* as soon as possible.
The children made this mess, so see that they *get it cleaned up* right away.

The difference between, for example, *I'll do it* and *I'll get it done*, when the speaker is in any case going to do the work himself, is in the *effort* which is suggested by the word **get**, and the idea of *completing the job*.

4 A similar idea to Section 2.10.3b is expressed with **want** as in the sentence:

I want my kitchen redecorated = I want to get/have my kitchen redecorated.

14 Contents

14 Sentence construction

The Spaniel and the Hedgehog
(Part 2)

Next, the spaniel threw a heavy sack over the hedgehog, but again he received a very nasty jab as the prickly spines poked through the material.

He then put a piece of wood under the hedgehog and managed to turn it over, but as soon as he approached, the creature rolled over, and once more the poor dog yelped with pain.

This went on for several hours, but in the end the spaniel, defeated and very very sore, looked down at the funny creature and muttered to himself:

'I'd like to get my hands on the stupid idiot who brought such a dangerous creature into the garden. Some people have no sense of responsibility!'

Moral: If at first you do not succeed, try, try, try again. Then blame someone.

A Conjunctions

14.1 Definition of conjunctions

Conjunctions are words which we use to join statements together.* they show the *relationship* between the facts contained in the statements:

	Fact 1		Fact 2	Statements joined
A1	I am poor	+	I am unhappy	I am poor *and* I am unhappy.
A2	It is raining	+	I am happy	It is raining *but* I am happy.
B1	I am poor	+	I am unhappy	*Because* I am poor, I am unhappy.
B2	It is raining	+	I am happy	*Although* it is raining, I am happy.

*They are also used to link smaller sentence elements, e.g. **and** – *The house and gardens are open to the public;* **either** . . . **or** *Either you or I will have to go.*

14.2 And, but, so, (n)either . . . (n)or, or

The conjunctions used in sentence **A1** and **A2** simply join the two statements; we have to work out the relationship (the connection) between the facts from the meaning. For example, the connection between the fact *I am poor* and the fact *I am unhappy* is probably that my unhappiness is caused by my poverty, i.e., sentence **A1** means the same as sentence **B1**, i.e. *Because I am poor, I am unhappy*. Similarly, the connection between the facts in **A2** – *It is raining* and *I am happy* – must be that I am happy and I do not mind if it is raining, i.e., **A2** means the same as **B2**, *Although it is raining, I am happy*.

The most useful and the commonest spoken forms are the patterns

A AND B	A BUT B
He drove too fast and had an accident.*	= He had an accident *because* . . .
Eat that and you'll be ill!	= You'll be ill *if* . . .
He gave her everything, and she left him!	= She left him *even though* . . .
He can speak Thai, and write it.	= *Not only* can he speak Thai, but . . .
He looked down at the creature and muttered.	= Action 1 followed by Action 2
I drink but I don't smoke.	= Action 1 contrasted with Action 2
It is late but I'm not tired.	= *although* it is late . . .

*Note that the subject pronoun is not repeated when the two statements are joined with and: He then put a piece of wood underneath and (~~he~~) managed to turn it over.

The conjunction **so** is similar in meaning to **and** in the sense of *because*:
e.g. It was late *so* I went to bed.
    There isn't much time, *so* we had better hurry.

The conjunction **(n)either** is used with **(n)or** to express alternatives or choices:
e.g. We can either stay in or go to the pictures.
    I neither smoke nor drink.

The word **either** can also express a kind of conditional:
    Either you go or I'll report you. = If you don't go I will report you.

Similarly with **or**:
    Sit still or I'll hit you! = If you don't sit still, I will hit you.

14.3   Other conjunctions

The conjunctions used in sentences **B1** and **B2** (**because, although**, sections 14.1 and 2) express the relationship or connection between the facts *more precisely*. For example, **because** expresses the idea *the reason for A is B* (*I am unhappy* [A], *because I am poor* [B]).

Here is a list of the commonest conjunctions.* The ones in bold type are the ones most often used in speaking.

*In the examples, we have put the clauses introduced by the conjunctions in the order in which they would usually appear. Where it is not possible to reverse the order, we have marked the conjunction with a (NR) = not reversible.

after — e.g. I felt much better after I had had a bath.
The word **after** can also be used as a preposition
e.g. I felt much better after having (had) a bath.

although (or **though**) — e.g. Although the weather was bad, everyone seemed to have a good time.
The commoner form in speaking is **even though**, which emphasizes the contrast: 'I went even though I didn't really feel like it.'
WARNING: the expressions *despite* and *in spite of*, which mean the same as **although**, are in fact prepositions only:
e.g. Despite/In spite of the weather, everyone...
To make them into conjunctions, add *the fact that*
(Despite/In spite of *the fact that* it was raining...)

as (= when) — e.g. He received a nasty jab as the prickly spines poked through the material.
To emphasize that two things happened at the same time, use **just as**: *He arrived just as I was about to leave the house.*

as (= because) — As you know John better than I do, could you ask him for me?

as far as(NR) (literal sense) — This is as far as I go.

as far as — In a different sense, **as far as** is used in expressions like *As far as I can see,... As far as I know...*, and *As far as I am concerned,...*

as long as(NR) (literal sense) — You can stay here as long as you like.

as long as (= provided that) — You can stay here as long as you don't make a noise.

as soon as — As soon as he approached, the creature rolled over...

as if (or **as though**)(NR) — He looked as if he had seen a ghost.

assuming (that) — They should be here by six, assuming everything goes well.

because — e.g. I study English because I have to.
Sentences with **because** can be ambiguous (i.e. have two meanings): *I didn't reply because I was angry* means either *I was angry so I did not reply* or *The reason I replied was not because I was angry but because...* + some other reason. In speaking, **because** is often replaced by such constructions as:
    I was tired. *That's why* I didn't go.
Or, simply:
    I was tired, *so* I didn't go.

before	e.g. Before I answer your question, please tell me why you want to know.
considering (that)	e.g. You have learned English very quickly, considering (that) you only started six months ago.
if	a e.g. If I were you, I'd wait. (← Section 10.9 for conditionals) b e.g. I wonder if you could help me. (→ Section 14.7)
in case	e.g. Take your key in case I am out when you get back.
now (that)	e.g. What are you going to do now (that) you have left school?
once (= after or as soon as)	You should be all right once you have had a bit more practice.
providing/provided (that) (= if)	e.g. You can stay here providing (that) you do not make a noise. (Compare *as long as*). A similar conjunction is *on condition that*.
seeing (that)	e.g. Seeing that you have all worked so hard today, you needn't start work until ten tomorrow. A similar idea is expressed by **because** or by the expression *in view of the fact that*.
since (= time)	e.g. I haven't seen either of them since they got married.
since (= because)	e.g. Since you will not tell me, I must find out for myself.
so that (= in order that, i.e., purpose)	e.g. Get an early night so that you will be fresh in the morning.
so + adj. (that) (= result)	e.g. The children were *so excited (that)* they could hardly sit still.
so + adv. (that)	e.g. He came in so *quietly (that)* nobody noticed him.
such +adj.+noun+that	e.g. America is $\begin{vmatrix} \text{so } big \text{ that} \\ \text{such a big country that} \end{vmatrix}$ it has several time zones.
such that (= of such a kind that)	e.g. His reaction was such that everyone assumed he was guilty. The conjunction *such that* is like *so + adjective that*, but is normally used only as a written form.
supposing (that)	e.g. FIRST MAN: 'I am very short of money. SECOND MAN: 'Well, supposing I lend you £20.00, and you . . .' i.e. 'Would it solve your problem if I lent you £20.00?'
that⁽ᴺᴿ⁾	e.g. I know that you do not believe me. (→ Section 14.4) **That** is also used in relative clauses: e.g. It's a nice car, but it isn't the car (that) I ordered. (→ Section 14.9)
unless	*Unless* and *if . . . not* are similar but not identical. There are **three** possibilities: a *Unless = if . . . not* In many cases you can use *unless* or *if . . . not* with only a

slight change of meaning or emphasis.
A I won't do it *if you don't want me to.*
B I won't do it *unless you want me to.*
Sentence B emphasizes that my action (*do it* must come from
your action (*want me to*).

b *if . . . not ≠ unless*
There are cases when you can use only *if . . . not*
A I am busy: if I were not busy, I would come with you.
B I was busy: if I had not been busy, I would have come
with you.
i.e. *unless* cannot be used instead of *if . . . not* with Type II
and III conditionals (← Section 10.9). Compare:
I may or I may not be busy later.

I'll see you later, $\begin{cases} \text{unless I am busy.} \\ \text{if I am not busy.} \end{cases}$

c I'll be | glad
| happy
I'll be | pleased | if they do not come.
| relieved
It will be better|
In this case, my state (*being glad*, etc.) is actually *caused* or
produced by something not happening (*their not coming*).

d *unless ≠ if . . . not*
There is a common use of *unless* as a spoken form, where
someone makes a suggestion or similar statement, but then
thinks of an objection or an alternative:
e.g. Let's go for a meal – unless you would rather stay in.
One of the children must have done it – unless it was the
dog.

General advice: except for **c**, which you should learn to recognize
but not use, we advise you to use *unless* only in the pattern
UNLESS A +, B ±
e.g. Unless you promise to behave [A]+, I will not let you go
[B]−.
Unless their demands are met [A]+, the men will go on
strike [B]+.
(The *unless* clauses can, of course, come second.)

until (or **till**)   e.g. I cannot afford it now. You will have to wait until I get
paid.

when   e.g. Give her my regards when you see her.

whenever (= every time)   e.g. I always seem to bump into someone I know whenever I go
to London.

where   e.g. He hid the book where nobody would think of looking.

whether ⊗   e.g. I don't know whether John has been in. (See ← 13.9.3c and→
14.7)

wherever/everywhere   e.g. They seem to cause trouble wherever/everywhere they go.

while   e.g. Please do not interrupt me while I am working.
While means *during the time that*. The word *during* is a preposition: ...*while I am at work* but *during working hours; while the programme is on* but *during the programme*. (see, also ◄—Section 6.4.2).

Note on the tense used in time clauses
In the following sentences, *the act or event* in the **time clauses** refers to a future time, but *the tense of the verb* is the present or present perfect (e.g., *am* not *will be; have finished* not *will have finished*). The tense of the verb in the **main clause** varies, but is often a future form.

Main clause	Conj.	Time clause
I shall meet you	when	I am next in London.
Shall we have something to eat	before	we got out?
You can go	as soon as	you finish/have finished.
Please wait here	until	you are called.
I cannot mark your work	until	you have written it out neatly.
I'll stay here	as long as	you need me.

The same *sequence of tenses* applies to conditional clauses beginning with **if, unless** and **in case**:

The men will go on strike	if	their demands are not met.
The men will go on strike	unless	their demands are met.
You should take your umbrella	in case	it rains.

(◄—Section 10.9)

B   *Sequence of tenses* in reported (indirect) speech and questions

For a list of *reporting verbs* and their patterns, see ◄— 13.9.)

Reported speech

14.4   Tense and other changes

When someone's words* are reported (*He says that*..., *He told us that*..., *It is said that*..., *Everyone assumed/knew/thought/ etc. that*...), certain changes are necessary:

*When reporting people's commands/instructions, we use the to-infinitive: 'Go away!' He told us to go away; 'Don't stare!' He told us not to stare. 'Let's' = 'Shall we...?': 'Let's go!' = 'Shall we go?' He suggested that we should go.

Actual words
CINDY: 'I have finished my work. I will make the tea.'

Reported words   ↓   ↓   ↓

A Cindy *says* (that) she *has finished* her work, and that she *will make* the tea.
B Cindy *said* (that) she *had finished* her work, and that she *would make* the tea.

The logical changes are that pronouns change (I→she, my→her) and that the inverted commas ('. . .') disappear (*Cindy*: 'I have finished . . .' →Cindy says that she has finished . . .)

The other important change is in the tense of the verbs in the reported speech. In sentence A, the reporting verb is in the present tense, so there is no change. In sentence B, the reporting verb is in the past tense, which causes the verbs in the reported speech to change to the past as well (= the so-called *sequence of tenses*). The sequence of tenses is as follows:

Reporting verb   *Reported verbs*

A ⎧ says ⎫
  ⎨ is saying ⎬ that   *has* finished   *will* make
  ⎩ has said ⎪
    will say ⎭

B ⎧ said ⎫
  ⎨ was saying ⎬ that *had* finished   *would* make
  ⎩ had said ⎪
    would say ⎭

In Type B, i.e., when the reporting verb is in one of the past tenses, the usual changes to reported verbs are:

am/is/are	⟶	was/were
do/does	⟶	did
can	⟶	could
will	⟶	would
has/have	⟶	had
may	⟶	might

Note on **shall**
I/we shall becomes *he/she/they will* (A) or *would* (B).
'*Shall I/we?*' as a simple question ('*Shall I need an umbrella?*') becomes *will* (A) or *would* (B):
A 'He wants to know if he will need an umbrella.'
B He wanted to know if he would need an umbrella.
'*Shall I/we?*' as an offer or as the equivalent of '*Ought I/we?*' becomes **should** in both A and B:
'Shall I carry that for you?' (offer)
'Shall I take an umbrella?' (= Ought I to take an umbrella?')
A He wants ⎫ to know if he should ⎧ carry it for her.
B He wanted ⎭   ⎩ take an umbrella.

Other examples of sequence of tenses (Type B = reporting verb in past tense)

Actual words	*Reporting verb*	*Reported words*
'I'm going out.'	He said	he was going out.
'I don't understand.'	She told us	he did not understand.
'She cannot do it.'	I realized (that)*	she could not do it.
'We'll (will) do it.'	They explained	they would do it.
'We'll (shall) see you later.'	They hoped	they would see us later.

*For the omission of **that**, see ◀ Section 13.9).

'I've had enough.'	He announced		he had had enough.
'You may be able to go.'	She thought	(that)*	we might be able to go.
'He works very hard.'	We all believed		he worked very hard.
'My car's been stolen.'	He reported		his car had been stolen.

14.5   Variations in the *sequence of tenses*

This sequence of tenses is usual when you are reporting someone's words. There are some exceptions, i.e., cases where the tense of the verb in the reported part of the sentence does not change even though the reporting verb is in the past. Most of these exceptions are quite logical.

14.5.1   The truth of the statement still holds

First example

I was told }
Somebody told me } that agencies | are / were | very expensive.

The actual words were 'Agencies are very expensive'. If I simply report the words without any *attitude* to them I would say 'Somebody told me that agencies were expensive'. If it is still true that agencies are expensive, or it is my attitude that they are expensive, I would say 'Somebody told me that agencies are expensive.'

Second example

Our teacher told us that the earth goes round the sun. The actual words were 'The earth goes round the sun.' In this case there is no doubt that this is a true statement, which we can only report as in the example, i.e., leaving the verb *goes* in the present tense. On the other hand, if the teacher told you about the existence of cannibals in Borneo, saying 'There are still cannibals in Borneo', you might feel less certain about the truth of the statement:

Our teacher told us that there | are (I believe her) / were (This is what she said) | cannibals in Borneo.

Third example

Cindy said that she | will / would | make the tea.

The actual words were 'I'll make the tea.' If we are reporting an immediate future event, we can leave the verb (will) in the present:

I'll make the tea — CINDY   JOE   ANNA

She said she'll make the tea — What did she say? — CINDY   JOE   ANNA

...and then she said that she would make the tea...

LATER, ANNA TELLS HER BOYFRIEND ABOUT WHAT HAPPENED...

Amazing!

i.e. Anna does not hear what Cindy has just said, so Joe repeats it. He could also have followed the usual sequence *'She said she would make the tea'*.

14.5.2 *Must→had to* or *must→must?*

If the obligation (*must*) still applies when you report it, it is not necessary to change *must* to *had to*. If the obligation no longer applies, we advise you to change *must* to *had to*:

TEACHER: 'For homework I want you to learn the equation

$$x = \frac{-b \pm \sqrt{b^2 - 4ac}}{2a}.'$$

Students A and B talk after the lesson:
A: 'What have we got to do for homework tonight?'
B: 'Mr Jones *said* that we *must* (or *have got to*) learn an equation.

Compare this with a father telling his children about his experiences when he was a soldier:
'...and then our Commanding Officer came up and *told* us that we *had to* stay where we were until daybreak...'

14.5.3 *Past→past perfect* (e.g. took→had taken) or *past→past* (took→took)?

In most cases the past tense (in the reported words) does not change, especially when you are reporting a simple narrative (story), i.e.:
A happened, then B happened, then C happened, ...

Actual words:
'I took my girlfriend home to meet my parents, and they all got on well together...'

Reported words:
He told me⎫ (that) he *took* his girlfriend home to meet his
He said   ⎭   parents, and (that) they all *got* on well together...
(Of course the present perfect *has done* changes to the past perfect *had done* in the usual way:
e.g. 'I have not finished.'→He complained that he *had not* finished).

14.5.4 Other verb forms

When you report statements containing *should, ought to* and *might*, you do not change them. For example:

Actual words: 'You look ill: you should see a doctor.'
Reported words: He thought I looked ill, and said I should see a doctor.
Actual words: 'It might rain.'
Reported words: He said that he thought it might rain.

Only use the past forms *should have (done), ought to have (done)* and *might have (done)* when you want to refer to something which did not in fact happen:

Actual words: 'You ought to fit new brakes.'
Later (see picture on left.)

i.e., you report his advice:
'He said I *ought to have fitted* new brakes, but I took no notice of him.'

The expression *used to* (← Section 8.3.3) does not change:
Actual words: 'I *used to play* a lot of sport when I was young.'
Reported words: My father told us that he *used to play* a lot of sport when he was young.

General notes

1 After certain verbs of suggesting and ordering, the present tense (*is*) changes to *should (be)* regardless of the tense of the reporting verb:
Actual words: 'Please see that everyone *is* informed.'

Reported words: He suggests/asks / suggested/asked that everyone *should be* informed.*

Other verbs like *suggest* and *ask* are: *command, demand, insist, order, propose, recommend.*

*The form *He suggests that everyone be informed* is now regarded as old-fashioned, except in the common question 'What do you suggest we (should) do?'

2 Other changes that may be needed in the reported part of the sentence are quite logical:
this → that; today → that day; tomorrow → the following day (or the next day); yesterday → the day before (or the previous day); yet → by then; ago → before
Depending on the meaning, you might also need to change other words in the same way that you change *this* to *that* (← Section 2.5.1). For example, *come* to *go*, *here* to *there*, *bring* to *take*, etc.

3 A *sequence of tenses* also occurs after the expressions *I wish*, *I'd rather* (-'d = had or would) and *It is (about/high) time*:

Actual words	*Reported words*
'Speak to him.'	I wish you *would speak* to him.
'What a pity you *did not speak* to him.'	I wish you *had spoken* to him.
'What a pity I *am not* with you.'	I wish I *were* with you.*
'I *do not know.*'	I wish I *knew.*
'I *did not know.*'	I wish I *had known.*
'I *cannot* swim.'	I wish I *could* swim.
'Go!'	It is (high/about) time you *went.*
'Don't *do* it.'	I'd ⎰ you *did not do* it.
'Stay here!'	I would ⎱ rather ⎰ you *stayed* here.
'You *went* out.'	I had ⎱ you *had not gone* out.

*See page 206 footnote.

Reported (indirect) questions

14.6 Question word = to-infinitive phrase

When someone is asking questions about himself/herself/themselves, and they are in effect asking for advice (= What should I do?), we can use a to-infinitive phrase to report their questions:

	Actual words			*Reported words*
Joe's questions	'How do I do it?' 'Where do I go?' 'When do I start?' 'How long should I stay?' 'Which do I choose?' 'What do I take?' 'Who do I report to?'	Joe {	wants to know asked me	how to do it. where to go. when to start. how long to stay. which to choose. what to take. who to report to.

Instead of the to-infinitive phrase, you could also use the form: Joe wants to know/asked me how he *should do* it, etc.

14.7 wh-clauses

In all other cases, we report questions with a **wh-clause**, and make the same changes of pronouns, tense, etc., as for reported speech. In addition the question pattern and the question mark disappear:

Actual question		*Reported question*
'Where *is he*?'	⟶	Tell me where *he is.*
'What *does she want*?'	⟶	Tell me what *she wants.*
'How *can they* be sure?'	⟶	Tell me how *they can* be sure.
'Who *did you see*?'	⟶	Tell me who *you saw.*
'What *have I done* wrong?'	⟶	Tell me what *I have done* wrong.

Other examples

Actual question	*Reporting verb present*	*Reporting verb past*
Joe:	Joe *wants* to know	Joe *wanted* to know
'How do they do it?'	how they *do* it.	how they *did* it.
'Where has she been?'	where she *has been.*	where she *had been.*
'Why are you staring?'	why they *are* staring	why they *were* staring.
'When will they pay me?'	when they *will pay* him.	when they *would pay* him.
'Who can you trust?'	whom you *can* trust.	whom you *could* trust.
'Who trusts you?'	who *trusts* you.	who *trusted* you.
'What did he say?'	what he *said.*	what he *said/had said.*
'What happened?'	what *happened.*	what *happened*/had *happened.*
'Can you help me?'	whether I can help him.	if I could help him.
'Do you know her?'	if I know her.	whether I knew her.
'Did it work?'	whether it worked.	if it worked/had worked.
'Have they come back?'	if they have come back.	whether they had come back.

When there is no question word (where, what, etc.), i.e., when the question is a *yes/no* question, use the conjunctions **whether** or **if** (◄ 13.9.3c):

Note:
To report *negative questions*, such as *'Aren't you afraid?'* or *'Don't you like meat?'*, i.e., questions which express surprise (◄—Section 7.6.2), we usually use a reporting expression like *I am surprised, I thought, he could not believe.*

e.g. 'Aren't you afraid?'   I am surprised that you are not afraid.

'Don't you like meat?'   I thought you liked meat.*

*Note the difference between
A 'I thought you didn't like meat' – 'You told me you didn't like meat . . .'
B 'I didn't think you like meat' – 'I had a wrong idea about you . . .'
i.e., sentence B is normal, sentence A is 'coloured'.

C   Relative clauses (defining and non-defining adjectival clauses)

14.8 Definition of relative clauses

Relative clauses are like adjectives (◄—Chapter 4) in that they give information about a noun or pronoun. They have the pattern:

NOUN/PRONOUN DESCRIBED	+	RELATIVE PRONOUN	i.e.	who(m) which whose that	or Ø	+ (Subj.) + VERB + compl.

Examples	Noun/pronoun described	Relative pronoun	(Subj.) + verb + compl.
a Is this	the dress	which/that/Ø	you bought in Paris?
b Tell me about	the old man	who(m)/that/Ø	you met in the park.
c Do you know	the woman	who/that	used to work here?
d What happened to	the big house	which/that	stood on the corner.
e I feel sorry for	the girl	whose	car you damaged.
f Let us consider	gold	, which	is a precious metal.

The clauses in sentences **a–e** actually identify or define the preceding noun/pronoun: these are called **defining** relative clauses.

Sentence **f** gives an example of a relative clause which does not define or identify the preceding noun (*gold*), but simply adds a piece of information. This kind of relative clause is called a *non-defining* relative clause.

The omission of the relative pronoun is dealt with in Section 5.8.

14.9 Defining relative clauses

14.9.1 Ways of identifying

We can use adjectival forms to help us to *identify* or to *define* which particular person or thing we are talking about.

e.g. *A dress* – this is not enough. We need to identify the dress.

Question:	Which dress?	
Answer:	The *blue* one.	*adjective*
or	The one *with the pretty ribbons.*	*adjectival phrase*
or	The one *which I bought in Paris.*	*defining relative*

A man – we need more information.

Question:	Which man?	
Answer:	An old man – this is still not enough to identify him	
Question:	Which old man?	
Answer:	The old man *sitting in the corner.*	*adjectival phrase*
or	The old man *who(m) you met in the park.*	*defining relative*

14.9.2 The form of defining relatives

We can analyse the form of defining relatives as follows:

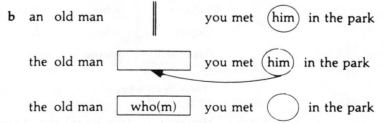

a a dress ‖ I bought it in Paris

the dress [＿＿＿] I bought (it) in Paris

the dress [which] I bought ( ) in Paris

= . . . the dress which I bought in Paris.

b an old man ‖ you met (him) in the park

the old man [＿＿＿] you met (him) in the park

the old man [who(m)] you met ( ) in the park

= . . . the old man who(m) you met in the park.

In sentences **a** and **b**, the relative pronoun replaces an object pronoun, i.e., I bought *it* ⟶ *which* I bought
I saw *him* ⟶ *who(m)* I saw

In sentences **c** and **d**, the relative pronoun replaces a subject pronoun, i.e., *she* used to work here → *who* used to work here
it stood . . . → *which* stood . . .

Subject →	Subject pronoun →	Relative pronoun
The woman . . . →	She . . . →	who . . .
The house . . . →	It . . . →	which . . .

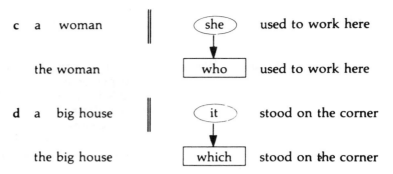

Sentence **e** gives an example of the use of the possessive pronoun (whose) to introduce a defining relative:

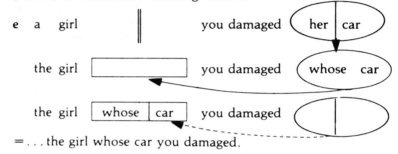

= . . . the girl whose car you damaged.

14.9.3 Who, whom, which, that or Ø?

If you are not sure which pronoun to choose, the safest course is to follow the traditional rule, i.e.:

	People	Things
Subject	who	which
Object	whom	which
Possessive	whose	of which

*These are the forms which you must use with non-defining relative clauses, see ➙ Section 14.10.

However, in defining relative clauses, the pronoun **that** is often used instead of **who(m)** and **which**, and it is common to use **Ø** for object pronouns:

	People and things	People	Things
	Ø	that/who	that/which
Subject	–	that or who	that or which
Object	Ø+	that or who(m)	that or which
Possessive	–whose+	(whose)	(whose)

The more popular forms are in bold type. In other words:

Defining relatives

subject relative pronoun: **that** or **who for people; that** or **which** for things

object relative pronoun: **Ø** (i.e. leave out the pronoun), or use **that/who** for people, **that/which** for things

possessive: **whose**, or a different construction (see Note 2 below).

Examples:

subject/people/who   I do not like *people who* talk about themselves all the time.

subject/people/that   I'd like to get my hands on *the idiot who* brought such a creature into the garden (or *the idiot that* brought . . .)

subject/thing/that   Is it *the car that** used to belong to Edwin? (or *which* used to belong . . .)

object/people/Ø   Tell me about *the people you met* when you were in Italy.

object/thing/Ø   Don't listen to *the things he says.*

poss./people/whose   I never argue with *people whose opinions* are different from my own.

poss./thing/(whose)   Fancy buying *a car whose engine* won't start! *or* a different construction, e.g., Fancy buying *a car with an engine* that won't start!

*The pronoun **that** is unstressed, i.e. [ðət], never [ðæt].

Notes

1   There are some cases where we prefer the use of *Ø* or **that** as object pronouns:

    a   *Superlatives* (← Section 4.5.1) *and similar words* (first, only, etc.)

       It is *the funniest* show (that) I have ever seen.

       She is *the biggest* liar (that) I know.

       Is this *the first time* (that) you have been to a zoo?

       It is *the only thing* (that) I am good at.

       And that is *all* (that) I can tell you about it.

    b   *Time expressions*

the day	I met you
the moment	she saw him
the year (that)*	Churchill became Prime Minister
the minute	you get back
the week	the new term began

*We prefer to leave out **that** in these time expressions

    c   *With indefinite pronouns* (← Section 5.10.)

       You can have *anything* (that) you like.

       People welcomed us *everywhere* (that) we went.

       I think she is *someone* (that) you will like.

2   The pronoun **whose** is often avoided in speaking. For example, instead of saying *'I feel sorry for the girl whose car you damaged'*, we would probably use two sentences: *'I feel sorry for that girl – you know, you damaged her car'*. Instead of saying *'I never argue with people whose opinions are different from mine'* we might say *'If I meet people who have different opinions from mine, I don't argue with them'*. The pronoun **whose** is, of course, used in writing. Similarly, when talking about things, we tend to avoid either **whose** or **of which**. Instead of *'I live in a house whose front garden is full of rose trees'*, we would probably say *'The house I live in, well, it's got a front garden that is full of rose trees'*.

3   Clauses beginning with *where* (and less commonly with *when*) can also be defining relative clauses when they identify the preceding noun phrase.
e.g. I need to find *a place where* I can work undisturbed.
(where = in which)

14.9.4 Prepositional verbs*
in defining relative clauses

In speaking and in informal writing, such sentences as the following would be very unusual:
(?)   Where is the man to whom you were talking?
(?)   Let me see the book at which you were looking.
(?) = this not a common form in everyday English
We would say:
a   Where is the man you were talking to?
b   Let me see the book you were looking at.

We can analyse the form of the sentences as follows:

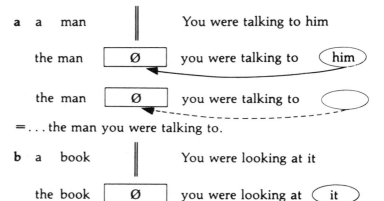

=...the man you were talking to.

=...the book you were looking at.

Note: Other forms are possible, e.g....*the man that you were talking to* or ...*the man who(m) you were talking to* but we advise you to use the Ø form, i.e. leave out the relative pronoun altogether.

14.10 Non-defining relative clauses

Sentence f (p 290) is an example of a non-defining relative clause:

Let us consider gold, *which is a precious metal.*

Non-defining relative clauses do not define or identify: they simply give additional information about something which is already defined or identified: For example:

14.10.1 Use of the non-defining relative clause

a My wife, *who is a heavy smoker*, catches cold very easily.
   My wife is already completely identified. (It would make no sense to ask the question *Which wife?*) The sentence gives two facts about my wife:
   1 she is a heavy smoker; 2 she catches cold very easily
   I could also have said *My wife is a heavy smoker and she catches cold very easily* (◄─Section 14.2.).

b The property is very attractive. The house, *which was built in 1770*, was once owned by the Duke of Royston. The gardens, *which were designed by the Duke himself*, contain over 150 species of trees.
   We already know which *house* and which *gardens* – they are part of *the property*. We are given two facts about each:

   1 the house was once owned by the Duke of Royston
   2 it was built in 1770
   1 the gardens were designed by the Duke himself
   2 they contain over 150 species of trees.

   We could also say 'The house was built in 1770 and was once owned by the Duke of Royston'; and 'The gardens were designed by the Duke himself and contain over 150 species of trees'.

We may decide to use the pattern   X is A, and has B,   or we may prefer the pattern   X, which is A, has B: it is mostly a matter of style. In speaking, we prefer the first, simpler pattern using **and** to join the ideas; the non-defining relative is mainly a formal written pattern.

14.10.2 The form of the non-defining relative clause

You must use the **relative pronouns** *who*, *whom*, *which* and *whose*, and you must separate the clause from the rest of the sentence by commas (. . . .,_____, ...)

(See the table at the beginning of Section 14.9.3).

Examples

Subject
a The Phoenicians, who were the greatest traders of their age, even traded with Britain.
b The new Metro, which was built in only eighteen months, now carries over twenty thousand commuters each day.

Object
c I was asked to write an article about Martin Luther King, whom I once met at a meeting in Alabama.

d   We always looked forward to Grandmother's cake, which she used to make in a huge baking tin.

Object after preposition

e   The Headmaster, of whom everyone was very afraid, always carried a large stick around with him.

f   The magazine *Punch*, to which he had long subscribed, was the only thing he ever read.

Possessive

g   We stayed with grandmother, whose cooking was the best in the world.

h   He showed me his new car, the wheels of which* were painted bright red.

*The variation ... *his new car, of which the wheels were* ... is unusual and best avoided.

14.10.3   Is it a defining or a non-defining clause?

The following sentences have exactly the same words. The only difference *in form* between them is that the first sentence (A) has a clause separated from the rest of the sentence by commas.*
There is, on the other hand, a big difference of meaning.

A   Children, who are untidy, do not take care of their things.

B   Children who are untidy do not take care of their things.

Sentence A is a statement about *all* children, and contains two facts (at least they are facts according to the man who wrote the sentence):

1   (all) children are untidy
2   (all) children fail to take care of their things

In other words, the clause ... ,*who are untidy*, ... is a non-defining clause.

Sentence B is a statement about *some* children, i.e. untidy children, and it states one fact about them: they fail to take care of their things. In other words, the clause ... *who are untidy* ... is a defining clause.

In diagram form:

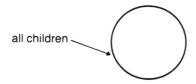

all children

These children (100%) do not take care of their things

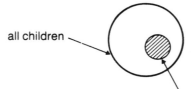

all children

The % of children who are untidy : these children (say 15%) do not take care of their things.

*In speaking, the commas are replaced by a marked pause or change of voice tone:

Children ‖ who are untidy ‖ fail to take care of their things.

15 Appendix   Notes on punctuation

1   The punctuation marks

Usual name	*Other names*	*Symbol*
Full stop	period	.
Comma		,
Semi-colon		;
Colon		:
Question mark		?
Exclamation mark		!
Apostrophe		'
Inverted commas	quotation marks	' ' or " "
Dash		–
Brackets	parentheses	( )
Hyphen		-

2   The use of punctuation marks

The purpose of punctuation marks is to make your meaning as clear and as immediately understandable as possible to your reader. Punctuation marks have four main uses:

a *To separate words or groups of words*
This is the function of the **full stop**, the **comma**, the **semi-colon**, the **colon**, and, in particular cases, the **dash** and **brackets.**

b *To indicate the type of sentence*
This is the function of the **question mark**, the **exclamation mark** and **inverted commas**.

c *(i) To show possession (ii) to show that a letter is missing from a word*
This is the function of the **apostrophe**.

d *To join words or parts of words*
This is the function of the **hyphen**.

Examples

Separation of words and groups of words:
Full stop: There was a knock at the door. We all waited silently for it to come again.
Comma: Tom, completely exhausted by this time, threw himself down on the sofa.
Semi-colon: The Government announced its plans for a third London airport; even the Opposition was taken by surprise.
Colon: The only true definition of friendship is this: a friend is someone in whose company you can happily remain silent.

Dashes: Perhaps the best thing to do – and this is only a suggestion – would be to stay here until the trial has finished.
Brackets: Martin Ramirez (better known as El Topo) is wanted by Interpol in connection with several kidnappings.

Indication of type of sentence:

Question mark: What is the use of worrying?
Exclamation mark: You'll never guess who I saw yesterday! Malcolm!
Inverted commas: 'Come on,' he said, 'or we shall be late.'

Possession and shortening of words

Apostrophe: John's idea and the publishers' response to it.
P'raps it's goin' to rain. (NB for the only generally accepted short forms see ← Section 7.5.2)

Joining words or parts of words

Hyphen: pseudo-intellectuals   well-educated people   prosperity

3 Are punctuation marks important?

a They are always important when they help to make your reader's task easier. For example, they are very important when they:

  i) *Remove ambiguity* (i.e. make sure that your words only mean one thing)
  { Mary thinks I know that John is abroad.
  { Mary thinks, I know, that John is abroad.
  { Women who drive carelessly are a danger to other road users. (Those women who . . .)
  { Women, who drive carelessly, are a danger to other road users.* (=all women drive carelessly)
  { She left me to talk to the tour leader. (I had to talk to him)
  { She left me, to talk to the tour leader. (. . . , because she wanted to talk to him)
  { He doesn't walk normally. (He walks in a strange way.)
  { He doesn't walk, normally. (Normally (Usually) he doesn't walk)
  { He left the room so that we could talk more freely. (he wanted to allow us to)
  { He left the room, so that we could talk more freely. (. . . , with the result that . . .)

Author's note: There is no suggestion that such a statement is true, of course.

ii) *Making something easier to read*
co-opt is easier than *coopt*.
Do-it-yourself is easier than *do it yourself*.
Where I had 'had had', John had 'had' is easier than
Where I had had had John had had! (This is an old
children's game)
Whatever she needs – and she needs a lot – she can have is
clearer than
Whatever she needs and she needs a lot she can have.

iii) *Change meaning or emphasis*

She is a pretty intelligent girl.	(=fairly intelligent)
She is a pretty, intelligent girl.	(she is both pretty and intelligent)
He is young and handsome and rich.	(three qualities of equal importance)
He is young and handsome – and rich.	(not only young and handsome, but rich as well!)

b In other cases, punctuation is very much a matter of *taste* or
personal style. For example, you could punctuate the following
in different ways, very much according to your personal taste
in these matters:
George Bridge, the technical advisor to the board, has been
called in.
George Bridge (the technical advisor to the board) has been
called in.
George Bridge – the technical advisor to the board – has been
called in.
Before the scheme can be completed, we need to conduct a
feasibility study, make a site inspection, do the costing, and
draw up a proposal.

Before the scheme can be completed, we need to: conduct a
feasibility study; make a site inspection; do the costing; and
draw up a proposal.
Sometimes, people develop a strong appetite for punctuation
marks and, especially in personal letters, produce texts which
seem to have contracted measles (a children's illness which
produces lots of spots and pimples on the face and body):

Dear Jane,
         It's me again, darling! Well, you'll never guess what
– I saw an old friend of yours the other day! I was in Harrod's
doing some shopping – what else? – when, believe it or not, I
ran into Charles; Charles, of all people! I couldn't believe it!
After all this time!
etc. etc. etc.
We advise you not to imitate this rather 'breathless' style of
over-dramatic writing.

4 Classes of use of punctuation marks

To help you to choose which punctuation marks you need in particular situations, and to help you decide which are more useful than others, we have classified them, in the table which follows, into four categories of use:

a *Obligatory* This means that you *must* use the punctuation mark in these cases. Not to do so would be a mistake.

b *Usual* This means that most people use the punctuation mark in these cases, and we advise you to do the same, even though it is not strictly necessary.

c *Taste* This means that, in these cases, it is a matter of personal taste or style. Whether you imitate these usages is up to you, but we advise you only to use punctuation marks when they are really needed.

d *No! no! no!* There are some cases where English usage is quite different and unexpected. We have drawn your attention to cases where, whatever you might expect, it would be completely wrong to use the punctuation mark in this way.

	Obligatory	Usual	Personal taste	No! No! No!
Full stop	1 *At the end of a sentence* 2 *Abbreviations of single letters:* i.e., e.g., p.a. 3 *Shortened words:* pron., Dept., Chem.Eng. adj., etc. 4 North, South, East, West and other *geographical terms used initially:* N. Africa, W. Indies, L. Geneva, U. Volta	1 *Abbreviations in addresses:* St., Ave., Rd., Cres., Sq. 2 *Initial letters of the names of organizations, esp. if new or not easy to say as one unit:* N.A.S.U.W.T., R.S.P.C.A.	1 *Titles* like Mr, Mrs, Dr, Prof, Rev. 2 *Acronyms,* that is, names formed from the initial letters of organizations NATO, UNO, UNICEF, CID	1 At the start of a letter we write Dear Sir, *not* ~~Dear Sir.~~ 2 Whole numbers of four or more figures are written, e.g. 175,000 and 1,000,000 *not* ~~175,000 or 1,000,000~~
Comma	1 *Non-defining relatives (see 14.10):* *Churchill, who was not liked by many colleagues, became very popular later.* 2 *Additional information which does not define:* Ted Heath, the former Prime Minister, ... (but not when it does define: My old friend Ted Heath ...	1 *Separating initial adverbials (12.19.1):* Personally, I never ... After dinner, we ... Finally, ... If you like, we can ... 2 *Separating final comment expressions:* You are a Welshman, I believe. I'm a Scot, as a matter of fact.	1 *Separating initial phrases without a main verb:* To end with (,) he ... Given the time (,) I would ... Sighing heavily (,) she ... 2 *In addresses:* 30, Main Street, Hathersage, Devon.	1 Decimals are written, e.g., 0.075 and 13.6 *not* ~~0,075 or 13,6~~ 2 We *never* mark off an object from its verb: I know you are tired *not* ~~I know, you are tired~~ He asked me who I was *not* ~~He asked me, who I was~~

	Obligatory	Usual	Personal taste	NO! NO! NO!
Comma	3 *Inserted comment phrases*, or *clauses or words*: It is, I believe, the first of its kind. I decided, after a lot of thought, to stay with her. It was not, however, an easy decision. 4 *To mark off quoted speech*: 'It is time,' he remarked, 'to go home.' 5 *Lists*: I need eggs, butter, baking powder, flour and salt. (Note no comma before *and*) 6 *Adjectives*: He is tall, strong and handsome (See 4.4.2) 7 *To avoid ambiguity*: (See 14.10.3).			
Semi-colon	It is never obligatory.	1 *To mark off a series of listed clauses or phrases* 2 *To mark off a final comment clause*	1 *Instead of a comma to separate items in a list*: The books were divided in several sections: geography; physics; history; classics.	*At the end of a question use a question mark*: Where is it? *not* ~~Where is it;~~
Colon	It is never obligatory.	1 *To introduce a list of items*: (See the examples in this table) 2 *To introduce a quote*: He said: 'Go away!'	1 *Instead of a conjunction, to introduce a second clause which expands or explains the first*: I don't like coaches: I much prefer trains.	*It is not used to start letters. We say* Dear Anna, *not* ~~Dear Anna:~~

	Obligatory	Usual	Personal taste	NO! NO! NO!
Inverted commas	1 *At the beginning and end of direct speech:* 'Tell me,' he said, 'if I am boring you.' 2 To show that words are being quoted: I believe in the beauty of holiness', as Laud described it.	1 *To show that a word is being used in a special way, i.e. not in its usual sense:* She is a very 'physical' person. 2 *To show that a word is slang or invented:* The 'in' thing to do. A 'bluesy' kind of song.	1 *When quoting the title of a book, play, etc:* 'Wuthering Heights' by Emily Bronte.	Do not use them round proper names or round numbers. He was born in 1845 *not* He was born in 1845'
Apostrophe	*Possession* (See 1.8) *Short forms* (See 7.5.2.)			
Exclamation mark	It is never obligatory.	1 *After directly quoted exclamations:* 'Good heavens!' he exclaimed. 2 *After strong imperatives:* Get out! Look out!	*To dramatize events,* to make them sound exciting or extraordinary: He had the biggest nose you have ever seen!	We never use it to begin a letter. We write Dear Sir, *not* Dear Sir!
Question mark	*After direct questions:* 'Where are you going?'	*In brackets, to express your doubt about the truth, etc., of something:* He says he is the best (?) in Europe.	You can leave it out when the question is really a request: Could I have some more tea.	Do not use it after reported questions. We write: He asked me who I was. *not* He asked me who I was?
Dash	It is never obligatory.		1 It can replace the comma *to mark off non-defining relatives or information.* (◄ 14.10.2) 2 After: to introduce items, *i.e. : – . . .*	Do not use dashes instead of quotation marks.
Brackets	1 *In cross-references and years:* Adverbials (see chapter 12) da Vinci (1452–1519)		Instead of commas *to mark off inserted additional information:* Ted Heath (the former PM)	

5 Special note on the use of hyphens

In many cases the use of hyphens is decided by individual printers or publishing houses, and even dictionaries do not agree on whether for example *dining room* should be written with a hyphen as *dining-room*. (See also ◄ 1.7.8c).

We recommend you to use hyphens in the following cases:

a *After certain prefixes which form new or long words*

Crypto-	crypto-fascist
Ex-	ex-boss, ex-girlfriend
Pseudo-	pseudo-intellectual, pseudo-scientific
Macro-/micro-	Macro-economics, micro-photography
Mini-	mini-revolution
Semi-	semi-detached, semi-automatic
Un-+adjective with initial capital	
	un-American activities, un-English behaviour

b *Compound adjectives*

   i) Adjectives formed from WELL- and BADLY- +A PAST PARTICIPLE are usually hyphenated when they are used attributively* (◄ Section 4.3.1.):
   well-dressed, well-educated, well-kept
   badly-dressed, badly-formed,
   Similarly, soft-spoken, hard-won, (ill-used), etc.

*People often write them with a hyphen whether they are used attributively or predicatively.

   ii) Adjectives formed like *blue-eyed* (see ◄ Section 4.2.1.) until they become very widely and commonly used, are best written with a hyphen.

   iii) Any adjectives which are formed from more than two elements:

a *cut-and-dried* case	a *now-or-never* opportunity
a *died-in-the-wool* conservative	
a *do-it-yourself* shop	an *on-the-spot* decision
a *give-and-take* relationship	an *out-of-the-way* place
a *hand-to-mouth* existence	a *take-it-or-leave-it* attitude
a *make-or-break* attempt	
a *nine-to-five* job	a *well-to-do* neighbourhood

   Warning: do not try to invent your own: you cannot say, for example, a *bought-in-London* dress.

c *To make words easier to recognize*

It is helpful to your reader if you put a hyphen after *co-* or *pre-* when they are followed by the same vowel. Also, in some cases, *re-*:

e.g. co-operate, co-ordinate, co-opt; pre-eminent; re-export, re-introduce

Notice, too, the convention which allows you to use two prefixes to the same noun:

e.g. The party was split into pro- and anti- nationalization groups.

d *At the end of a line, to show that the word is incomplete*
If you need to split a word at the end of a line, try to make the break at a point where an affix occurs,

e.g. *depart-ure, govern-ment, impress-ed, interest-ing, realiz-ation.*

Otherwise, try to leave enough of the word to make it recognizable.

e.g. *hou-se* rather than *ho-use, hus-band* rather than *hu-sband.*

Try not to split a word in such a way that only one letter is left,

e.g. split *house* into *hou-se*, not *h-ouse* or *hous-e.*

Index

a(n)   see *articles*, 2.1–2.3

-a (suffix)   plural of nouns of foreign origin, 1.3.5

a- (prefix)   adjs. with prefix *a-* used predicatively, 4.3.3

ABBREVIATIONS   plural of abbreviated words, e.g., *photo*, 1.3.1: of modals, 7.5.2: *viz., e.g., i.e.,* etc., 12.20

ABILITY   prepositions to express level of ability e.g. *at* (good at games), 6.5.1d; intro. to modals, 10.1; modals of ability: *can, could, able to,* 10.7

-ability   formation of abstract nouns from **-able** adjs., 1.7.5

-able   adj. to noun, 1.7.5; adj. suffix, 4.2.1; more/most *-able*, 4.5.3b; to form advbs. of manner: *-able* to *-ably,* 12.14.1

about (prep. and advb.)   6.5.1 d, 6.5.2 (note 1); 6.5.3; 6.7; 11.3; 11.5

above (preposition)   6.3.3

absolutely   12.21. 2, (note 4)

ABSTRACT NOUNS   mass nouns, 1.6; formation of, 1.7.5; 2.3.1a; 7.7.4

ABSTRACT (IDEAS)   and use of articles, 2.2.1b (note); 2.2.3d

accident   *by accident,* 12.16.3

ACCOMPANIMENT   preps. *with/without* to express accompaniment 6.5.1d

according to   6.5.3

across (prep./advb)   6.3.4–5; 6.6.1; 11.3.3; 11.5; 12.5

ACTIONS   endings to express small/repeated actions 1.7.3; *every*+*time* to express repeated action, 3.8.2c; vbs which refer to actions, 7.1; vbs which suggest small or repeated actions, 7.7.2; Past simple to focus on action 8.3.1; performer of action (agent) in passive, 8.9; *going to* when future action depend on present facts, 9.8; *base-infinitive* or *present participle* to describe complete or incomplete action, 13.7.2

ACTIVE   *active* and *passive* participles (e.g., *boring/bored*), 4.2.2 (note); 5.4.2; of verbs, 7.3; relationship between *active* and *passive,* 8.9

ACTIVITIES   formation of gerunds to describe *sporting/healthy* activities, 1.7.6; verbs in phrasal vbs refer to physical activities, 11.1; go+activity. (e.g., *go dancing*), 13.2.4

actor   1.7.1b; 1.7.4

actress   1.7.1b

addendum/addenda   1.3.5

ADDITION   in addition, 12.20

ADJECTIVAL CLAUSES   see *clauses*

ADJECTIVAL PHRASES   2.3.1 (note 1); 3.1; 5.11; 14.9.1

ADJECTIVAL PHRASES   in particular statements, 2.3.1 (note); describing quantity, 3.1: *the ones* +ap (e.g., *the ones I like best*), 5.11.1; ap to help to identify or define, 14.9.1

ADJECTIVES   capital letters for adjectives in titles, 1.2, (note 2); nationality adj. in *-ish* with plural meaning, 1.3.6b; adj. to identify whether noun refers to male or female, 1.7.1c; to describe size, 1.7.2; in formation of nouns, esp. from *-able* or *-ible,* 1.7.5; adj + noun when not a compound noun, 1.7.8b; in formation of compound nouns, 1.7.8d; list of common adjs. formed from phrasal verbs, 1.10; use of *the* with superlative, 2.2.3c; *the* + adj. = the whole class (*the rich*), 2.2.3e; adj. + noun to form particular statements, 2.3.1, (note 1); demonstrative + adj. + noun, 2.4.5; describing quantity, 3.1; e.g., *no bread left,* 3.5.2; *every* = adj., 3.8.2b; *either/neither* as adjs., 3.10; ADJECTIVES, Chapter 4, see Contents; *whose?* as adj., 5.7; *which?* as adj., 5.7 (see also 4.1); adj. + *one(s),* e.g., *the blue one(s),* 5.11.1; use of adj. *other/another* 5.11.2; adj. + prep., e.g., *afraid of,* 6.5.1a; irregular past participles to form adjectives (e.g., *molten* for *melted*), 7.4.4 (note); adj. + *-en* to form vbs. (e.g., *black* ⟶ *blacken*), 7.7.3; past participle = part of passive or adj. ?, 8.11 (note); adj. derived from phrasal vbs., 1.10, 11.1.3; adj. + *-ly* to form advbs. of manner, 12.14.1; adj. in *-ly* used adverbially in *in a _____ manner/way* (e.g., *in a friendly way*), 12.16.1; advbs used to modify adjs., e.g. *fairly good,* 12.21; adjectival expression as complement of sentence, Chapter 13A, adjs. in intransitive verb sentence patterns, 13.1–13.4.2; adjs. in transitive sentence patterns, 13.10; adjs. to identify or define, 14.9.1

admit   13.8.2, 13.9.2

ADVERBIALS   in formation of compound nouns, 1.7.8d; adjs., with adverbial meaning, e.g. *a heavy smoker,* 4.3.4c; adverbials associated with present simple and continuous tenses, 8.2.4, with past tenses, 8.3.4, with perfect tenses, 8.4.5; ADVERBIALS, Chapter 12, see Contents; adverbials in intransitive verb patterns, 13.1–13.4.1, and in transitive verb patterns, 13.10